Clerical Payroll Procedures

Robert W. Fuller

EIGHTH EDITION

K52 Published by
SOUTH-WESTERN PUBLISHING CO.
CINCINNATI WEST CHICAGO, ILL. DALLAS PELHAM MANOR, N.Y. PALO ALTO, CALIF.

ISBN: 0-538-11520-3

Library of Congress Catalog Card Number: 78-65088

2 3 4 5 6 7 8 H 5 4 3 2 1 0

Printed in the United States of America

CONTENTS

(continued)

INTRODUCTION

As you study CLERICAL PAYROLL PROCEDURES, assume that you have just been employed by Solarheat Systems Inc. as a General Office Clerk. One of your responsibilities will be the preparation of the weekly payroll. Solarheat Systems Inc. is a small company with 14 employees that manufactures solar heating units. The employees are: a general manager, 2 office employees, 2 salespersons, 7 production workers on an hourly-rate pay basis, and 2 production workers on a piece-rate pay basis.

Under the Social Security Act, every employee must have a social security number before starting to work in a business. Form SS-5 (Illustration 1) is the form used to apply for a social security number. A person without this number must file Form SS-5 no later than 7 days after being hired by a company. This form can be filed with any field office of the Social Security Administration.

The person who files Form SS-5 will receive from the Social Security Administration a card showing the social security number that has been given only to that employee. The card for a social security number (Illustration 2) is shown at the right. The employee must inform the employer of the number and keep the card in a safe place. It is a good idea to make a note of the number and to carry it with you at all times. If you change your job, inform your new employer of this number. Generally, your social security number remains the same for the rest of your life. This social security number will be used no matter how many times a person changes jobs.

Illustration 2 Card for a Social Security Number

ID: CN: DO: DO NOT WRITE IN THE ABOVE SPACE

APPLICATION FOR A SOCIAL SECURITY NUMBER

See Instructions on Back. Print in Black or Dark Blue Ink or Use Typewriter.

1 Print FULL NAME YOU WILL USE IN WORK OR BUSINESS — (First Name) Judith (Middle Name or Initial—if none, draw line) F. (Last Name) Mahle

2 Print FULL NAME GIVEN YOU AT BIRTH — Judith Frances Mahle

3 PLACE OF BIRTH — (City) Cincinnati (County if known) Hamilton (State) Ohio

4 MOTHER'S FULL NAME AT HER BIRTH (Her maiden name) — Grace Margaret Schumacher

5 FATHER'S FULL NAME (Regardless of whether living or dead) — Clarence Francis Mahle

6 YOUR DATE OF BIRTH (Month) (Day) (Year) — Aug. 24, 196

7 YOUR PRESENT AGE (Age on last birthday)

8 YOUR SEX — MALE ☐ FEMALE ☒

9 YOUR COLOR OR RACE — WHITE ☒ NEGRO ☐ OTHER ☐

10 HAVE YOU EVER BEFORE APPLIED FOR OR HAD A UNITED STATES SOCIAL SECURITY, RAILROAD, OR TAX ACCOUNT NUMBER? — NO ☒ DON'T KNOW ☐ YES ☐ (If "Yes" Print State in which you applied and Date you applied and Social Security Number if known)

11 YOUR MAILING ADDRESS — (Number and Street, Apt. No., P.O. Box, or Rural Route) 5609 Alomar Drive (City) Clovis (State) California (Zip Code) 93612

12 TODAY'S DATE — Nov. 15, 19--

13 TELEPHONE NUMBER — 863-9214

NOTICE: Whoever, with intent to falsify his or someone else's true identity, willfully furnishes or causes to be furnished false information in applying for a social security number, is subject to a fine of not more than $1,000 or imprisonment for up to 1 year, or both

14 Sign YOUR NAME HERE (Do Not Print) — Judith F. Mahle

DHEW, Social Security Administration
Form **SS-5**

☐ RESCREEN ☐ ASSIGN ☐ DUP ISSUED

Return completed application to nearest SOCIAL SECURITY ADMINISTRATION OFFICE

Illustration 1 Form SS-5—Application for a Social Security Number

An employee must also furnish the employer with Form W-4, a signed withholding allowance (exemption) certificate (Illustrations 3 and 4). This form is needed by an employer to determine the marital and tax filing status of each employee for income tax deductions from wages. The employer must have this form for each employee. If there is any change in the number of withholding allowances claimed by the employee, a new Form W-4 should be filed with the employer.

Your first responsibility as the General Office Clerk of Solarheat Systems Inc. is to become familiar with the duties of your job. Therefore, you should read carefully Sections 1, 2, and 3 which explain the various laws that affect a company's payroll records, the different methods for paying salaries and wages, and the basic payroll records that are used in most businesses. After you have studied these sections, you will be given instructions for preparing the first week's payroll.

ACTIVITY 1

Practice applying for a social security number by filling out Form SS-5 on page 47.

If your teacher asks for your completed Form SS-5, check it to see that you have properly filled in all the information. Be sure your name appears at the top of the page.

ACTIVITY 2

As a new employee of Solarheat Systems Inc., you must fill out a Form W-4. For this activity, assume that you are single and claim 1 withholding allowance (exemption) for yourself. Complete Form W-4 on page 48.

If your teacher asks for your completed Form W-4, be sure that you have filled in all the information properly.

Form **W-4**

Department of the Treasury
Internal Revenue Service

Employee's Withholding Allowance Certificate

(Use for Wages Paid After December 31, 19--)

This certificate is for income tax withholding purposes only. It will remain in effect until you change it. If you claim exemption from withholding, you will have to file a new certificate on or before April 30 of next year.

Type or print your full name: Judith Frances Mahle		Your social security number: 239-76-3077
Home address (number and street or rural route): 5609 Alomar Drive	Marital Status	[X] Single [ ] Married
		[ ] Married, but withhold at higher Single rate
City or town, State, and ZIP code: Clovis, CA 93612		Note: *If married, but legally separated, or spouse is a nonresident alien, check the single block.*

1 Total number of allowances you are claiming	1
2 Additional amount, if any, you want deducted from each pay (if your employer agrees)	$ None
3 I claim exemption from withholding (see instructions). Enter "Exempt"	

Under the penalties of perjury, I certify that the number of withholding allowances claimed on this certificate does not exceed the number to which I am entitled. If claiming exemption from withholding, I certify that I incurred no liability for Federal income tax for last year and I anticipate that I will incur no liability for Federal income tax for this year.

Signature ► *Judith F. Mahle* Date ► December 3, 19--

Detach along this line

▲ *Give the top part of this form to your employer; keep the lower part for your records and information* ▲

Instructions

The explanatory material below will help you determine your correct number of withholding allowances, and will assist you in completing the Form W-4 at the top of this page.

See **Publication 505** for more information on withholding.

Avoid Overwithholding or Underwithholding

By claiming the number of withholding allowances you are entitled to, you can fit the amount of tax withheld from your wages to your tax liability. In addition to the allowances for personal exemptions to be claimed in item (a), be sure to claim any additional allowances you are entitled to in item (b), "Special withholding allowance," and item (c), "Allowance(s) for credit(s) and/or deduction(s)." While you may claim these allowances on Form W-4 for withholding purposes, you may not claim them under "Exemptions" on your tax return Form 1040 or Form 1040A.

You may claim the special withholding allowance if you are single with only one employer, or married with only one employer and your spouse is not employed. If you have unusually large itemized deductions, make alimony payments, or credit(s) for child care expenses, earned income, credit for the elderly, or residential energy credits, you may claim additional allowances to avoid having too much income tax withheld from your wages.

If you and your spouse are both employed or you have more than one employer, you should make sure that enough has been withheld. If you find that you need more withholding, claim fewer allowances or ask for additional withholding or request to be withheld at the higher "Single" status. If you are currently claiming additional withholding allowances based on itemized deductions, check the worksheet on the back to see that you are claiming the proper number of allowances.

How Many Withholding Allowances May You Claim?

Use the schedule below to determine the number of allowances you may claim for tax withholding purposes. In determining the number, keep in mind these points: if you are single and hold more than one job, you may not claim the same allowances with more than one employer at the same time; or, if you are married and both you and your spouse are employed, you may not both claim the same allowances with your employers at the same time. A nonresident alien, other than a resident of Canada, Mexico, or Puerto Rico, may claim only one personal allowance.

Completing Form W-4

If you find you are entitled to one or more allowances in addition to those you are now claiming, increase your number of allowances by completing the form above and filing it with your employer. If the number of allowances you previously claimed decreases, you must file a new Form W-4 within 10 days. (If you expect to owe more tax than will be withheld, you may increase your withholding by claiming fewer or "0" allowances on line 1, or by asking for additional withholding on line 2, or both.)

You may claim exemption from withholding of Federal income tax if you had no liability for income tax for last year, and you anticipate that you will incur no liability for income tax for this year. You may not claim exemption if your joint or separate return shows tax liability before the allowance of any credit for income tax withheld. If you are exempt, your employer will not withhold Federal income tax from your wages. However, social security tax will be withheld if you are covered by the Federal Insurance Contributions Act.

You must revoke this exemption (1) within 10 days from the time you anticipate you will incur income tax liability for the year or (2) on or before December 1 if you anticipate you will incur Federal income tax liability for the next year. If you want to stop or are required to revoke this exemption, you must file a new Form W-4 with your employer showing the number of withholding allowances you are entitled to claim. This certificate for exemption from withholding will expire on April 30 of next year unless a new Form W-4 is filed on or before that date.

The Following Information is Provided in Accordance with the Privacy Act of 1974

The Internal Revenue Code requires every employee to furnish his or her employer with a signed withholding allowance certificate showing the number of withholding allowances that the employee claims (section 3402(f)(2)(A) and the Regulations thereto). Individuals are required to provide their Social Security Number for proper identification and processing (section 6109 and the Regulations thereto).

The principal purpose for soliciting withholding allowance certificate information is to administer the Internal Revenue laws of the United States.

If an employee does not furnish a signed withholding allowance certificate, the employee is considered as claiming no withholding allowances (section 3401(e)) and shall be treated as a single person (section 3402(l)).

The routine uses of the withholding allowance certificate information include disclosure to the Department of Justice for actual or potential criminal prosecution or civil litigation.

Figure Your Total Withholding Allowances Below

(a) Allowance(s) for exemption(s)—Enter 1 for each personal exemption you can claim on your Federal income tax return* . . .	1
(b) Special withholding allowance—Enter 1 if single with 1 employer, or married with 1 employer and spouse not employed** . . .	-0-
(c) Allowance(s) for credit(s) and/or deduction(s)—Enter number from tables on page 2	-0-
(d) Total (add lines (a) through (c) above)—Enter here and on line 1, Form W-4, above	1

*If you are in doubt as to whom you may claim as a dependent, see the instructions that came with your last Federal income tax return or call your local Internal Revenue Service office.

**This allowance is used solely for purposes of figuring your withholding tax, and cannot be claimed when you file your tax return.

Illustration 3 Form W-4—Employee's Withholding Allowance Certificate (Front)

Form W-4 Page 2

TABLE A.—Table for Determining Number of Withholding Allowances Based on Tax Credits

Figure the number of additional withholding allowances for the amount of tax credits for child care expenses, earned income credit, credit for the elderly, or residential energy credits, from the appropriate column (see line (c) on other side). For an explanation of these credits, see the Instructions for Form 1040.
Note: *Watch for announcements that could affect the number of withholding allowances you may claim.*

Allowances ▶	0	1		2		3		4		5		6	
Estimated salaries and wages from all sources:	If the amount of estimated tax credits is:												
	Under	At least	But less than	At least	But less than	At least	But less than	At least	But less than	At least	But less than	At least	But less than
Part I Single Employees													
Under $5,000	No additional allowances												
5,000–15,000	250	250	500	500	700	700	900	900 or more					
15,001–25,000	350	350	700	700	1,000	1,000 or more							
25,001–35,000	550	550	950	950 or more									
Part II Head of Household Employees													
Under $5,000	No additional allowances												
5,000–20,000	150	150	400	400	650	650	900	900 or more					
20,001–35,000	1	1	300	300	650	650	1,000	1,000 or more					
35,001–45,000	450	450	850	850 or more									
Part III Married Employees (When Spouse is Not Employed)													
Under $8,000	No additional allowances												
8,000–15,000	200	200	350	350	500	500	700	700	800	800	950	950 or more	
15,001–25,000	250	250	500	500	700	700	950	950 or more					
25,001–35,000	300	300	650	650	950	950 or more							
35,001–45,000	650	650	1,050	1,050 or more									
Part IV Married Employees (When Both Spouses are Employed)													
Under $8,000	No additional allowances												
8,000–15,000	250	250	400	400	450	450 or more							
15,001–25,000	550	550	800	800	950	950 or more							

How to Use Table A

1 Find your filing status under Part I, II, III, or IV.
2 Using your filing status, find your estimated salaries and wages in the left column.
3 Read the shaded amounts to the right until you get to the amount of your estimated tax credits.
4 Look to the top of the column to find the number of allowances you may take for your estimated tax credits.
5 Enter this number on page 1, line (c), together with the number of allowances from Table B for itemized deductions, and alimony payments.

Example: *A taxpayer who expects to file a Federal income tax return as a single person estimates annual wages of $12,000 and tax credits of $650. The taxpayer uses Part I for single employees. The $12,000 falls in the wage bracket of $5,000 to 15,000 in the left column. Reading in the shaded area to the right, $650 falls within the estimated tax credits bracket of At least 500 But less than 700. Looking to the top of the column, the taxpayer finds that 2 allowances are permitted. The taxpayer adds "2" to the number of any allowances from Table B below and enters the total on page 1, line (c).*

TABLE B.—Table for Determining Number of Withholding Allowances Based on Itemized Deductions and Alimony Payments, if Any*

Estimated salaries and wages from all sources:	Column (A) Single Employees (only one job)	Column (B) Married Employees (one spouse working and one job only)	Column (C) Married Employees (both spouses working or employees with more than one job)
Under $10,000	$2,800	$3,900	$4,000
10,000–30,000	2,800	3,900	5,800
30,001–40,000	3,500	3,900	8,000
Over $40,000	15% of estimated salaries and wages	13% of estimated salaries and wages	23% of estimated salaries and wages

*If you are paying alimony but will not itemize deductions, figure the number of withholding allowances by dividing the estimated alimony payments by $1,000 (round off fractions to the nearest whole number) and enter on page 1, line (c).

How to Use Table B

1 Enter the amount of your estimated itemized deductions, including alimony payments, for the year . . . . . . ______
2 Find your total estimated salary and wage amount in the left column. Read to the right and enter the amount from column (A), (B), or (C) for your filing status . . . . ______
3 Subtract line 2 from line 1 . . . . ______
4 Divide the amount on line 3 by $1,000. Enter here and on page 1, line (c) together with the number of any allowances for tax credits from Table A, above. (Round off fractions to the nearest whole number.) . . . . . . ______

Illustration 4 Form W-4—Employee's Withholding Allowance Certificate (Back)

1 LAWS AND REGULATIONS AFFECTING A PAYROLL

Various federal and state laws require that most businesses keep records to provide information about salary and wage payments and to help in preparing reports. The laws that affect many companies are described here.

THE SOCIAL SECURITY ACT

The Social Security Act became a federal law on August 14, 1935. Although there are many phases of this Act that affect millions of people, the parts that require businesses to keep payroll records are:

1. *The old-age, survivor, disability, and hospital insurance benefits and the taxes imposed for these benefits under the Federal Income Contributions Act (FICA)*—generally known as the FICA tax but sometimes OAB (old-age benefits) tax is used.
2. *The unemployment provisions of the Social Security Act and the taxes imposed under the Federal Unemployment Tax Act*—known as the FUTA tax.
3. *The state unemployment compensation laws*—providing for unemployment benefits and in some states providing for sickness benefits to workers; taxes are levied to provide funds from which these benefits are paid.

FICA Tax. Under the Social Security Act, most businesses must pay a FICA tax on salaries and wages paid to employees besides collecting this tax from the employees. The FICA tax is levied so that benefits will be available to retired workers, to survivors of such workers, and to disabled workers. The 1965 amendments to the Social Security Act also set up a health-insurance program (Medicare) for persons who are age 65 or older, and part of the FICA taxes collected by the federal government is for this purpose. Although the rate of FICA tax on both the employer and employee is changed often by Congress, the principle of keeping payroll records is always the same. The present FICA tax rate is 6.13% which is collected from both the employee and the employer on $22,900 of salary or wages paid to an employee during a calendar year. Both the FICA tax rate and the base amount may be changed by Congress. Under the Social Security Act, a business must keep records showing this information:

1. The name, address, date of birth, and social security number of each employee.
2. The total amount and the date of each salary or wage payment along with the time period worked by each employee.
3. The amount of such salary or wage payment that is taxable.
4. The amount of tax withheld or collected.
5. The reason why and the date when an employee left the company.

After the FICA tax has been deducted from the salary or wages of each employee, the employer must send to the federal government the total amount of these collected FICA taxes along with the FICA tax that is contributed by the employer.

Under the 1978 legislation, the FICA tax rates and the salary or wages subject to the FICA tax during the next few years for both the employee and employer are:

FICA TAX RATES AND WAGE BASES FOR THE EMPLOYER AND THE EMPLOYEE

Year	*Tax*	*Taxable Wage Base*
1979	6.13%	$22,900
1980	6.13	25,900
1981	6.65	29,700
1982-84	6.70	Automatic cost-of-living adjustments in the wage base
1985	7.05	
1986-89	7.15	
1990 and later	7.65	

Unemployment Taxes. Many businesses are also subject to federal taxes under the Social Security Act that pay for the operating costs of state unemployment compensation plans. The Federal Unemployment Tax Act (FUTA) sets the federal rate for unemployment taxes under the Social Security Act. This FUTA tax is for most employers who pay wages of $1,500 or over during any calendar quarter in the previous or present calendar year.

The FUTA tax rate now is 3.4%. A credit of 2.7% is allowed for state contributions in paying the federal tax. With a FUTA tax of 3.4%, this means that for a business with a credit of 2.7% for state contributions, the FUTA tax rate actually amounts to 0.7% (3.4% − 2.7% = 0.7%). The taxable wage ceiling for the FUTA tax is $6,000. This means that this tax applies only to the first $6,000 of an employee's earnings.

If an employer's tax liability is more than $100, deposits are made quarterly to the federal government. Contributions to state unemployment funds are usually paid quarterly. A few states also require contributions for an unemployment compensation fund from the employees as well as from the employers. Here, the employer deducts the employees' part of the contributions from wages paid and sends the amount of these deductions when the employer's contributions are paid.

The Federal Unemployment Tax Act requires an employer to keep these records:

1. The total amount of wage payments paid to each employee during the calendar year.
2. The total amount of such wage payments that is taxable.
3. The amount of contributions paid into each state unemployment compensation fund that shows separately
   (a) The payments made and not deducted from the employees' wage payments and
   (b) The payments made and deducted from the employees' wage payments.
4. All of the above information must be shown on Form 940, the annual federal tax return for reporting unemployment taxes.

THE FAIR LABOR STANDARDS ACT

The Fair Labor Standards Act, known as the Wage and Hour Law, set up certain rules for businesses engaged in interstate commerce. The definition of "interstate commerce" has been expanded to include many workers under this Act. The minimum wage for 1979 is $2.90 for the first 40 hours worked during a work week (a regular repeated period of 168 hours in the form of 7 consecutive 24-hour periods). The work week does not need to be at the same time as the calendar week. It may begin any day of the week and any hour of the day.

For any work beyond 40 hours during a work week, this Act states that the rate be 1½ times the hourly rate for excess hours worked over 40. More information about the Fair Labor Standards Act is explained in Section 3.

INCOME TAX WITHHOLDING

In 1943, the federal government enacted a law that required businesses to withhold from wages of all employees amounts that would pay the federal income taxes of employees. The rates of income tax are determined by the Internal Revenue Code.

The law states that employers must keep records and give statements under oath as the Commissioner of Internal Revenue may require under the regulations prescribed by him with the approval of the U.S. Secretary of the Treasury. No specific records are required by an employer, but records must be kept to show the number of persons employed during the calendar year whose wages are subject to income tax withholding, the periods of employment, the amounts paid, and the dates of payment. It is only by keeping good records that an employer will have the needed information to prepare the reports that are required.

Some states and cities have laws that require the withholding of state and city income taxes. The procedure for collecting these taxes is about the same as that for the withholding of federal income tax.

THE WALSH-HEALEY PUBLIC CONTRACTS ACT

Under the Walsh-Healey Public Contracts Act, certain labor standards are set up for work done on federal government contracts. The U.S. Secretary of Labor has the authority to establish minimum wage rates based on those already in effect in a certain industry. The part of the law that affects payroll computation requires the payment of overtime wages at a rate of 1½ times the regular hourly rate for over 40 hours weekly or 8 hours daily.

WORKMEN'S COMPENSATION LAWS

In most states, a business pays into a state fund an amount of money that is used to pay accident, disability, or death benefits to workers (or their families) who may be injured or killed while working on a regular job. While most of these laws do not state the types of payroll records or information required of an employer, it is important that certain records be kept.

The amount paid into the fund is usually a certain percentage of the total payroll. For a claim made by an employee, the employer usually must file a report of the wages received by that employee over a period of time before the accident. Accurate payroll records must be kept to show this information.

FAIR EMPLOYMENT PRACTICES

Many federal, state, and local laws have been enacted for fair employment practices that prevent discrimination in the employment and promotion of employees based on age, race, color, sex, religion, or national origin. While these laws do not directly affect payroll records, they do require that businesses keep personnel records to show that such practices are being enforced.

OTHER REASONS FOR KEEPING PAYROLL RECORDS

Besides the need for payroll records, there are other laws, regulations, or requirements that make it necessary for businesses to keep such records. Local taxes have been imposed in some areas based on salaries and wages. For businesses with unions, dues are often deducted at the time wage payments are made. Such a practice is known as the check-off system in paying dues. Under this plan, a business deducts the dues from wages when they are paid and then sends the total of these deductions to the union.

A business needs the data shown on its payroll records. Certain figures are needed to determine manufacturing or department costs. Only by keeping good wage records can this data be obtained. In many businesses, plans for life insurance, sick benefits, medical care, and retirement benefits are based on the payroll records. Whether the employer pays all the costs of these plans or whether the costs are shared by the employer and the employees, it is necessary to have accurate payroll information.

Several states have laws that provide sick benefits for workers. The money to pay these benefits usually is from a fund to which contributions are made by employees, employers, or both. When employees must contribute a part of their wages, the amounts collected by the employer are sent to the state at certain times to be creditied to a sick-benefit fund.

It is very clear that most businesses have no choice in deciding whether or not payroll records should be kept. Today all businesses must keep certain payroll records to provide the data needed for preparing the forms and reports that are required not only for the federal, state, and local governments but also to meet the requirements of the businesses themselves.

ACTIVITY 3

On pages 49 and 50 is a study guide for this section. In completing this guide, determine whether you have learned the basic reasons why a business must keep payroll records. If your teacher asks you for your completed study guide, be sure your name appears in the proper place.

2 BASES FOR SALARY AND WAGE PAYMENTS

Many different methods are used to determine the wages paid to employees. Solarheat Systems Inc. uses several different ways of determining the wages and salaries of its employees. An important part of payroll work is the understanding of the different methods of wage payments and the ability to compute hourly rates when other payment methods are used for quoting salaries. This section presents the basic methods of paying wages or salaries.

SALARIES AND WAGES

A *wage payment* is often based on the amount of time an employee works. Wages may be stated by different time periods, such as by the hour or by the week. A *salary payment*, on the other hand, is usually stated semimonthly (twice a month), monthly, or by the year.

Hourly (Regular) Rate. The regular rate of pay for an employee who is paid by the hour is known as the *hourly rate*. This rate is then quoted as "so much per hour"—for example, $3.20 per hour. An employee who works more than 40 hours in a work week at a business under the Fair Labor Standards Act is paid at least 1½ times the hourly rate for each hour worked over 40.

> *Example:* John Yin is paid $3.20 per hour at the regular rate. He is paid 1½ times $3.20, or $4.80 for each hour over 40. John's wage payment for a 44-hour week is $128 for the first 40 hours plus $19.20 (4 × $4.80) for the 4 overtime hours, or a total of $147.20 ($128 + $19.20).

Weekly Rate. A *weekly rate* is the amount that is paid to an employee by the week for a certain number of hours per week. The hourly rate for this employee is obtained by dividing the weekly wage payment by that number of hours.

> *Example:* Linda Carter is paid $132 for a 40-hour week. Her hourly rate is $132 divided by 40 hours, or $3.30 an hour. If she works overtime, she earns 1½ times the

$3.30, or $4.95 for each hour worked over 40 hours. For a 45-hour week, Linda receives $132 for the first 40 hours plus $24.75 (5 × $4.95) for the 5 overtime hours, or a total of $156.75 ($132 + $24.75).

The last two columns in the table of Illustration 5 show the hourly and overtime rates based on the weekly wage payments of a typical employee.

AN EMPLOYEE'S WAGE PAYMENTS FOR DIFFERENT TIME PERIODS

Yearly	*Monthly*	*Weekly*	*Hourly Rate* (40-hour week)*	*Overtime Rate (Over 40 hours)*
$ 7,200	$ 600	$138.46	$3.462	$5.19
7,500	625	144.23	3.606	5.41
7,800	650	150.00	3.750	5.63
8,400	700	161.54	4.039	6.06
9,000	750	173.08	4.327	6.49
9,600	800	184.62	4.616	6.92
10,200	850	196.15	4.904	7.36
10,800	900	207.69	5.192	7.79
11,400	950	219.23	5.481	8.22
12,000	1,000	230.77	5.769	8.65

Illustration 5
Hourly and Overtime Rates Based on an Employee's Weekly Wage Payments

* **NOTE:** In this textbook, compute the hourly rate by dividing the wage payment by the hours worked and then rounding the result to 3 decimal places as shown for the first example in the above table:

$138.46 ÷ 40 hours worked = $3.4615 or *$3.462 hourly rate*

Figure the overtime rate by multiplying the hourly rate by 1.5 and then rounding the result to 2 decimal places:

$3.462 × 1.5 = $5.193 or *$5.19 overtime rate*

Other Wages. Salaries and wages may also be paid annually, monthly, semimonthly (twice a month), or biweekly (every two weeks). If earnings are paid on another basis other than weekly, the weekly amount must be figured first in order to compute the hourly rate and the overtime rate. For the weekly pay rate (if earnings are paid twice a month), the semimonthly amount is first multiplied by 24 and then the product is divided by 52.

Example: If wages of $360 are paid twice a month, the hourly rate and the overtime rate would be:
$360 × 24 = $8,640 per year
$8,640 ÷ 52 = $166.1538 or $166.15 per week
$166.15 ÷ 40 hours = $4.1537 or $4.154 per hour (*hourly rate*)
$4.154 × 1.5 = $6.231 or $6.23 per hour (*overtime rate*)

To find the weekly pay rate, a monthly salary should be first multiplied by 12 and then the product is divided by 52.

Example: If a salary of $720 per month is paid, the hourly rate and the overtime rate would be:
$720 × 12 = $8,640 per year
$8,640 ÷ 52 = $166.1538 or $166.15 per week
$166.15 ÷ 40 hrs. = $4.1537 or $4.154 per hour (*hourly rate*)
$4.154 × 1.5 = $6.231 or $6.23 per hour (*overtime rate*)

An annual salary or wages may be quoted as a certain stated amount to a person who applies for a job. However, the amount quoted is always changed to a monthly, semimonthly, biweekly, or weekly amount after the person is hired. Illustration 5 shows how the different rates of wage payments are computed from the yearly amount.

PIECE RATE

The earnings of an employee paid by the *piece rate* are determined by multiplying the number of pieces produced by the rate per piece. For example, a worker who produces 2,400 pieces at 7¢ per piece during a 40-hour week is paid $168 (2,400 × $0.07) for the week.

The hourly rate for an employee paid on a piece-rate basis is obtained by dividing the total weekly earnings by the total number of hours worked in the same week. In the above example, the hourly rate is $168 divided by 40 hours, or $4.20 per hour. Under the Fair Labor Standards Act, the hourly rate of a piece-rate worker must be at least the minimum wage rate of $2.90.

The Fair Labor Standards Act provides that on a piece-rate basis the hourly rate is computed by totaling all weekly earnings of piece-rate workers and all other sources (such as production bonuses). This sum is then divided by the total hours worked during the week to arrive at the "hourly rate" for that week.

A piece-rate worker with overtime beyond 40 hours a week is entitled to the hourly rate (as figured above) for all hours worked plus half of the hourly rate for hours worked over 40 per week. In this textbook, this is the procedure that is to be used when figuring the weekly earnings for a piece-rate worker who has overtime.

Example: During the week, Raul Chavez worked 45 hours and produced 2,120 units at a piece rate of 7¢ for each unit. His piece-rate earnings for that week were $148.40 (2,120 × $0.07) while his hourly rate for that week was $3.30 ($148.40 ÷ 45 hours). Besides his hourly rate, he is entitled to $1.65 (half of his hourly rate—$3.30 ÷ 2) for each hour worked over 40—or $8.25 ($1.65 × 5 overtime hours). His total earnings for the week were $156.65 ($148.40 + $8.25).

NOTE: In computing his hourly piece-rate earnings, the 5 overtime hours were included. Therefore, Raul is entitled to only half of his hourly rate for the 5 overtime hours. This gives him 1½ times the hourly rate for the 5 overtime hours as required by law.

Another way to pay piece-rate workers for overtime (when it is agreed upon before the work is begun) is to pay 1½ times the piece rate for each unit produced during the overtime hours. The piece rate must be the one actually paid during nonovertime hours and must be enough to yield at least the minimum wage per hour.

COMMISSION

In some businesses, all salary or wage payments of certain employees are made on a *commission* basis. This is true for a salesperson who is often paid a certain percentage of sales as a commission. For example, a salesperson may receive a 10% commission on all sales. If the yearly sales amount to $93,000, the commission is $9,300. Sometimes the commission is "graduated"—which means the percentage changes at various levels. In the same way, a salesperson might have an estimated sales quota of $100,000 to be reached during a certain year. Besides the base salary or wage payment, a commission of 5% is to be paid on sales above $100,000. If the salesperson's sales for the year were $120,000, the commission is $1,000 ($20,000 × 0.05) plus the base salary or wage payment. In keeping payroll records, a commission is figured as part of a wage or a salary payment.

BONUS

If a *bonus* payment is to be a part of the hourly rate at which a worker is employed, it must be included when computing the hourly and overtime rates of pay. No problem arises in computing overtime if the bonus is for only one weekly pay period. The amount of the bonus is just added to the other earnings of the employee, and the total is divided by the total hours worked.

In many bonus plans, however, the calculation of the bonus must be delayed over a period of time longer than a work week. It is often difficult to figure the bonus until some time later. When the bonus can be determined, it must be distributed over the work weeks of the period during which it was earned. The employee must then receive an extra amount of earnings for each week that was worked overtime during the period equal to half the hourly rate of pay that applied to the bonus for that week, multiplied by the number of overtime hours worked during the week.

A bonus payment does not need to be included as part of earnings in figuring overtime pay (1) if it is paid without a previous promise or agreement, (2) if the employee has no contract to receive a bonus, and (3) if the bonus payment and the amount determined is not decided until the end of the period for which the bonus is paid. Such a bonus payment is known as a "discretionary bonus." A business paying such a bonus should obtain a ruling from the Wages and Hours Division of the U.S. Department of Labor to be sure that the bonus is not needed in computing overtime. A business often pays such bonuses as gifts or holiday presents. These amounts usually are not included in computing the hourly rate for overtime.

EMPLOYEE PROFIT-SHARING PLANS

Regulations have been set up under the Fair Labor Standards Act for payments to employees under profit-sharing, thrift, or savings plans. These rules cannot be explained here. In general, however, the amount received by an employee under most profit-sharing plans need not be thought of as a part of the hourly pay rate in computing overtime. The Wages and Hours Division should advise a company in such cases.

ACTIVITY 4

On pages 51 and 52 is a study guide for this section. Be sure you know all the answers to these questions and problems before you begin the next section. If your teacher asks for your completed study guide, be sure your name appears in the proper place.

---

3 BASIC PAYROLL RECORDS AND REQUIRED DATA

Accurate records are kept by businesses that follow good accounting practices. Every employer must keep certain records about each worker who is covered by the minimum wage and overtime pay requirements of the Fair Labor Standards Act. This Act does not require certain forms for keeping these records but does specify that the records provide the following information:

1. *Identifying information*—includes an employee's full name, address, birth date, sex, and job description.
2. *Hourly records*—to show the time of day and the day of the week when the work week begins, the hours worked each day, and the total hours worked each work week.
3. *Wage or salary information*—includes the basis on which wages are paid (hourly, weekly, piecework, etc.), hourly pay rate for any week when overtime is worked, total daily or weekly straight-time earnings, total overtime earnings, additions or deductions from the employee's wages for each pay period, total wages paid each pay period, and the dates of payment and of the pay period covered by the payment.

An employer must keep a record of the hours worked for each day and work week by all employees except those who are exempt from the overtime rate of pay as required by law. Management, administrative, supervisory personnel, and commission salespersons are usually exempt under provisions of the law.

TIME CARDS

Any method of keeping time that provides the needed data is satisfactory if it is complete and accurate. An employee may ring in on a *time card* that is inserted in a time clock which records the time (such as the time cards shown in Illustration 6). The card at the left is the kind used in most businesses and shows two 12-hour periods from midnight until noon and from noon until midnight. The card at the right uses a consecutive 24-hour period starting at midnight and ending the next midnight. The hours from midnight until noon are from 1 to 12 and the hours from noon to the next midnight are from 13 to 24.

As you examine these time cards, note that the left card lists the days of the week down the card from top to bottom with Morning, Afternoon, and Overtime hours printed across the card. In the card at the right, the days of the week are listed across the bottom while the time is recorded from the bottom to the top each day. For this course, the time cards used will be like the one on the left which uses two 12-hour periods for each day.

OTHER TIME RECORDS

If time cards are not used, another kind of record must be kept of hours worked by each employee if the business is under the Fair Labor Standards Act. A departmental *time record* such as the one in Illustration 7 may be used. This record is signed by each employee under the supervision of a department head. Or the supervisor, department head, or timekeeper can keep the record. All time records upon which wage-and-hour computations are based must be kept for 3 years.

PRODUCTION RECORDS

In a company with employees who work on production (especially when such employees are paid on a piece-rate basis), some record of the production for each employee must be kept. Illustration 8 shows two daily cost cards that are often used for computing the earnings of such employees. These records are also used by a business to compute job or production costs. If employees work on a piece-rate basis, the hours worked and the amount produced are both needed by the payroll department to compute earnings.

From this discussion, it can be seen that much information must be given to meet the requirements of the various laws. If a business tried to keep separate records to meet the requirements of each law, there would be much confusion. Every business therefore should try to design records that will provide all the data in one basic set of forms.

In most businesses, all payroll information can be kept in these three basic forms:

1. A personnel record
2. A payroll register
3. An employee's earnings record

Each form will be discussed and illustrated as its use is explained. Obviously, the forms kept by different businesses are not the same and are often known by different names.

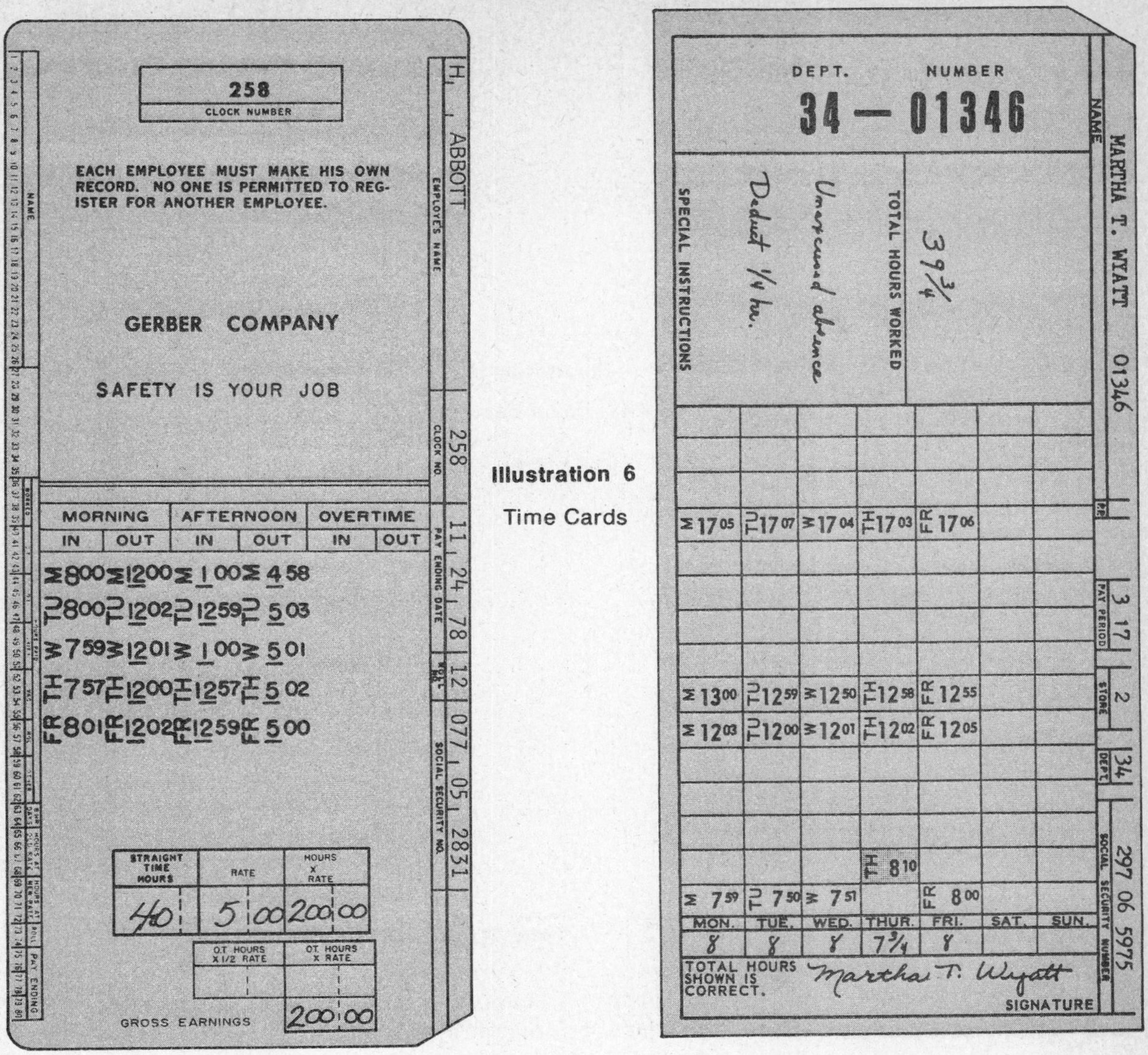

258
CLOCK NUMBER

EACH EMPLOYEE MUST MAKE HIS OWN RECORD. NO ONE IS PERMITTED TO REGISTER FOR ANOTHER EMPLOYEE.

GERBER COMPANY

SAFETY IS YOUR JOB

EMPLOYE'S NAME: H. ABBOTT
CLOCK NO: 258
PAY ENDING DATE: 11 24 78
ROLL NO: 12
SOCIAL SECURITY NO: 077 05 2831

MORNING IN	MORNING OUT	AFTERNOON IN	AFTERNOON OUT	OVERTIME IN	OVERTIME OUT
M 8 00	M 12 00	M 1 00	M 4 58		
TU 8 00	TU 12 02	TU 12 59	TU 5 03		
W 7 59	W 12 01	W 1 00	W 5 01		
TH 7 57	TH 12 00	TH 12 57	TH 5 02		
FR 8 01	FR 12 02	FR 12 59	FR 5 00		

STRAIGHT TIME HOURS	RATE	HOURS X RATE
40	5.00	200.00

O.T. HOURS X 1/2 RATE	O.T. HOURS X RATE

GROSS EARNINGS 200.00

DEPT. 34 — NUMBER 01346

NAME: MARTHA T. WYATT 01346

TOTAL HOURS WORKED: 39¾

SPECIAL INSTRUCTIONS: Unexcused absence Deduct ¼ hr.

PAY PERIOD 3 17 · STORE 2 · DEPT. 34 · SOCIAL SECURITY NUMBER 297 06 5975

M 17 05 · TU 17 07 · W 17 04 · TH 17 03 · FR 17 06

M 13 00 · TU 12 59 · W 12 50 · TH 12 58 · FR 12 55

M 12 03 · TU 12 00 · W 12 01 · TH 12 02 · FR 12 05

TH 8 10

M 7 59 · TU 7 50 · W 7 51 · FR 8 00

MON.	TUE.	WED.	THUR.	FRI.	SAT.	SUN.
8	8	8	7¾	8		

TOTAL HOURS SHOWN IS CORRECT. Martha T. Wyatt SIGNATURE

Illustration 6

Time Cards

TIME RECORD

DEPARTMENT *Assembly* FOR WEEK ENDING *March 20, 19--*

EMPL. NO.	NAME	M	Tu	W	Thu	F	Sat	Sun	REGULAR HOURS	OVERTIME HOURS	TOTAL HOURS WORKED
6	Bruegman, Joan	8	8	8	8	8			40		40
3	Chavez, Raul	8	8	8	8	4	8		40	4	44
7	Hammond, Richard	—	8	8	8	8			32		32
4	Pavick, Dorothy	8	8	4	8	8	4		40		40
1	Sanchez, Phillip	8	8	8	10	8			40	2	42
5	Toyota, Mary	8	8	8	8	8			40		40
2	Turner, Roosevelt	8	8	8	8	8	8		40	8	48
6	Wade, Pamela	8	8	8	8	8			40		40

Illustration 7

Departmental Time Record

DAILY COST CARD

No. 43

NAME PETERS, GREG DATE 7/1/--

CLOCK	LAPSED TIME	OPERATION & ORDER NO.		NO. PIECES	RATE PER C	AM'T EARNED
			OFF			
			ON			
			OFF			
			ON			
M 4.9	0.9	3799	OFF	150	0.80	1.20
M 4.0			ON			
M 4.0	0.7	3796	OFF	75	1.20	0.90
M 3.3			ON			
M 3.3	1.8	3784	OFF	200	1.40	2.80
M 1.5			ON			
M 12.5	2.4	3772	OFF	250	1.40	3.50
M 10.1			ON			
M 10.1	2.1	3761	OFF	50	5.20	2.60
M 8.0			ON			
TOTAL	7.9				TOTAL	11.00

Illustration 8

Production Records

JOB COST CARD

No. 749 Date 4/6/--

Name RILEY, PEGGY

CLOCK TIME RECORD	TIME		JOB NO.
		OFF	
		ON	
		OFF	
		ON	
		OFF	
		ON	
TU PM 5:00	1 30	OFF	18
TU PM 3:30		ON	
TU PM 3:30	42	OFF	22
TU PM 2:48		ON	
TU PM 2:48	1 47	OFF	96
TU PM 1:01		ON	
TU PM 12:00	54	OFF	96
TU AM 11:06		ON	
TU AM 11:06	42	OFF	235
TU AM 10:24		ON	
TU AM 10:24	1 09	OFF	15A
TU AM 9:15		ON	
TU AM 9:15	1 15	OFF	26
TU AM 8:00		ON	
TOTAL	7 HRS. 59 MIN.		

PERSONNEL RECORD

The employee *personnel record* is needed by every business—both large and small. This record is usually prepared at the time an employee is hired. Some businesses use the application of the employee as the personnel record. Usually more information than that shown on the application is needed in a personnel record. In most companies, a personnel record takes the form of a card or sheet on which detailed information is shown.

Personnel records may be in the form of sheets or cards that are kept in a visible file or in a ring binder. Usually the personnel record is kept in the personnel department or in the payroll department.

ACTIVITY 5

Since you will be responsible for keeping the payroll records of Solarheat Systems Inc. in your new position, your next step is to complete your own personnel record (on page 53). List *General Office Clerk* as your job description, *3* as your employee number, and *$135* as your wages per week. Figure your hourly and overtime rates. Enter *$17 per mo.* for your deduction of medical insurance.

PAYROLL REGISTER

Various types of forms for keeping a record of the hours worked by each employee have already been described. A *payroll register* is a form or record that is used to summarize for each pay period information pertaining to the salary or wages paid to all employees. This form is also known as a payroll journal, a payroll record, a payroll report, or a payroll sheet.

A payroll register should supply the following information:

1. The title of the form
2. The department or branch indicated—(Some large businesses with many departments or branches prepare separate payroll registers for each department or branch on each payday. In such cases, it is best that a company design the payroll register so that this can be shown.)
3. The period covered by the payroll and the date on which the employee is paid
4. A column for the employee's identifying number—(usually the time clock number)
5. The name of each employee
6. A column for the marital status and the tax withholding allowances claimed by each employee—("M" for Married and "S" for

PERSONAL AND EMPLOYMENT DATA

Solarheat Systems Inc.

NAME MAHLE (Last) JUDITH (First) FRANCES (Middle) SOC. SEC. NO. 239-76-3077

ADDRESS 5609 ALOMAR DRIVE (Street Address) CLOVIS, CA. 93612 (City, State, ZIP Code) TELEPHONE NO. (209) 863-2914

PERSON NOTIFIED IN CASE OF EMERGENCY C.F. MAHLE (Name); 475 KERN RD.; FRESNO, CA 93706 (Address); (209) 299-5107 (Telephone Number)

LAST EMPLOYER DANTE INC.; 2200 N. ILA AVENUE; FRESNO, CA 93705 (Company Name and Address); (209) 829-1233 (Telephone Number); OFFICE CLERK (Your Job Description)

REASON FOR LEAVING LIMITED OPPORTUNITY FOR ADVANCEMENT

PHYSICAL DESCRIPTION (Complete only if work related) ____ Height ____ Weight ____ Other Description

DATE EMPLOYED NOVEMBER 25, 19--

JOB DESCRIPTION GENERAL OFFICE CLERK

DEPARTMENT OFFICE

EMPLOYEE CLOCK NO. 3

INCOME TAX WITHHOLDING ALLOWANCES 1

MARITAL STATUS SINGLE

HIRED AS: [X] Full Time [ ] Part Time [ ] Temporary

SALARY/WAGES PER WEEK $ 125.00

Hourly Rate $ 3.125 Overtime Rate $ 4.69

DEDUCTIONS: Credit Union .... $____

Group Insurance ..... $____

Medical Insurance .... $ 17 PER MO.

Union Dues .... $____

U.S. Savings Bond .... $____

Other .... $____

DATE OF BIRTH AUGUST 24, 196

DATE LEFT EMPLOYMENT DECEMBER 1, 19--

Remarks: JOINED THE U.S. NAVY

Illustration 9 Personnel Record

Single; this information affects the amount of income tax withheld)

7. A record of the time worked—(Some companies show detailed information in the payroll register as to hours worked each day by each employee when separate time records are not available for this data. If it is not shown in detail, it must be given on the employee's time record.)
8. A column for the amount earned by the employee at the regular rate of pay
9. A column for the amount earned by the employee at the overtime rate of pay
10. A separate column to record the total earnings for each employee
11. Separate columns for each amount deducted from total earnings and a column that shows the total deductions
12. A column that shows the net pay, which is the amount paid to each employee (TOTAL EARNINGS − TOTAL DEDUCTIONS = NET PAY)—(When salaries or wages are paid by check, this column is usually followed by a column for the number of the check given to the employee.)
13. A special column that shows the part of an employee's salary or wages which is taxable under the Federal Insurance Contributions Act and other laws that require payment of the tax only on earnings up to a certain amount—(This column is often omitted in the payroll register and is added to the employee's earnings record, as discussed on page 14).

For example, an employee earning over $22,900 yearly will have no deductions made from wages for FICA tax purposes after these deductions were made on the first $22,900 earned during the year. If a part of the earnings received for one pay period brings the total up to $22,900 (the maximum), the rest of the earnings for the period will not be taxed.

The Payroll Register for Solarheat Systems Inc. for the week ending December 2 is shown on page 14 (Illustration 10). The forms that you will use to prepare the payroll for the four weeks are on pages 57 to 135.

PAYROLL REGISTER

WEEK ENDED *December 2, 19--*

DATE OF PAYMENT *December 5, 19--*

	EMPL NO.	EMPLOYEE'S NAME	MARITAL STATUS	ALLOW-ANCES	TOTAL HOURS	EARNINGS REGULAR	EARNINGS OVERTIME	EARNINGS TOTAL	DEDUCTIONS FEDERAL INC. TAX	DEDUCTIONS FICA TAX	DEDUCTIONS GROUP INSURANCE	DEDUCTIONS MEDICAL INSURANCE	DEDUCTIONS OTHER	DEDUCTIONS TOTAL	PAID NET PAY	PAID CK NO.	
1	1	Flores, Jesse	M	4		460 00		460 00	73 90	28 20				102 10	357 90		1
2	2	Jackson, Paula	M	0	40.0	180 00		180 00	21 10	11 03				32 13	147 87		2
3	12	Klaus, Elsie	M	2		381 39		381 39	59 60	23 38				82 98	298 41		3
4	13	Hirasuna, James	M	4		398 69		398 69	54 90	24 44				79 34	319 35		4
5	22	Salazar, Ruben	M	2	42.5	276 00	25 88	301 88	39 60	18 51			U 5 00	63 11	238 77		5
6	23	Brown, Leroy	M	5	43.7	174 68	26 40	201 08	11 70	12 33			U 5 00	29 03	172 05		6
7	24	McLaughlin, Darlene	S	1	39.0	195 00		195 00	27 20	11 95			U 5 00	44 15	150 85		7
8	25	Vukovich, Diane	M	2	42.0	216 00	16 20	232 20	24 90	14 23			U 5 00	44 13	188 07		8
9	26	Riley, Sam	M	2	42.0	236 00	17 70	253 70	28 60	15 55			U 5 00	49 15	204 55		9
10	27	Neufeld, Sara	M	0	41.8	226 86	17 10	243 96	32 80	14 95			U 5 00	52 75	191 21		10
11	28	Leonardo, Mike	M	2	40.5	180 00	3 38	183 38	15 90	11 24			U 5 00	32 14	151 24		11
12	42	Baker, Edna	M	0	40.0	230 02		230 02	30 60	14 10			U 5 00	49 70	180 32		12
13	43	Svenson, Karl	S	1	40.0	208 20		208 20	29 60	12 76			U 5 00	47 36	160 84		13
14																	14
15																	15
16																	16
17																	17
18		TOTAL				3,362 84	106 66	3,469 50	450 40	212 67			U 45 00	708 07	2,761 43		18

Other Deductions: B—U.S. Savings Bonds; C—Credit Union; U—Union Dues; UF—United Fund

Illustration 10

Payroll Register

EMPLOYEE'S EARNINGS RECORD

An *employee's earnings record* is an additional record that is needed to provide a summary of information about each employee. If this form is properly designed, anyone who works in the payroll department can obtain most of the data needed about each employee's earnings. Information for quarterly and annual reports under various laws is obtained from this form. While employee's earnings records may change slightly in different businesses, the one used by Solarheat Systems Inc. is like the forms found in most companies (see Illustration 11). The Employees' Earnings Records, with entries already made for the first nine weeks of the present quarter (including the week ending December 2), are on pages 107 to 135.

Solarheat Systems Inc. pays salaries or wages to each of its employees every week. Therefore, a separate line is provided on the Employee's Earnings Record to record the information from the Payroll Register for each weekly pay period. There are also two lines at the bottom of the Employee's Earnings Record on which the quarter and yearly totals are entered. Separate sheets are kept for each employee, which provide a one-year payroll summary for that employee. In a business that pays salaries or wages monthly, only 12 lines (3 for each quarter) are needed to record the data for the 12 pay periods. In the same way, for a business on a semimonthly payroll, only 24 lines (6 for each quarter) are needed to record the data for the year.

An employee's earnings record usually shows:

1. The title of the form
2. The number of the pay period in each quarter
3. The date on which the pay period ends
4. Separate columns to record the earnings (regular; overtime; total) for each pay period—(Some employee's earnings records also include a column to record the days or hours worked in the pay period.
5. Separate columns to record the amounts of the deductions and a column to show the total deductions—(Although a column is not needed for the total of all deductions, having such a column makes it easier to figure net earnings and to balance the record.)
6. A column that shows the net pay, which is the amount paid to each employee on every payday—(This amount is the difference between the TOTAL EARNINGS column and the TOTAL DEDUCTIONS column.)
7. A column that accumulates the amount of taxable earnings for each pay period on each line—(This information is needed when an employee is being paid wages over the maximum amount that is taxable under various laws.)

For example, the maximum taxable amount of wages under the FICA Act is $22,900 while it is only $6,000 for unemployment tax. Some businesses include a separate column to accumulate taxable earnings under each law. This is not needed, however, since the column is used only as a reminder to show when this maximum is reached under the various laws so that no other taxes are deducted.

EMPLOYEE'S EARNINGS RECORD

NAME *Flores, Jesse* EMPL. NO. *1*

ADDRESS *912 Elm Street; Clovis, CA 93612*

SOC. SEC. NO. *123-16-7048* ALLOWANCES *4* MARRIED *X* SINGLE ____

DEPARTMENT *Administration*

OCCUPATION *General Manager*

DATE EMPLOYED *January 3, 1977* DATE TERMINATED ____

DEDUCTIONS:
Credit Union ____
Group Insurance *$10 per mo.*
Medical Insurance *$27 per mo.*
U.S. Savings Bond ____
Union Dues ____
United Fund ____
Other ____

EARNINGS:
Yearly *$23,920*
Monthly ____
Weekly *$460*
Hourly ____
Commission ____
Piece Rate Per Unit ____

PAY PERIOD		EARNINGS			DEDUCTIONS								
WEEK	WEEK ENDED	REGULAR	OVERTIME	TOTAL	FEDERAL INC. TAX	FICA TAX	GROUP INSURANCE	MEDICAL INSURANCE	OTHER	TOTAL	NET PAY	ACCUMULATED TAXABLE EARNINGS	WEEK
TOTALS 3 QUAR.		17,940 00		17,940 00	2,882 10	1,099 80	90 00	243 00		4,314 90	13,625 10	17,940 00	
1	10/7	460 00		460 00	73 90	28 20				102 10	357 90	18,400 00	1
2	10/14	460 00		460 00	73 90	28 20		27 00		129 10	330 90	18,860 00	2
3	10/21	460 00		460 00	73 90	28 20				102 10	357 90	19,320 00	3
4	10/28	460 00		460 00	73 90	28 20	10 00			112 10	347 90	19,780 00	4
5	11/4	460 00		460 00	73 90	28 20				102 10	357 90	20,240 00	5
6	11/11	460 00		460 00	73 90	28 20		27 00		129 10	330 90	20,700 00	6
7	11/18	460 00		460 00	73 90	28 20				102 10	357 90	21,160 00	7
8	11/25	460 00		460 00	73 90	28 20	10 00			112 10	347 90	21,620 00	8
9	12/2	460 00		460 00	73 90	28 20				102 10	357 90	22,080 00	9
13													13
QUARTER TOTALS													
YEARLY TOTALS													

Illustration 11

Employee's Earnings Record

8. Separate lines to show the quarter and yearly totals that are needed for the various federal, state, and local reports.
9. Information about each employee that is needed to prepare the payroll—(Some businesses include most of this information in the employee's personnel record.)

Having the right data in the employee's earnings record saves much time in preparing payrolls. Note that the Employee's Earnings Record used by Solarheat Systems Inc. (Illustration 11) shows the:

a. Name, address, job description, social security number, time clock number, and salary or wage data.
b. The marital status and the number of tax withholding allowances claimed by the employee for income tax purposes.
c. Deductions, other than those deductions for income and FICA taxes, that are to be made each pay period for the employee.

After the payroll register is completed for each pay period, the data for each employee is recorded on that employee's earnings record. These figures are placed on the line that shows the pay period in which the salaries or wages were paid. While the payroll register is a summary of the amounts paid to all employees on each payday, the employee's earnings record is a summary for gathering each employee's payroll data during the entire year.

In many businesses a system of forms is used so that the payroll register, the employee's earnings record, and the payroll check are written at the same time. Some of these systems are described in Section 10.

In Section 4 you will be given the data for the payroll work that was completed for the week ending December 2 and for the payroll to be prepared for the week ending December 9.

ACTIVITY 6

Use the Employee's Earnings Record on page 111 to enter your own payroll data as follows: your name; your employee number, 3; your street address; for the city, state, and ZIP code, use *Clovis, CA 93612*; social security number, *384-28-8971*; allowances, *1*; marital status, *X* for *Single*; department, *Office*; occupation, *General Office Clerk*; date employed, *December 3, 19–*; deduction for medical insurance, *$17 per mo.*; and weekly earnings, *$135.* Figure the hourly rate.

ACTIVITY 7

On pages 55 and 56 is a study guide for this section. Be sure you know all the answers to these questions and problems before you begin the next section. If your teacher asks for your completed study guide, be sure your name appears in the proper place.

4 PREPARING THE PAYROLL

As a new employee of Solarheat Systems Inc., you are responsible for preparing the weekly payroll. Therefore, you will need specific information about the payroll policies of the company. The person whom you replaced prepared a summary of payroll data to help you. This section gives basic information for preparing each weekly payroll.

BASIC PAYROLL INFORMATION

EMPLOYEE IDENTIFICATION

Each employee of Solarheat Systems Inc. is given an identifying number. These numbers appear on the time cards and on the payroll records. The numbers that are presently being used in the different groups may be given to new employees as they are hired.

NOS.

1-10 *ADMINISTRATIVE AND OFFICE EMPLOYEES*

[1] Jesse Flores, the General Manager, receives a salary of $23,920 per year or $460 per week. He is exempt from the overtime provisions of the Fair Labor Standards Act.

[2] Paula Jackson, a secretary, receives wages of $180 per week and overtime pay when she works over 40 hours during a week.

[3] As General Office Clerk, you will receive wages of $135 per week and overtime pay when you work over 40 hours during a week.

11-20 ***SALESPERSONS (Exempt from the Overtime Provisions of the Fair Labor Standards Act)***

[12] Elsie Klaus—8% commission on sales

[13] James Hirasuna—8% commission on sales

21-40 ***PRODUCTION WORKERS ON AN HOURLY BASIS (Subject to Overtime Rate Over 40 Hours Per Week)***

[22] Ruben Salazar—$6.90 per hour

[23] Leroy Brown—$4.40 per hour

[24] Darlene McLaughlin—$5 per hour

[25] Diane Vukovich—$5.40 per hour

[26] Sam Riley—$5.90 per hour

[27] Sara Neufeld—$5.70 per hour

[28] Mike Leonardo—$4.50 per hour

41-50 ***PRODUCTION WORKERS ON A PIECE-RATE BASIS (Subject to Overtime Provisions of the Fair Labor Standards Act and the Minimum Hourly Rate of $2.90)***

[42] Edna Baker—14¢ per unit produced

[43] Karl Svenson—12¢ per unit produced

RECORDING THE TIME WORKED

You will need information about the methods followed by Solarheat Systems Inc. to keep a record of the time worked by the employees. This data is given for each type of employee.

Administrative and Office Employees. Since Mr. Flores, the General Manager, is exempt from overtime pay, he does not record his time worked. On each Monday, the other office employees will give you a record that shows the hours worked for each day of the previous week.

Salespersons. No record of the time worked is kept by the salespersons, but each Monday you will receive a report of sales made by each salesperson during the previous week. This is done so that you can figure the commissions.

Production Workers. All of the production workers use a time clock to record the hours they work each day.

Working Hours. The work week is from Sunday through Saturday. The working hours are from 8 a.m. to 12 noon and from 1 p.m. to 5 p.m. with an hour for lunch. The contract between Solarheat Systems Inc. and the union for the production workers states that for any time worked after 5 p.m. on weekdays or for any time worked on Saturday each employee is paid at 1½ times the regular hourly rate.

The penalty to an employee for being late to work is in 10ths of an hour—1/10th of an hour for each 6 minutes or fraction of 6 minutes. For example, if a time card showed 8:03 a.m., the penalty is 1/10th (0.1) of an hour or a time credit of 7.9 hours (8.0 − 0.1 = 7.9 hours) if the employee worked the rest of a normal day. In other words, an employee is given a penalty of 1/10th (0.1) of an hour for being late 1 to 6 minutes, 2/10ths (0.2) of an hour for 7 to 12 minutes, 3/10ths (0.3) of an hour for 13 to 18 minutes, etc. An employee who leaves work early is penalized in the same way. Leaving a few minutes after 5 p.m. does not make up the time for being late in the morning or coming back late after the lunch hour.

The time cards for Solarheat employees show their starting time at a few minutes before 8 a.m. and their quitting time at a few minutes after 5 p.m. Overtime is not paid unless an employee works at least 30 minutes after 5 p.m. except on Saturday.

TIME AND METHOD FOR PAYING SALARIES AND WAGES

The payroll is prepared on the Monday following each work week, and employees are paid in cash on Tuesday. Detailed instructions for the payroll procedures are given in the information that follows.

SUMMARY OF PROCEDURES FOR PREPARING THE WEEKLY PAYROLL

Although detailed instructions for each weekly payroll are given in Section 5, the following summary will help you to understand the various steps as you complete the work for each week.

1. *Determine the earnings of the General Manager and the office employees*. Mr. Flores earns a weekly salary of $460. The earnings of the two office employees (including yourself) are determined from the weekly time records.
2. *Figure the earnings of the salespersons*. You will be given weekly sales reports by the salespersons to use in figuring their commissions.
3. *Figure the earnings of the hourly production workers*. A time card for each employee will give you the hours worked.
4. *Figure the earnings of the production piece-rate workers*. The data for figuring these earnings are given in the piece-rate production reports.
5. *List the earnings of the employees in the payroll register*. After Step 4, you will have the data for recording the employee number, name, marital status, exemptions, total hours worked, and the earnings of each employee (both regular and overtime) in the payroll register.
6. *Figure the deductions for income tax*. For each pay period, a deduction is made for income tax to be withheld from the earnings of each employee. This amount is entered in the payroll register.
7. *Figure the deductions for FICA tax*. Like Step 6, a deduction is made for FICA tax from each employee's earnings and is entered in the payroll register.
8. *List the other deductions*. All of the other deductions that are to be withheld from the earnings of each employee are entered in the payroll register. These may be for group insurance, medical insurance, union dues, etc.
9. *Figure the total deductions and the net pay*. In this step, the deductions for each employee are totaled. Then the DEDUCTIONS columns are balanced with the column showing the total deductions. The net pay is computed for each employee as follows: Total Earnings − Total Deductions = Net Pay.
10. *Total and balance the payroll register*. The entire payroll register is balanced to be sure that all the amounts have been properly entered and totaled.
11. *Pay the payroll*. This step involves the actual money payment to each employee.
12. *Enter data from the payroll register to each employee's earnings record*. Here all the payroll figures are entered on each employee's earnings record from the payroll register.

The next section will show how the last employee followed these steps to complete the payroll for the week ending December 2. You will then follow similar steps to complete the payroll for the week of December 3-9.

5 PREPARING THE PAYROLL FOR DECEMBER 3-9

As explained in Section 4, there are certain steps to be followed in completing the payroll for each week. In this section, you are given the instructions for each step.

First, you will be shown the instructions and the illustrations of the payroll for the week ending December 2 as it was prepared by the last employee. Next, you will be given similar information for preparing the payroll for the week of December 3-9. The instructions for December 3-9 are indicated by a border around the information for this week.

The forms on pages 57 to 135 are the ones you will need to complete the payroll for the week of December 3-9 and for the remaining weeks in December.

STEP 1—DETERMINE THE EARNINGS OF THE GENERAL MANAGER AND THE OFFICE EMPLOYEES

For the week ending December 2, Jesse Flores, the General Manager, was paid his regular salary of $460 per week. The office employees were paid their regular weekly wages unless they were asked to work overtime or if they were absent for personal reasons other than illness. Each Monday, the office employees report the hours they have worked on a Weekly Time Record. Below is the Weekly Time Record for Ms. Paula Jackson (Illustration 12) for the week ending December 2. Since she had no time lost and did not work overtime, she had worked 40 hours—earning her regular wages of $180. Now, you are to complete Step 1 for the week of December 3-9 as explained below.

WEEKLY TIME RECORD — Solarheat Systems Inc.

For week ending *December 2* 19--

Name *Paula Jackson*

Dept. *Office* Employee No. *2*

DAY WORKED	REGULAR HOURS	OVERTIME HOURS	TOTAL HOURS WORKED
Monday	8.0		8.0
Tuesday	8.0		8.0
Wednesday	8.0		8.0
Thursday	8.0		8.0
Friday	8.0		8.0
Saturday			
Sunday			
		TOTAL HOURS ...	40.0

Illustration 12 Weekly Time Record

> **STEP 1—for December 3-9.**
> **Determine the Earnings of the General Manager and the Office Employees**
>
> Mr. Flores has no time record but received his regular salary this week. Use the Weekly Time Records for Ms. Jackson and yourself on page 57. Since there was no overtime or time lost for any reason, no special computation is necessary for these employees. Their regular weekly earnings are entered in the Payroll Register as you will be directed to do later in Step 5.

STEP 2—FIGURE THE EARNINGS OF THE SALESPERSONS

The earnings of the salespersons are figured from a Weekly Sales Report that shows their sales for the week. Both salespersons receive a commission of 8% of their sales. The Weekly Sales Report for the week ending December 2 (Illustration 13) is on the next page. Based on sales of $4,767.40, the commission of Elsie Klaus is $381.39. The commission of James Hirasuna on sales of $4,983.62 amounts to $398.69.

> **STEP 2—for December 3-9.**
> **Figure the Earnings of the Salespersons**
>
> Use the Weekly Sales Report for December 3-9 on page 57 to determine the commissions earned by both salespersons for this week.

WEEKLY SALES REPORT

Solarheat Systems Inc.

For week ending December 2 19--

NO.	SALESPERSON	SALES	X % RATE	= COMMISSION EARNED
12	Klaus, Elsie	$ 4,767.40	8%	$ 381.39
13	Hirasuna, James	4983.62	8%	398.69

TOTAL SALES $ 9,751.02 TOTAL COMMISSIONS $ 780.08

Illustration 13

Weekly Sales Report

STEP 3—FIGURE THE EARNINGS OF THE HOURLY PRODUCTION WORKERS

The time worked each day must be determined for each hourly production employee. The time card for Leroy Brown (Illustration 14) is shown below.

Note that Leroy Brown's time card showed he arrived at 7:56 a.m. on Monday morning and that he left at 12:03 p.m. for lunch. This meant that he worked a total of 4 hours—the normal morning schedule from 8 a.m. to 12 noon. He returned from lunch at 12:58 (1 p.m.) and left work at 5:06 p.m. (5 p.m.).Therefore, he worked from 1 p.m. to 5 p.m., or 4 more hours in the afternoon for a total of 8 hours for the day. This is entered on the time card as 8.0 regular hours. He did not work any overtime on Monday.

NAME LEROY BROWN

CLOCK NO. 23

SOC. SEC. NO. 263 23 3724

PERIOD WEEK ENDING DECEMBER 2, 19--

	MORNING In	MORNING Out	AFTERNOON In	AFTERNOON Out	NIGHT In	NIGHT Out	REGULAR HOURS	OVERTIME HOURS
M	7:56	12:03	12:58	5:08			8.0	
T	7:59	12:01	12:57	5:06			8.0	
W	7:54	12:05	12:59	6:00			8.0	1.0
T	8:15	12:03	12:56	5:03			7.7	
F	7:57	12:06	12:58	5:05			8.0	
S	8:57	12:03						3.0
S								
						TOTAL HOURS	39.7	4.0

TYPE	RATE	HOURS	EARNINGS
Regular	$4.40	39.7	$174.68
Overtime	6.60	4.0	26.40
Special			
TOTAL		43.7	$201.08

FOR PAYROLL USE ONLY

Illustration 14 Time Card

On Tuesday, he also worked a normal 8-hour day. Wednesday morning was normal, but Leroy worked until 6 p.m. in the afternoon or 1 hour overtime. This is then recorded as 8.0 hours regular time and 1.0 hour overtime.

On Thursday morning, Leroy Brown had car trouble on the way to work and did not arrive until 8:15 a.m. An employee who is late at Solarheat Systems is penalized 1/10th (0.1) of an hour for each 6 minutes, or a fraction of 6 minutes. Since Leroy was 15 minutes late, he is penalized for 3/10ths (0.3) of an hour. In other words, the 15 late minutes can be broken down into 6 + 6 + 3 = 15 minutes. Leroy is then penalized 2/10ths (0.2) of an hour for the two 6-minute segments and another 1/10th (0.1) of an hour for the 3-minute segment for a total penalty of 3/10th (0.3) of an hour. Therefore, Leroy's time for Thursday is recorded as 7.7 hours (8.0 − 0.3 = 7.7).

On Friday, Leroy Brown worked the usual 8-hour day but was asked to come in on Saturday to do some maintenance work on the equipment. He worked from 8:57 a.m. (9 a.m.) until 12:03 p.m. (12 noon) for a total of 3 hours. Since he received overtime pay (1½ × his regular hourly rate) for work on Saturday, his time of 3.0 hours is recorded in the O.T.(Overtime) HRS. column.

Leroy Brown's hours were then totaled to show that he had worked 39.7 regular hours and 4.0 overtime hours. His earnings for the week were determined by multiplying his hourly rate of $4.40 by 39.7 (the regular hours worked) for a regular earnings figure of $174.68

($4.40 × 39.7 = $174.68). His overtime rate of $6.60 ($4.40 × 1.5) was multiplied by 4.0 (the overtime hours) for an overtime earnings figure of $26.40 ($6.60 × 4.0 = $26.40). His total earnings for the week were $201.08 ($174.68 + $26.40 = $201.08).

STEP 3—for December 3-9.
Figure the Earnings of the Hourly Production Workers

Use the Time Cards for the hourly production workers on pages 58 and 59 to figure the weekly earnings as explained in the above procedure. As an example, use the time card on page 19. A summary of the hourly rates for these workers is given on page 16. The regular and overtime hours worked by each of these employees should be recorded on each time card.

STEP 4—FIGURE THE EARNINGS OF THE PRODUCTION PIECE-RATE WORKERS

The total production of each piece-rate employee must be determined by adding the units produced for each day on the Piece-Rate Production Report. Illustration 15 below shows that Edna Baker's production was 1,643 units (310 + 324 + 336 + 341 + 332 = 1,643). Edna is paid 14¢ per unit produced so by multiplying 1,643 (her units produced) by $0.14 (the rate per unit) gives a weekly earnings figure of $230.02 (1,643 × $0.14 = $230.02).

You must be sure that the hourly rate for each piece-rate worker (earnings ÷ hours worked) at least equals or exceeds the minimum wage of $2.90 per hour. For example, Edna Baker's hourly rate is $5.75 per hour ($230.02 ÷ 40 hours = $5.75). If Edna's hourly rate were less than $2.90, she would have been paid $2.90 per hour instead of the piece rate.

Remember that any time worked over 8 hours in one day must be paid at the overtime rate. See page 9 for instructions on figuring the overtime rate for a piece-rate worker.

STEP 4—for December 3-9.
Figure the Earnings of the Production Piece-Rate Workers

Use the Piece-Rate Production Report on page 60 to determine the earnings of the production piece-rate workers. Remember that the regular hourly earnings of each employee for the week must be at least $2.90 per hour.

STEP 5—LIST THE EARNINGS OF THE EMPLOYEES IN THE PAYROLL REGISTER

After figuring the earnings of all the employees in Steps 1 through 4, you are ready to enter employee numbers, names, marital statuses, allowances, total hours worked, and earnings in the Payroll Register. The Payroll Register on page 21 (Illustration 16) shows these entries for the week ending December 2.

STEP 5—for December 3-9.
List the Earnings of the Employees in the Payroll Register

Use the form on page 61 to prepare the Payroll Register as follows:

1. At the top of the form, enter *December 2, 19—* after WEEK ENDED. Then enter *December 12, 19—* after DATE OF PAYMENT.

(continued)

PIECE-RATE PRODUCTION REPORT

Solarheat Systems Inc.

For week ending *December 2* 19— —

NO.	NAME	MON.	TU.	WED.	THU.	FRI.	TOTAL PRODUCTION	X RATE	= GROSS PAY
42	*Baker, Edna*	310	324	336	341	332	1,643	$0.14	$230.02
43	*Svenson, Karl*	356	348	338	353	340	1,735	0.12	208.20

Illustration 15

Piece-Rate Production Report

PAYROLL REGISTER

WEEK ENDED *December 2, 19--* DATE OF PAYMENT *December 5, 19--*

	EMPL. NO.	EMPLOYEE'S NAME	MARITAL STATUS	ALLOW-ANCES	TOTAL HOURS	EARNINGS: REGULAR	EARNINGS: OVERTIME	EARNINGS: TOTAL	DEDUCTIONS: FEDERAL INC. TAX	DEDUCTIONS: FICA TAX	DEDUCTIONS: GROUP INSURANCE	DEDUCTIONS: MEDICAL INSURANCE	DEDUCTIONS: OTHER	DEDUCTIONS: TOTAL	PAID: NET PAY	PAID: CK. NO.	
1	1	Flores, Jesse	M	4		460.00		460.00									1
2	2	Jackson, Paula	M	0	40.0	180.00		180.00									2
3	12	Klaus, Elsie	M	2		381.39		381.39									3
4	13	Hirasuna, James	M	4		398.69		398.69									4
5	22	Salazar, Ruben	M	2	42.5	276.00	25.88	301.88									5
6	23	Brown, Leroy	M	5	43.7	174.68	26.40	201.08									6
7	24	McLaughlin, Darlene	S	1	39.0	195.00		195.00									7
8	25	Vukovich, Diane	M	2	42.0	216.00	16.20	232.20									8
9	26	Riley, Sam	M	2	42.0	236.00	17.70	253.70									9
10	27	Neufeld, Sara	M	0	41.8	226.86	17.10	243.96									10
11	28	Leonardo, Mike	M	2	40.5	180.00	3.38	183.38									11
12	42	Baker, Edna	M	0	40.0	230.02		230.02									12
13	43	Svenson, Karl	S	1	40.0	208.20		208.20									13
14																	14
15																	15
16																	16
17																	17
18		TOTAL				3,362.84	106.66	3,469.50									18

Other Deductions: B—U.S. Savings Bonds; C—Credit Union; U—Union Dues; UF—United Fund

Illustration 16
Payroll Register with Earnings Listed

STEP 5 (*continued*)

2. List the employees in number order by their identification or clock number with their last names first. Then show *M* or *S* in the third column for "Married" or "Single" filing status. In the fourth column, show the number of withholding allowances as shown on the Employee's Earnings Record for each employee.

 REMINDER: Since this is the first week you have worked as General Office Clerk, be sure to list your employee number and name on the third line of the Payroll Register.

3. In the TOTAL HOURS column, enter the total hours worked by each employee as shown on the time cards.
4. In the EARNINGS section, enter the regular, overtime, and total earnings for each employee.
5. Then total each of the columns in the EARNINGS section vertically. Check these totals by adding the Regular Earnings total and the Overtime Earnings total, which should equal the Total Earnings

(*continued*)

STEP 5 (*concluded*)

total. If these totals are not correct, locate your error now. Check the additions again or your figures to see if they were written correctly in the Payroll Register.

NOTE: The checking of totals on a payroll form is called "proving." This is a very important payroll procedure.

After you have completed Step 5, you are ready to figure the deductions for each employee. The employees of Solarheat Systems Inc. have money deducted from their weekly pay for income and FICA taxes, group and medical insurance, and union dues. Deductions for income and FICA taxes must be made by the company under federal law. Before the company can make deductions for group insurance or medical insurance, each employee must sign certain forms. The deduction of union dues for each production worker is provided for as a part of the union contract between Solarheat Systems Inc. and the union. The procedure for handling each of these deductions is explained in Steps 6, 7, and 8.

NOTE: When figuring deductions on a payroll register, it is easier to work vertically down the columns instead of working across them. For example, figure the income tax to be withheld for each employee first; then figure the FICA tax, etc.

STEP 6—FIGURE THE DEDUCTIONS FOR INCOME TAX

This step involves the figuring of the amount of income taxes to be withheld from the salaries and wages of all employees. The amount to be deducted is based on each employee's earnings, filing status, and allowances claimed as shown on the Employee's Earnings Record.

Below is part of the income tax withholding table (Illustration 17) that was used to figure the deduction for income tax to be withheld from the wages of Leroy Brown for the week ending December 2.

WEEKLY Payroll Period—Employee MARRIED

And the wages are—		And the number of withholding allowances claimed is—						
At least	But less than	0	1	2	3	4	5	6
		The amount of income tax to be withheld shall be—						
145	150	14.30	11.70	9.10	6.50	4.40	2.20	.10
150	160	15.70	13.10	10.50	7.90	5.50	3.30	1.20
160	170	17.50	14.90	12.30	9.70	7.10	4.80	2.70
170	180	19.30	16.70	14.10	11.50	8.90	6.30	4.20
180	190	21.10	18.50	15.90	13.30	10.70	8.10	5.70
190	200	22.90	20.30	17.70	15.10	12.50	9.90	7.30
200	210	24.70	22.10	19.50	16.90	14.30	11.70	9.10
210	220	26.50	23.90	21.30	18.70	16.10	13.50	10.90
220	230	28.40	25.70	23.10	20.50	17.90	15.30	12.70
230	240	30.60	27.50	24.90	22.30	19.70	17.10	14.50
240	250	32.80	29.60	26.70	24.10	21.50	18.90	16.30
250	260	35.00	31.80	28.60	25.90	23.30	20.70	18.10
260	270	37.20	34.00	30.80	27.70	25.10	22.50	19.90
270	280	39.40	36.20	33.00	29.80	26.90	24.30	21.70
280	290	41.80	38.40	35.20	32.00	28.90	26.10	23.50

Illustration 17 Income Tax Withholding Table

During the week ending December 2, Leroy Brown earned $201.08 (as explained in Step 3). He is married and claims 5 withholding allowances. The table above shows that his earnings of $201.08 are located on the line labeled **At least** ***$200*** **But less than** *$210*. This means that the amount of $201.08 is between $200 and $210. Follow across the line to the allowances column headed 5. There the income tax to be withheld from Leroy Brown's weekly wages of $201.08 is $11.70. This amount is entered in the FEDERAL INC. TAX column of the Payroll Register (Illustration 18).

STEP 6—for December 3-9.

Figure the Deductions for Income Tax

Use the tax tables on pages 151 and 152 to figure the income tax to be deducted from the earnings of each employee. Refer to the ALLOWANCES column on the Payroll Register for the number of withholding allowances to be used in figuring these deductions. Then record each amount in the FEDERAL INC. TAX column of the Payroll Register.

STEP 7—FIGURE THE DEDUCTIONS FOR FICA TAX

The FICA tax may be figured by either of two methods—by using the Federal Social Security-Medicare Tax Table or by using a calculator. Both methods are explained on page 23.

The Federal Social Security-Medicare Tax Table is used to figure the amount of FICA tax to be withheld from the earnings of each employee. A part of this tax table is shown on the next page (Illustration 19).

PAYROLL REGISTER

WEEK ENDED *December 2, 19--* DATE OF PAYMENT *December 5, 19--*

	EMPL. NO.	EMPLOYEE'S NAME	MARITAL STATUS	ALLOWANCES	TOTAL HOURS	EARNINGS: REGULAR	EARNINGS: OVERTIME	EARNINGS: TOTAL	DEDUCTIONS: FEDERAL INC. TAX	FICA TAX	GROUP INSURANCE	MEDICAL INSURANCE	OTHER	TOTAL	PAID: NET PAY	CK. NO.	
1	1	Flores, Jesse	M	4		460 00		460 00	73 90								1
2	2	Jackson, Paula	M	0	40.0	180 00		180 00	21 10								2
3	12	Klaus, Elsie	M	2		381 39		381 39	59 60								3
4	13	Hirasuna, James	M	4		398 69		398 69	54 90								4
5	22	Salazar, Ruben	M	2	42.5	276 00	25 88	301 88	39 60								5
6	23	Brown, Leroy	M	5	48.7	174 68	26 40	201 08	11 70 ←								6
7	24	McLaughlin, Darlene	S	1	39.0	195 00		195 00	27 20								7
8	25	Vukovich, Diane	M	2	42.0	216 00	16 20	232 20	24 90								8
9	26	Riley, Sam	M	2	42.0	236 00	17 70	253 70	28 60								9
10	27	Neufeld, Sara	M	0	41.8	226 86	17 10	243 96	32 80								10
11	28	Leonardo, Mike	M	2	40.5	180 00	3 38	183 38	15 90								11
12	42	Baker, Edna	M	0	40.0	230 02		230 02	30 60								12
13	43	Svenson, Karl	S	1	40.0	208 20		208 20	29 60								13
14																	14
15																	15
16																	16
17																	17
18		TOTAL				3,362 84	106 66	3,469 50									18

Other Deductions: B—U.S. Savings Bonds; C—Credit Union; U—Union Dues; UF—United Fund

Illustration 18 Payroll Register Showing Income Tax Deductions

Social Security and Hospital Insurance Tax Table - 6.13%

$ Wages less than	$ Tax	$ Wages less than	$ Tax	$ Wages less than	$ Tax
190.95	11.70	200.74	12.30	210.53	12.90
191.11	11.71	200.90	12.31	210.69	12.91
191.28	11.72	201.07	12.32	210.85	12.92
191.44	11.73	201.23	12.33	211.02	12.93
191.60	11.74	201.39	12.34	211.18	12.94
191.77	11.75	201.55	12.35	211.34	12.95
191.93	11.76	201.72	12.36	211.51	12.96
192.09	11.77	201.88	12.37	211.67	12.97
192.26	11.78	202.04	12.38	211.83	12.98
192.42	11.79	202.21	12.39	212.00	12.99

Using the Federal Social Security-Medicare Tax Table. For the week ending December 2, the earnings of Leroy Brown were $201.08. To find the FICA tax on this table, look at the column labeled **$ Wages less than** that shows the figure that is more than $201.08. This figure is *$201.23*. Then follow across on the same line to the next column labeled **$ Tax** that shows the figure of *$12.33*. The FICA tax on Leroy Brown's earnings of $201.08 is *$12.33*. (See Illustration 20 below.)

Using a Calculator. If you use a calculator, the FICA tax can be easily figured by entering 0.0613 as a constant amount and then multiplying 0.0613 by the earnings of each employee. To figure Leroy Brown's FICA tax, enter 0.0613 as the constant and multiply this amount by his earnings of $201.08. The FICA tax is $12.32620, which is rounded to the nearest cent or $12.33.

Use this same procedure to figure the FICA tax for each of the other employees. If 0.0613 is entered as a constant in the calculator, you do not need to reenter it again for each employee. As you figure the FICA tax for each employee, enter it in the FICA TAX column as shown in Illustration 20 below.

The FICA taxes that an employee must pay apply only to the first $22,900 earned from an employer during the year. When the earnings reach $22,900, no further deductions are made that year.

NOTE: If an employee works for more than one employer during the year and earns over $22,900 in total earnings but less than that amount from other employers, the FICA taxes deducted from all the total earnings will result in an overpayment. Credit may be claimed for this overpayment of FICA tax on the employee's income tax return. The overpayment is either applied against the employee's income tax liability or is included in the refund.

Keep a careful check on the ACCUMULATED TAXABLE EARNINGS column of the Employee's Earnings Record to determine when an employee's net pay reaches the $22,900 limit for tax liability. When the net-pay amount reaches this point, no other deductions are made for FICA tax. During the week in which this amount reaches the $22,900 limit, only a part of the

Illustration 20

Payroll Register Showing FICA Tax Deductions

PAYROLL REGISTER

WEEK ENDED *December 2, 19--* DATE OF PAYMENT *December 5, 19--*

	EMPL. NO.	EMPLOYEE'S NAME	MARITAL STATUS	ALLOW-ANCES	TOTAL HOURS	EARNINGS: REGULAR	EARNINGS: OVERTIME	EARNINGS: TOTAL	DEDUCTIONS: FEDERAL INC. TAX	DEDUCTIONS: FICA TAX	DEDUCTIONS: GROUP INSURANCE	DEDUCTIONS: MEDICAL INSURANCE	DEDUCTIONS: OTHER	DEDUCTIONS: TOTAL	PAID: NET PAY	PAID: CK. NO.	
1	1	Flores, Jesse	M	4		460 00		460 00	73 90	28 20							1
2	2	Jackson, Paula	M	0	40.0	180 00		180 00	21 10	11 03							2
3	12	Klaus, Elsie	M	2		381 39		381 39	59 60	23 38							3
4	13	Hirasuna, James	M	4		398 69		398 69	54 90	24 44							4
5	22	Salazar, Ruben	M	2	42.5	276 00	25 88	301 88	39 60	18 51							5
6	23	Brown, Leroy	M	5	43.7	174 68	26 40	201 08	11 70	12 33 ←							6
7	24	McLaughlin, Darlene	S	1	39.0	195 00		195 00	27 20	11 95							7
8	25	Vukovich, Diane	M	2	42.0	216 00	16 20	232 20	24 90	14 23							8
9	26	Riley, Sam	M	2	42.0	236 00	17 70	253 70	28 60	15 55							9
10	27	Neufeld, Sara	M	0	41.8	226 86	17 10	243 96	32 80	14 95							10
11	28	Leonardo, Mike	M	2	40.5	180 00	3 38	183 38	15 90	11 24							11
12	42	Baker, Edna	M	0	40.0	230 02		230 02	30 60	14 10							12
13	43	Svenson, Karl	S	1	40.0	208 20		208 20	29 60	12 76							13
14																	14
15																	15
16																	16
17																	17
18		TOTAL				3,362 84	106 66	3,469 50									18

Other Deductions: B—U.S. Savings Bonds; C—Credit Union; U—Union Dues; UF—United Fund

earnings may be subject to a deduction of FICA tax for that week.

> **STEP 7—for December 3-9.**
> **Figure the Deductions for FICA Tax**
>
> Use a calculator or the FICA tax tables on pages 153 to 156 to figure the amount of FICA tax to be withheld from each employee's earnings. Record this amount in the FICA TAX column of the Payroll Register.

STEP 8—LIST THE OTHER DEDUCTIONS

The employee's portion of the cost of group insurance and medical insurance is deducted each month. These deductions will be explained during the pay period in which they occur. Union dues for the factory production workers are $5 per week for each employee. Illustration 21 shows the deductions for union dues in the Payroll Register for the week ending December 2.

> **STEP 8—for December 3-9.**
> **List the Other Deductions**
>
> The only other deductions for this week are for union dues. Record these amounts in the OTHER column for each production worker. Before each amount, write the letter *U* to show that this deduction is for union dues.

STEP 9—FIGURE THE TOTAL DEDUCTIONS AND THE NET PAY

After all deductions are entered in the Payroll Register (Steps 6, 7, and 8), you are ready to figure the total deductions and the net pay for each employee as follows:

1. For each employee, add all the deductions and enter the total amount in the TOTAL column in the DEDUCTIONS section.
2. Subtract the total deductions from the total earnings, and enter this amount in the NET PAY column for each employee.

After making these entries for the week ending December 2, the Payroll Register appeared as shown in Illustration 22.

Using an Adding Machine. If an adding machine is available, use it to figure the total deductions and the net pay as follows:

1. If the machine has a NON-ADD key, use it to enter the identifying number of each employee. This shows the amounts for each employee on the adding-machine tape. If your machine does not have this key, go to the next step.
2. Using the ADD (+) key, enter all the deductions for each employee from the Payroll Register. Then, use the SUB-TOTAL key to find the amount for the total deductions.
3. Enter the amount for the total earnings from the Payroll Register, using the MINUS (−) key.

PAYROLL REGISTER

WEEK ENDED *December 2, 19--* DATE OF PAYMENT *December 5, 19--*

	EMPL. NO.	EMPLOYEE'S NAME	MARITAL STATUS	ALLOW-ANCES	TOTAL HOURS	EARNINGS			DEDUCTIONS						PAID		
						REGULAR	OVERTIME	TOTAL	FEDERAL INC. TAX	FICA TAX	GROUP INSURANCE	MEDICAL INSURANCE	OTHER	TOTAL	NET PAY	CK. NO.	
1	1	Flores, Jesse	M	4		460 00		460 00	73 90	28 20							1
2	2	Jackson, Paula	M	0	40.0	180 00		180 00	21 10	11 03							2
3	12	Klaus, Elsie	M	2		381 39		381 39	59 60	23 38							3
4	13	Hirasuna, James	M	4		398 69		398 69	54 90	24 44							4
5	22	Salazar, Ruben	M	2	42.5	276 00	25 88	301 88	39 60	18 51			U 5 00				5
6	23	Brown, Leroy	M	5	43.7	174 68	26 40	201 08	11 70	12 33			U 5 00				6
7	24	McLaughlin, Darlene	S	1	39.0	195 00		195 00	27 20	11 95			U 5 00				7
8	25	Vukovich, Diane	M	2	42.0	216 00	16 20	232 20	24 90	14 23			U 5 00				8
9	26	Riley, Sam	M	2	42.0	236 00	17 70	253 70	28 60	15 55			U 5 00				9
10	27	Neufeld, Sara	M	0	41.8	226 86	17 10	243 96	32 80	14 95			U 5 00				10
11	28	Leonardo, Mike	M	2	40.5	180 00	3 38	183 38	15 90	11 24			U 5 00				11
12	42	Baker, Edna	M	0	40.0	230 02		230 02	30 60	14 10			U 5 00				12
13	43	Svenson, Karl	S	1	40.0	208 20		208 20	29 60	12 76			U 5 00				13
14																	14
15																	15
16																	16
17																	17
18		TOTAL				3,362 84	106 66	3,469 50									18

Other Deductions: B—U.S. Savings Bonds, C—Credit Union, U—Union Dues, UF—United Fund

Illustration 21

Payroll Register Showing Deductions for Union Dues

PAYROLL REGISTER

WEEK ENDED *December 2, 19--* DATE OF PAYMENT *December 5, 19--*

	EMPL. NO.	EMPLOYEE'S NAME	MARITAL STATUS	ALLOW-ANCES	TOTAL HOURS	EARNINGS: REGULAR	EARNINGS: OVERTIME	EARNINGS: TOTAL	DEDUCTIONS: FEDERAL INC. TAX	DEDUCTIONS: FICA TAX	DEDUCTIONS: GROUP INSURANCE	DEDUCTIONS: MEDICAL INSURANCE	DEDUCTIONS: OTHER	DEDUCTIONS: TOTAL	PAID: NET PAY	PAID: CK. NO.	
1	1	Flores, Jesse	M	4		460 00		460 00	73 90	28 20				102 10	357 90		1
2	2	Jackson, Paula	M	0	40.0	180 00		180 00	21 10	11 03				32 13	147 87		2
3	12	Klaus, Elsie	M	2		381 39		381 39	59 60	23 38				82 98	298 41		3
4	13	Hirasuna, James	M	4		398 69		398 69	54 90	24 44				79 34	319 35		4
5	22	Salazar, Ruben	M	2	42.5	276 00	25 88	301 88	39 60	18 51			U 5 00	63 11	238 77		5
6	23	Brown, Leroy	M	5	43.7	174 68	26 40	201 08	11 70	12 33			U 5 00	29 03	172 05		6
7	24	McLaughlin, Darlene	S	1	39.0	195 00		195 00	27 20	11 95			U 5 00	44 15	150 85		7
8	25	Vukovich, Diane	M	2	42.0	216 00	16 20	232 20	24 90	14 23			U 5 00	44 13	188 07		8
9	26	Riley, Sam	M	2	42.0	236 00	17 70	253 70	28 60	15 55			U 5 00	49 15	204 55		9
10	27	Neufeld, Sara	M	0	41.8	226 86	17 10	243 96	32 80	14 95			U 5 00	52 75	191 21		10
11	28	Leonardo, Mike	M	2	40.5	180 00	3 38	183 38	15 90	11 24			U 5 00	32 14	151 24		11
12	42	Baker, Edna	M	0	40.0	230 02		230 02	30 60	14 10			U 5 00	49 70	180 32		12
13	43	Svenson, Karl	S	1	40.0	208 20		208 20	29 60	12 76			U 5 00	47 36	160 84		13
14																	14
15																	15
16																	16
17																	17
18		TOTAL				3,362 84	106 66	3,469 50									18

Other Deductions: B—U.S. Savings Bonds; C—Credit Union; U—Union Dues; UF—United Fund

Illustration 22

Payroll Register Showing Total Deductions and Net Pay

4. To find the amount for the net pay, use the TOTAL key.

Illustration 23 below shows the adding-machine tape that was used to find the total deductions and the net pay of Leroy Brown for the week ending December 2.

	0.	*	
EMPLOYEE NO. →	23.	#	NON-ADD
	0.	*	
DEDUCTIONS:			
Income Tax →	11.70	+	ADD (+)
FICA Tax →	12.33	+	
Union Dues →	5.00	+	
TOTAL DEDUCTIONS →	29.03	#	SUB-TOTAL
TOTAL EARNINGS →	201.08	-	MINUS (-)
NET PAY →	172.05	*	TOTAL

Illustration 23 Adding-Machine Tape Showing Total Deductions and Net Pay

STEP 9—for December 3-9.

Figure the Total Deductions and the Net Pay

Follow the explanation just given to figure the total deductions and the net pay for each employee, and record these amounts in the Payroll Register.

STEP 10—TOTAL AND BALANCE THE PAYROLL REGISTER

When all lines of the Payroll Register have been extended, total all of the remaining columns. Check ("prove") the accuracy of these totals as follows:

1. The sum of all the totals in each deduction column should equal the total in the TOTAL column of the DEDUCTIONS section. If these two totals are not equal, an error was made when these columns were added horizontally or vertically.

2. If the above totals are equal, subtract the total in the TOTAL column of the DEDUCTIONS section from the total in the TOTAL column of the EARNINGS section. This figure should be equal to the total of the NET PAY column. If the DEDUCTIONS section "proved" as shown in Step 1 and if these figures are not equal, an error was made either in the totaling of the NET PAY column or in the figuring of each employee's net pay. Recheck your work in this area to find any errors.

WORK HINT: If you use an adding machine, do not repeat the work to look for mistakes. Check the amounts on your tape against those on the Payroll Register to find the cause of the error or errors.

Illustration 24 on page 26 shows the completed Payroll Register for the week ending December 2 after it was totaled and balanced.

PAYROLL REGISTER

WEEK ENDED *December 2, 19--* DATE OF PAYMENT *December 5, 19--*

	EMPL. NO.	EMPLOYEE'S NAME	MARITAL STATUS	ALLOW-ANCES	TOTAL HOURS	EARNINGS			DEDUCTIONS						PAID		
						REGULAR	OVERTIME	TOTAL	FEDERAL INC. TAX	FICA TAX	GROUP INSURANCE	MEDICAL INSURANCE	OTHER	TOTAL	NET PAY	CK. NO.	
1	1	Flores, Jesse	M	4		460 00		460 00	73 90	28 20				102 10	357 90		1
2	2	Jackson, Paula	M	0	40.0	180 00		180 00	21 10	11 03				32 13	147 87		2
3	12	Klaus, Elsie	M	2		381 39		381 39	59 60	23 38				82 98	298 41		3
4	13	Hirasuna, James	M	4		398 69		398 69	54 90	24 44				79 34	319 35		4
5	22	Salazar, Ruben	M	2	42.5	276 00	25 88	301 88	39 60	18 51			U 5 00	63 11	238 77		5
6	23	Brown, Leroy	M	5	43.7	174 68	26 40	201 08	11 70	12 33			U 5 00	29 03	172 05		6
7	24	McLaughlin, Darlene	S	1	39.0	195 00		195 00	27 20	11 95			U 5 00	44 15	150 85		7
8	25	Vukovich, Diane	M	2	42.0	216 00	16 20	232 20	24 90	14 23			U 5 00	44 13	188 07		8
9	26	Riley, Sam	M	2	42.0	236 00	17 70	253 70	28 60	15 55			U 5 00	49 15	204 55		9
10	27	Neufeld, Sara	M	0	41.8	226 86	17 10	243 96	32 80	14 95			U 5 00	52 75	191 21		10
11	28	Leonardo, Mike	M	2	40.5	180 00	3 38	183 38	15 90	11 24			U 5 00	32 14	151 24		11
12	42	Baker, Edna	M	0	40.0	230 02		230 02	30 60	14 10			U 5 00	49 70	180 32		12
13	43	Svenson, Karl	S	1	40.0	208 20		208 20	29 60	12 76			U 5 00	47 36	160 84		13
14																	14
15																	15
16																	16
17																	17
18		TOTAL				3,362 84	106 66	3,469 50	450 40	212 67			U 45 00	708 07	2,761 43		18

Other Deductions: B—U.S. Savings Bonds; C—Credit Union; U—Union Dues; UF—United Fund

Illustration 24

Completed Payroll Register

> **STEP 10—for December 3-9.**
> **Total and Balance the Payroll Register**
>
> Use the procedure just described to total and balance the Payroll Register for the week of December 3-9.

STEP 11—PAY THE PAYROLL

The work week at Solarheat Systems Inc. begins on Sunday and ends on Saturday. The payroll is prepared on the following Monday, and employees are paid on Tuesday for the last work week.

At the present time, the company pays its employees in cash. This means that the exact amount of currency and change needed to make these payments must be figured and obtained. A *currency analysis* like the one at the right (Illustration 25) is prepared. The net pay of each employee is listed, and the number of bills and coins needed to make the payment is figured. For example, Leroy Brown's net pay is $172.05. This payment will require eight $20 bills, one $10 bill, two $1 bills, and one nickel ($160 + $10 + $2 + $0.05 = $172.05). Each employee's net pay is broken down in this way, and the largest denominations are always used first where possible.

After the analysis for each payment is completed, each column is totaled to find the number of each denomination that is needed.

A *payroll change requisition* (Illustration 26) is then prepared using these totals to show the number and amount needed in bills and coins. The next step is to write a check for the total amount of net pay. The check and its voucher (Illustration 27) is taken to the bank along with the payroll change requisition and is cashed to obtain the currency and coins needed to make the payments to the employees. Each employee's pay is then placed in a pay envelope.

The federal government requires employers to give each employee an annual statement that shows the

CURRENCY ANALYSIS

Solarheat Systems Inc.

For week ending *December 2* 19*--*

EMPLOYEE'S NAME	AMOUNT TO BE PAID	BILLS				COINS				
		$20	$10	$5	$1	50¢	25¢	10¢	5¢	1¢
Flores, Jesse	357 90	17	1	1	2	1	1	1	1	
Jackson, Paula	147 87	7		1	2	1	1	1		2
Klaus, Elsie	298 41	14	1	1	3		1	1	1	1
Hirasuna, James	319 35	15	1	1	4	1	1	1		
Salazar, Ruben	238 77	11	1	1	3		1			2
Brown, Leroy	172 05	8	1		2				1	
McLaughlin, Darlene	150 85	7	1			1	1	1		
Vukovich, Diane	188 07	9		1	3				1	2
Riley, Sam	204 55	10			4	1			1	
Neufeld, Sara	191 21	9	1		1			2		1
Leonardo, Mike	151 24	7	1		1			2		4
Baker, Edna	180 32	9					1		1	2
Svenson, Karl	160 84	8				1	1		1	4
TOTAL →	2,761 43	131	8	6	25	6	8	9	7	18

Illustration 25 Currency Analysis

PAYROLL CHANGE REQUISITION

CALIFORNIA NATIONAL BANK
of Clovis, CA 93612

FIRM *Solarheat Systems Inc.*
December 5 19--

	NO.	AMOUNT
BILLS: $20	131	$ 2,620.00
$10	8	80.00
$5	6	30.00
$1	25	25.00
COINS: 50¢	6	3.00
25¢	8	2.00
10¢	9	.90
5¢	7	.35
1¢	18	.18
TOTAL		$ 2,761.43

Illustration 26 Payroll Change Requisition

Solarheat Systems Inc.
901 Arcade Street
Clovis, CA 93612

NO. 93159 90-085/1211

DATE *December 5* 19--

Cash

AMOUNT $ *-2,761.43-*

PAY *Two thousand seven hundred sixty-one 43/100* DOLLARS

CALIFORNIA NATIONAL BANK
of Clovis, CA 93612

⑆121100858⑆ 2381⑉4576⑈346

Solarheat Systems Inc.
Jesse Flores
AUTHORIZED SIGNATURE

Solarheat Systems Inc. 901 Arcade Street Clovis, CA 93612 NO. 93159 DETACH BEFORE DEPOSITING CHECK

DATE	DESCRIPTION	AMOUNT	DISCOUNT %	DISCOUNT AMOUNT	OTHER DEDUCTIONS	NET AMOUNT
19-- Dec. 5	Total earnings	3,469.50				
	Less deductions:					
	Income tax				450.40	
	FICA tax				212.67	
	Union dues				45.00	
	Total deductions				708.07	
	Net pay					2,761.43

Illustration 27 Voucher Check

total earnings subject to income and FICA tax withholdings and the amounts of the deductions for these purposes. Most employers also find it easy to prepare similar statements and to present them to their employees along with their regular earnings.

When the payroll is paid by cash, this statement (or receipt) is usually prepared on the front of the pay envelope in which the money is placed when it is given to the employee. A separate slip may also be prepared and enclosed in this envelope. Illustration 28 below shows Leroy Brown's pay envelope for the week ending December 2.

NO. *23* FOR WEEK ENDING *12/2* 19--
NAME *Brown, Leroy* DEPT. *Production*

EXPLANATION	HOURS	RATE	AMOUNT
Regular Hours	39.7	$ 4.40	$ 174.68
Overtime Hours	4.0	6.60	26.40

LESS TOTAL DEDUCTIONS: TOTAL EARNINGS $ *201.08*

Income Tax	11.70
FICA Tax	12.33
Union Dues	5.00
	29.03

NET PAY DUE $ *172.05*

APPROVED *J. F.*

RECEIVED IN FULL FOR SERVICES TO DATE

Illustration 28 Pay Envelope

STEP 11—for December 3-9.
Pay the Payroll

Prepare the payment of the payroll for the week of December 3-9 as follows:

1. Use the Currency Analysis on page 63 to list the employees' names and the amount of their net pay. Complete the analysis, and determine the number of bills and coins that will be needed.
2. Enter this information on the Payroll Change Requisition on page 63, and figure the amounts of each denomination.
3. Prepare the Voucher Check on page 64 for the amount of the net pay to be cashed to obtain the money needed.
4. Use the forms on pages 65 to 68 to prepare pay envelopes for the employees.

STEP 12—POSTING FROM THE PAYROLL REGISTER TO EACH EMPLOYEE'S EARNINGS RECORD

The information on the Payroll Register must now be posted to each Employee's Earnings Record. These forms are on pages 107 to 135.

NOTE: The procedure that is used for transferring entries from one payroll record to another is called *posting*.

Each line of the Payroll Register should be posted to the proper Employee's Earnings Record. Note that each Employee's Earnings Record covers 13 weeks, or 1/4th of a year. Each Line 1 through 13 represents a week of that quarter year. The data from the Payroll Register is posted to the line for the current week of the quarter.

For example, if an employee (like yourself) began work at Solarheat Systems Inc. during the 10th week, the first week's payroll data would be entered on Line 10. Lines 1-9 are not filled in. Note that the entries shown in the Payroll Register for the week ending December 2 have been posted to Leroy Brown's Employee's Earnings Record (Illustration 29).

STEP 12—for December 3-9.
Posting from the Payroll Register to Each Employee's Earnings Record

Post the Payroll Register you have just completed for the week ending December 9 to each Employee's Earnings Record on pages 107 to 135. After finishing this posting, give your teacher these forms: Time Cards, Payroll Register, Currency Analysis, Payroll Change Requisition, Voucher Check, and Pay Envelopes.

In the following sections, you will prepare the payroll for the remaining weeks of December.

PAYROLL REGISTER

WEEK ENDED *December 2, 19--* DATE OF PAYMENT *December 5, 19--*

	EMPL. NO.	EMPLOYEE'S NAME	MARITAL STATUS	ALLOW-ANCES	TOTAL HOURS	EARNINGS: REGULAR	EARNINGS: OVERTIME	EARNINGS: TOTAL	DEDUCTIONS: FEDERAL INC. TAX	FICA TAX	GROUP INSURANCE	MEDICAL INSURANCE	OTHER	TOTAL	PAID: NET PAY	CK. NO.	
1	1	Flores, Jesse	M	4		460 00		460 00	73 90	28 20				102 10	357 90		1
2	2	Jackson, Paula	M	0	40.0	180 00		180 00	21 10	11 03				32 13	147 87		2
3	12	Klaus, Elsie	M	2		381 39		381 39	59 60	23 38				82 98	298 41		3
4	13	Hirasuna, James	M	4		398 69		398 69	54 90	24 44				79 34	319 35		4
5	22	Salazar, Ruben	M	2	42.5	276 00	25 88	301 88	39 60	18 51			U 5 00	63 11	238 77		5
6	23	Brown, Leroy	M	5	43.7	174 68	26 40	201 08	11 70	12 33			U 5 00	29 03	172 05		6
7	24	McLaughlin, Darlene	S	1	39.0	195 00		195 00	27 20	11 95			U 5 00	44 15	150 85		7
8	25	Vukovich, Diane	M	2	42.0	216 00	16 20	232 20	24 90	14 23			U 5 00	44 13	188 07		8
9	26	Riley, Sam	M	2	42.0	236 00	17 70	253 70	28 60	15 55			U 5 00	49 15	204 55		9
10	27	Ne[illegible]	[illegible]	[illegible]	[illegible]	[illegible]	[illegible]	[illegible]	[illegible]	[illegible]			[illegible]	[illegible]	[illegible]		10
11	28	Leo[illegible]															11
12	42	Ba[illegible]															12
13	43	Sir[illegible]															13
14																	14
15																	15
16																	16
17																	17
18																	18

Other Deduc[illegible]

EMPLOYEE'S EARNINGS RECORD

NAME *Brown, Leroy* EMPL. NO. *23*
ADDRESS *610 Beech Road; Clovis; CA 93612*
SOC. SEC. NO. *263-23-3724* ALLOWANCES *5* MARRIED *X* SINGLE
DEPARTMENT *Production*
OCCUPATION *Production Worker-Hourly Basis*
DATE EMPLOYED *August 15, 1977* DATE TERMINATED

DEDUCTIONS:
Credit Union
Group Insurance *$10 per mo.*
Medical Insurance *$27 per mo.*
U.S. Savings Bond
Union Dues *$5 per wk.*
United Fund
Other

EARNINGS:
Yearly
Monthly
Weekly
Hourly *$4.40*
Commission
Piece Rate
Per Unit

WEEK	WEEK ENDED	EARNINGS: REGULAR	EARNINGS: OVERTIME	EARNINGS: TOTAL	DEDUCTIONS: FEDERAL INC. TAX	FICA TAX	GROUP INSURANCE	MEDICAL INSURANCE	OTHER	TOTAL	NET PAY	ACCUMULATED TAXABLE EARNINGS	WEEK
TOTALS 3 QUAR.		6,859 60	79 20	6,938 80	245 70	425 35	90 00	243 00	U 195 00	1,199 05	5,739 75	6,938 80	
1	10/7	176 00	6 60	182 60	8 10	11 19			U 5 00	24 29	158 31	7,121 40	1
2	10/14	171 60		171 60	6 30	10 52		27 00	U 5 00	48 82	122 78	7,293 00	2
3	10/21	175 12		175 12	6 30	10 73			U 5 00	22 03	153 09	7,468 12	3
4	10/28	176 00		176 00	6 30	10 79	10 00		U 5 00	32 09	143 91	7,644 12	4
5	11/4	176 00	13 20	189 20	8 10	11 60			U 5 00	24 70	164 50	7,833 32	5
6	11/11	176 00		176 00	6 30	10 79		27 00	U 5 00	49 09	126 91	8,009 32	6
7	11/18	175 56		175 56	6 30	10 76			U 5 00	22 06	153 50	8,184 88	7
8	11/25	176 00	13 20	189 20	8 10	11 60	10 00		U 5 00	34 70	154 50	8,374 08	8
9	12/2	174 68	26 40	201 08	11 70	12 33			U 5 00	29 03	172 05	8,575 16	9
10													10
11													11
12													12
13													13
QUARTER TOTALS													
YEARLY TOTALS													

Illustration 29
Posting from the Payroll Register to an Employee's Earnings Record

6 PREPARING THE PAYROLL FOR DECEMBER 10-16

The payroll for the week of December 10-16 is prepared in the same way as the payroll for the pay period ending December 9 with one exception. As stated earlier, the employees of Solarheat Systems Inc. make payments for medical insurance once a month. The amount to be deducted for each employee can be found on the Employee's Earnings Record. The amount for medical insurance should be deducted from each employee's earnings during this pay period.

In preparing the payroll for the week of December 10-16, follow the same procedures that were used in the previous week and as outlined below. The forms you will need for this week are on pages 69 to 76.

1. The General Manager and the office employees are paid the same weekly salary and wages as last week.
2. Figure the commissions earned by the salespersons by completing the Weekly Sales Report.
3. Figure the time worked each day on the Time Cards, and find the total regular and overtime hours for the week.
4. Figure the regular, overtime, and total earnings on the Time Cards.
5. Figure the earnings of the production workers on a piece-rate basis by completing the Piece-Rate Production Report for the week.

This week Karl Svenson worked overtime. In addition to his piece-rate earnings, he is paid overtime for these extra hours. The explanation for the figuring of overtime pay for production workers on a piece-rate basis is given in Section 2.

6. Complete the Payroll Register as follows:
   a. In the first four columns, enter each employee's number, name (with the last name first), marital status, and allowances.
   b. In the next column, enter the total hours worked. This information is obtained from the time cards.
   c. In the EARNINGS section, enter the regular, overtime, and total earnings in the proper columns.
   d. Total the three columns in the EARNINGS section. Then "prove" these totals this way:

      Total regular earnings + Total overtime earnings = Total earnings

   e. Use the Income Tax Withholding Tables on pages 151 and 152 to figure the amount of income tax to be withheld from the earnings of each employee. Enter these amounts in the FEDERAL INCOME TAX column of the DEDUCTIONS SECTION.
   f. Use the Federal Social Security-Medicare Tax Table (pages 153-156) to figure the FICA tax to be withheld from the earnings of each employee. Enter these amounts in the FICA TAX column of the DEDUCTIONS section.

This week the earnings of Jesse Flores, the General Manager, will exceed the limit for FICA taxable wages during a year of $22,900. This means that only part of his earnings for this week are subject to the deduction for FICA tax. Figure the deduction for FICA tax on only that part of Mr. Flores' earnings that is needed to reach this limit. The rest of his earnings for this week and for the next two weeks are no longer subject to FICA tax deductions.

HINT: To know when each employee's earnings reach the $22,900 taxable limit so that further FICA tax deductions can be stopped, always check the ACCUMULATED TAXABLE EARNINGS column of the Employee's Earnings Record.

   g. Enter the deductions for medical insurance in the MEDICAL INSURANCE column of the DEDUCTIONS section.
   h. Enter the deductions for union dues in the OTHER column of the DEDUCTIONS section.
   i. For each employee, add the deductions to find the amounts for the total deductions and the net pay. Enter these amounts in the TOTAL DEDUCTIONS and NET PAY columns.
   j. Total the remaining columns and "prove" these totals this way:

All DEDUCTION columns = TOTAL DEDUCTIONS column

TOTAL DEDUCTIONS column + NET PAY column = TOTAL EARNINGS column

7. Prepare the Currency Analysis, the Payroll Change Requisition, and the Voucher Check.
8. In preparing the payroll for the week of December 3-9, a pay envelope was prepared for each employee that showed total earnings, total deductions, and net pay. Since Paula Jackson, the other office employee, has some extra time, she offers to prepare the pay envelopes this week. Therefore, do not prepare the pay envelopes for the week of December 10-16.
9. "Post" the amounts on each line of the Payroll Register to each Employee's Earnings Record.
10. Give your teacher these forms: Time Cards, Payroll Register, Currency Analysis, Payroll Change Requisition, and Voucher Check.

PREPARING THE PAYROLL FOR DECEMBER 17-23

The forms needed for this week are on pages 77 to 97. Follow the same payroll procedures that were used last week with these exceptions:

1. Darlene McLaughlin, Employee No. 24, left the company at the end of the last pay period because of health problems. On the line space for DATE TERMINATED on her Employee's Earnings Record, write *December 16, 19—(health problems)*.
2. Another person was hired to replace Darlene McLaughlin. Prepare the Employee's Earnings Record on page 135 from this information: name, *Gloria Leshen;* employee number, *29*; address: *1216 Sunset Blvd.*; *Clovis, CA 93612*; social security number, *473-28-6925*; allowances, *3*; marital status, *X* for *Married*; department, *Production*; occupation, *Production Worker–Hourly Basis*; date employed, *December 17, 19—*; deductions (group insurance, *$10 per mo.*; medical insurance, *$27 per mo.*; union dues, *$5 per wk.*); hourly earnings, *$5*.
3. A Holiday bonus is paid to all employees. Jesse Flores, the General Manager, receives $450 while all of the other employees receive a bonus based on 2% of their total earnings for the previous 50 weeks. This means they will receive an extra 2% of all their earnings this year up to and including last week's payroll.

   Darlene McLaughlin does not receive a bonus as she is no longer employed at the company. Since Gloria Leshen is a new employee and did not work for the company during the first 50 weeks of the year, she will not receive a bonus.

NOTE: To figure the Holiday bonus, refer to the amount in the ACCUMULATED TAXABLE EARNINGS column of each Employee's Earnings Record for the week ended December 16.

The Holiday bonus must be included in the figuring of the total earnings and the tax deductions for this pay period and is shown on the forms as follows:

1. On each Weekly Time Record, write the word *Bonus* with the amount directly under the words TOTAL HOURS (which appear at the bottom).
2. On the Weekly Sales Report, write *Bonus* close to the = sign of the column heading. Then, figure the bonus for each salesperson and write the amounts under *Bonus*. Add the bonus figure to the commission figure to find the total weekly earnings.
3. At the bottom of each Time Card, write *Bonus* to the right of the word *Special* in the RATE column. Then, write the amount of the bonus payment in the EARNINGS column so that it will be included in the total weekly earnings.

In the Payroll Register, remember to write the amount in the REGULAR column of the EARNINGS section which is the total of both the regular earnings and the bonus payment for each employee. Remember also that the only other deductions for this week are the union dues for the production workers.

When "posting" the data from the Payroll Register to the Employee's Earnings Record, the holiday bonus should be included in the REGULAR column of the EARNINGS section. Some businesses have a special column for "Other" earnings in which such different payments are entered. There are so few of these payments at Solarheat Systems Inc., however, that all special bonuses are included with regular earnings. Of course, since the holiday bonus is included as taxable earnings, the amount received should be considered when deductions are made for FICA and state tax contributions. The deductions for income and FICA taxes and for disability benefits are figured on the total pay for the week including the bonus. Before preparing the Payroll Register, look at each Employee's Earnings Record to see if the $22,900 limit on FICA taxes has been reached during the year.

The remaining procedures to be followed for completing the December 17-23 payroll are:

1. Today most companies pay employees by check. Since this method is more efficient and safer, Solarheat Systems Inc. decided to change its payroll procedure. Beginning with this week, each employee is to be paid by payroll check rather than with cash.
2. After completing the Payroll Register, write a Voucher Check for the amount of the NET PAY total plus $500. This check will be used to open a special payroll account at the bank. The extra $500 is added to provide a balance in the payroll bank account and is also used when a payroll check must be written at some time other than the end of the pay period. This may occur if an employee leaves the company during a pay

	DOLLARS	CENTS
BALANCE BROUGHT FORWARD	-0-	
DEPOSIT 12/26/-- (DATE)	5,230	68
TOTAL	5,230	68
NO. 1		
DATE December 26 19--		
TO Jesse Flores		
FOR net pay for week ending 12/23/--		
AMOUNT THIS CHECK	679	10
BALANCE CARRIED FORWARD	4,551	58

Solarheat Systems Inc.
901 Arcade Street
Clovis, CA 93612

NO. 1 90-085/1211

DATE December 26 19--

PAY TO THE ORDER OF Jesse Flores $679.10

Six hundred seventy-nine 10/100 DOLLARS

CALIFORNIA NATIONAL BANK
of Clovis, CA 93612

SOLARHEAT SYSTEMS INC. — PAYROLL ACCOUNT

(Student's Name)
AUTHORIZED SIGNATURE

⑆121100858⑆ 4276⑈3391⑈721

Solarheat Systems Inc. STATEMENT OF EMPLOYEE EARNINGS AND PAYROLL DEDUCTIONS

WEEK ENDED	EARNINGS: REGULAR	OVERTIME	TOTAL	DEDUCTIONS: FEDERAL INC. TAX	FICA TAX	GROUP INSURANCE	MEDICAL INSURANCE	OTHER	TOTAL	PAID: NET PAY	CK. NO
19-- 12/23	910.00		910.00	230.90					230.90	679.10	1

Illustration 30
Payroll Check

period rather than at the end of the work week. If this happens, the employee must be paid immediately. The extra $500 is deposited at the bank only once and is not included in future payroll deposits.

3. Use the forms on pages 85 to 97 to prepare the employees' payroll checks for this pay period. Begin with Check No. 1 for Jesse Flores, the General Manager, by copying from his completed payroll check and stub shown above (Illustration 30). Be sure to make the right entries on the check stub at the left and on the summary stub at the bottom of each payroll check. Sign all of the payroll checks for the company. Note that the number of each check and its stub has already been preprinted.

PREPARING THE PAYROLL FOR DECEMBER 24-30

The forms needed for this week are on pages 99 to 105. Follow the same steps outlined previously in preparing this payroll with these changes:

1. Even though the employees of Solarheat Systems Inc. do not work on December 25, they are to receive full pay for that day. The word *Holiday* should be written on each time card for Monday. For December 25, the pay for the piece-rate workers (Edna Baker and Karl Svenson) is figured by multiplying 8 hours times the hourly rate for the four days that were actually worked. (See pages 7-8 for the procedure used to determine the hourly rate.)
2. Note that three hourly employees worked 8 hours on Saturday while two worked 2½ hours each. This time was necessary to take inventory at the end of the year. Also, the two office employees each worked 6 hours on Saturday to assist with the inventory and to prepare the payroll.

   To determine the office employees' overtime pay, first find the hourly rate for each. Then multiply the 6 overtime hours by 1½ times the hourly rate.
3. Some of the employees asked to be paid this week on Saturday instead of Tuesday so that they would have extra money over the New Year holiday. Since employees who worked overtime on Saturday had agreed to a certain number of hours on Saturday, the payroll was prepared on Saturday morning.

   The week ending on December 30 is the last pay period of the year (52 weeks). Any wages earned on December 31 will be paid to the employees on the first payday in January and will be considered taxable earnings of the next year.
4. Deductions are made this week for group insurance. The amount of the deduction for each employee is obtained from the Employee's Earnings Record.
5. Paula Jackson volunteered to prepare the payroll checks for this week so you will not need to prepare the checks for this pay period.

(*continued*)

WORK AT THE END OF THE YEAR

At the end of the year, after the data from the Payroll Register has been posted to each Employee's Earnings Record, the columns on each Record are totaled to find the quarterly and yearly totals. The procedure for totaling and proving the columns of each Employee's Earnings Record is given below.

1. Total the three EARNINGS columns, and prove these totals.

REGULAR EARNINGS Total	+	OVERTIME EARNINGS Total	=	TOTAL EARNINGS Total

2. Total the five DEDUCTIONS columns, and prove these totals.

INCOME TAX Total	+	FICA TAX Total	+	GROUP INS. Total	+	MEDICAL INS. Total	+	OTHER Total	=	TOTAL DEDUCTIONS Total

3. Total the NET PAY column, and prove this total.

NET PAY Total	+	TOTAL DEDUCTIONS Total	=	TOTAL EARNINGS Total

9 FEDERAL PAYROLL RETURNS AND PAYMENTS

As explained earlier, an important reason for keeping the payroll records for a company is to provide the information needed to prepare reports and payments under the various federal, state, and local laws. The purpose of this section is to describe the different federal returns and payment forms needed and to explain briefly how they are prepared. All of the information to be reported on these returns or forms such as total wages, taxable wages, and other deductions can be obtained from the payroll records that have already been prepared.

THE REPORTING AND THE PAYMENT OF INCOME AND FICA TAX WITHHOLDINGS

The following forms are used by an employer for reporting and paying income and FICA tax withholdings to the federal government:

Form 941 ...... Employer's Quarterly Federal Tax Return
Form 501 ...... Federal Tax Deposit

Form 941. The form used to report withheld income and FICA taxes during each quarter of a taxable year under the Federal Insurance Contributions Act for old-age, survivor, and disability benefits is *Form 941–Employer's Quarterly Federal Tax Return.*

The federal government requires a company to make four quarter-monthly deposits each month if the accumulated undeposited amount at the end of any quarter-monthly period (for the employees' income taxes + the employer's and employees' share of FICA taxes) is $2,000 or more. A quarter-monthly period is the period ending on the 7th, 15th, 22d, and last days of any month. If at the end of any quarter-monthly period the undeposited taxes are $2,000 or more, they must be deposited within three (3) banking days after the end of that quarter-monthly period. Such a tax deposit is mailed or delivered by check or money order with a federal tax deposit form (Form 501) to a qualified commercial bank or to a Federal Reserve Bank in the company's geographical area.

Illustration 31 shows Solarheat's record of tax deposits on the Form 941 that was prepared by the last General Office Clerk for the third quarter of the taxable year ending on September 30. These tax deposits were for the periods ending on the 22d day of July, the 15th day of August, and the 7th and last days of September. All of these amounts were deposited within the three-banking-days time limit requirement. Note

Form **941**

Department of the Treasury
Internal Revenue Service

Employer's Quarterly Federal Tax Return

Your name, address, employer identification number, and calendar quarter of return. (If not correct, please change)

Name (as distinguished from trade name): Solarheat Systems Inc.

Date quarter ended: September 30, 19--

Trade name, if any:

Employer identification number: 94-186438

Address and ZIP code: 901 Arcade Street, Clovis, CA 93612

T	
FF	
FD	
FP	
I	
T	

If address is different from prior return, check here ▶ ☐

Line	Description	Amount	¢
1	Number of employees (except household) employed in the pay period that includes March 12th (complete for first quarter only)		
2	Total wages and tips subject to withholding, plus other compensation →	40,397	28
3	Total income tax withheld from wages, tips, annuities, gambling, etc. (see instructions)	5,320	25
4	Adjustment of withheld income tax for preceding quarters of calendar year	-0-	
5	Adjusted total of income tax withheld →	5,320	25
6	Taxable FICA wages paid $40,397.28 multiplied by 12.26% = TAX	4,952	71
7	Taxable tips reported $ multiplied by 6.13% = TAX	-0-	
8	Total FICA taxes (add lines 6 and 7) →	4,952	71
9	Adjustment of FICA taxes (see instructions)	-0-	
10	Adjusted total of FICA taxes →	4,952	71
11	Total taxes (add lines 5 and 10)	10,272	96

Record of Federal Tax Deposits (See instructions on page 4)

Deposit period ending:		I. Tax liability for period	II. Date of deposit	III. Amount deposited
Overpayment from previous quarter				
First month of quarter	1st through 7th day			
	8th through 15th day			
	16th through 22d day	2,313.52	7/25/--	2,313.52
	23d through last day			
A First month total	A	2,313.52		2,313.52
Second month of quarter	1st through 7th day			
	8th through 15th day	2,423.72	8/15/--	2,423.72
	16th through 22d day			
	23d through last day			
B Second month total	B	2,423.72		2,423.72
Third month of quarter	1st through 7th day	2,403.82	9/5/--	2,403.82
	8th through 15th day			
	16th through 22d day			
	23d through last day	3,131.90	10/3/--	3,131.90
C Third month total	C	5,535.72		5,535.72
D Total for quarter (add items A, B, and C)		10,272.96		10,272.96
E Final deposit made for quarter. (Enter zero if the final deposit made for the quarter is included in item D)				-0-

Line	Description	Amount	¢
12	Total deposits for quarter (including final deposit made for quarter) and overpayment from previous quarter. (See instructions on page 4)	10,272	96
13	Undeposited taxes due (subtract line 12 from line 11—this should be less than $200). Pay to Internal Revenue Service and enter here →	-0-	

Note: *If undeposited taxes at the end of the quarter are $200 or more, deposit the full amount with an authorized financial institution or a Federal Reserve bank according to the instructions on the back of the Federal Tax Deposit Form 501. Enter this deposit in the Record of Federal Tax Deposits and include it in line 12.*

14 If line 12 is more than line 11, enter overpayment here ▶ $ and check if to be: ☐ Applied to next return, or ☐ Refunded.

15 If you are not liable for returns in the future, write **"FINAL"** (See instructions) ▶ Date final wages paid ▶

Under penalties of perjury, I declare that I have examined this return, including accompanying schedules and statements, and to the best of my knowledge and belief it is true, correct, and complete.

Date ▶ October 3, 19-- Signature ▶ *Jesse Flores* Title ▶ General Manager

Form **941**

Illustration 31 Form 941—Employer's Quarterly Federal Tax Return

that the last tax deposit of $3,131.90 (made on October 3) is larger than the other deposits as it includes withheld taxes for four weekly payroll periods instead of three.

Preparing Form 941.

Use Form 941 on page 139 for filing the employer's quarterly federal tax return for the withheld income and FICA taxes that are to be deposited for this last quarter of the taxable year. Complete the top part of Form 941. Line 1 does not apply since this is not the first quarterly report of the year. The amounts for Lines 2 and 3 are obtained from the payroll data in the QUARTER TOTALS lines of the Employee's Earnings Records. To aid you in obtaining these amounts, use the top part of page 137.

On Line 2, enter the amount of the total salaries and wages subject to withholding during this last quarter. On Line 3, show the total income tax withheld from salaries or wages during the quarter. Line 4 does not apply since there were no errors that needed adjustment for the preceding three quarters of the calendar year. The amount on Line 5 is the adjusted total of income tax withheld and is the same as the Line 3 amount.

Use the bottom part of page 137 to figure the amount to be entered in the middle of Line 6. This amount is for the taxable FICA wages paid for this taxable year and is less than the amount on Line 2 because Form 941 is being filed for the final quarter. This means that each employee's earnings must be checked to see at which point the FICA tax limit of $22,900 has been reached. Multiply this amount by 12.26% (6.13% for the employee's FICA taxes + 6.13% for the employer's FICA tax contribution) for the total taxable FICA taxes paid for this final quarter. Line 7 does not apply. Complete Lines 8 to 11 as instructed on Form 941.

The tax deposits that were made during the quarter have already been entered on Form 941 for you. Complete Lines 12 to 15 as instructed on the form. Then date Form 941 and have it signed by Jesse Flores, the General Manager.

Form 501. The form that is used for the payment of all the income and FICA taxes withheld by an employer during a certain period is *Form 501–Federal Tax Deposit.* Under the Federal Tax Deposit System, the employer enters the correct deposit amount on Form 501. This deposit form is sent automatically by mail to all employers with the basic information already printed on the form through the automatic data processing system of the Internal Revenue Service. Form 501, together with the check or money order for the amount of tax deposited, is mailed or delivered to an authorized commercial bank depositary or a Federal Reserve Bank. The Federal Reserve Bank forwards the tax deposit to the Office of the Treasurer of the United States. Then the Treasurer's office will send along the deposit data by magnetic tape to the Internal Revenue Service so that it may be recorded in the employer's account. The time requirements for the employer's deposits were discussed on page 32.

Form 501 (Illustration 32) shows the first federal tax deposit that was paid to the federal government by Solarheat Systems Inc. for the last quarter of the taxable year ending on December 31. The total amount of $2,417.20 for both income and FICA taxes withheld ($1,246.00 income tax + $585.60 employees' FICA taxes withheld + $585.60 employer's FICA tax contribution) must be paid at the time Form 501 is filed. This form, along with a $2,417.20 check, must be filed within three (3) banking days after the end of the quarter-monthly period to which the payment applies.

Preparing Form 501.

Use Form 501 on page 138 for the payment of the last tax deposit for the final fourth quarter of the taxable year. Form 501 is to be mailed together with Form 941 (which you have just completed) and with a Solarheat voucher check written for the proper amount of the tax deposit. Under the space labeled NAME OF BANK, enter *CALIFORNIA NATIONAL BANK.* Under the space labeled AMOUNT OF DEPOSIT, enter the amount shown for the quarter-monthly period ended December 31 on Form 941. This amount was already recorded for you on the line "23d through last day" in the Record of Federal Tax Deposits.

REPORTING TO THE EMPLOYEE

On or before January 31 of each year, an employer must furnish each employee with two copies (Copies B and C) of *Form W-2–Wage and Tax Statement.* This

FEDERAL TAX DEPOSIT OF: WITHHELD INCOME AND FICA TAX

REPORT ON IRS RETURN

941

501
FTD Form

NAME OF BANK	AMOUNT OF DEPOSIT	
CALIFORNIA NATIONAL BANK	2,417	20
	DOLLARS	CENTS

SOLARHEAT SYSTEMS INC
901 ARCADE ST
CLOVIS CA 93612

Employer Identification Number
94-186438
488
SEPT 22 --
Tax Period Ending

ENTER AMOUNT OF DEPOSIT AND NAME OF BANK WHERE DEPOSITED IN SPACE ABOVE
The space below may be used by depositaries for MICR encoding

Bank Name-Date Stamp

DEPARTMENT OF THE TREASURY · FISCAL SERVICE
Bureau of Government Financial Operations · FTD Form Rev Oct 1977

Illustration 32 Form 501—Federal Tax Deposit

form must be prepared if an employee is paid $600 or more during the taxable year. Copy B is filed by the employee along with the income tax return while Copy C is kept as a record. The employer must prepare four copies of the Form W-2 for each employee. All of the original copies (Copies A) are sent along with Form W-3—Transmittal of Income and Tax Statements (*not described here*) to the Social Security Administration by February 28. Copy D, the fourth copy, is kept by the employer for the payroll records.

The federal government requires an employer to furnish an employee who stops working with a company the proper copies of a Form W-2 within 30 days after the last wage payment. Shown below is the Form W-2 (Illustration 33) that was prepared for Darlene McLaughlin who left the company two weeks ago because of health problems.

Preparing Forms W-2.

For practice, use the three forms on page 141 to prepare the Form W-2 wage and tax information for these employees: Jesse Flores, Paula Jackson, and Elsie Klaus. In any business, these Form W-2s would be prepared and given to each employee on or before January 31 of the next year. Note that the amounts for the FICA tax withheld and the total FICA wages to which the FICA tax applies are entered in Boxes 11 and 12 of Form W-2. This information is obtained very easily from the YEARLY TOTALS line of each Employee's Earnings Record.

1 Control number: 222
2 Employer's State number: 31-0450660
For Official Use Only

3 Employer's name, address, and ZIP code
SOLARHEAT SYSTEMS INC.
901 ARCADE STREET
CLOVIS, CA 93612

4 Subtotal ☐ Correction ☐ Void ☐
5 Employer's identification number: 94-186438
6 Advance EIC payment
7

8 Employee's social security number	9 Federal income tax withheld	10 Wages, tips, other compensation	11 FICA tax withheld	12 Total FICA wages
147-62-6118	$1,461.60	$10,108.25	$619.64	$10,108.25

13 Employee's name (first, middle, last): Darlene McLaughlin
14 Pension plan coverage? Yes/No: No
15*
16 FICA tips

511 Delhi Pike
Clovis, CA 93612
17 Employee's address and ZIP code

Copy A For Social Security Administration
*See Instructions for Forms W-2 and W-2P and back of Copy D

Form W–2 Wage and Tax Statement 19– –
Department of the Treasury—Internal Revenue Service

Illustration 33 Form W-2—Wage and Tax Statement

NOTE: Solarheat Systems Inc. withholds only federal income tax from each employee's earnings. When a company withholds state and local income taxes in addition to the federal income tax from each employee's earnings, a different Form W-2 must be used. This Form W-2 is not described here. As General Office Clerk, you should be aware that there are always changes in the rates, forms, and rules of withholding taxes by the various governments.

THE REPORTING AND THE PAYMENT OF THE FEDERAL UNEMPLOYMENT TAX

Form 940. Every employer who during the current or preceding calendar year paid salaries or wages of $1,500 in any calendar quarter or at any time had one or more employees in any 20 calendar weeks must file *Form 940–Employer's Annual Federal Unemployment Tax Return*. This form is used for the annual reporting of tax under the Federal Unemployment Tax Act (FUTA), which is paid only by the employer. The tax rate is 3.4% (0.034) on the first $6,000 of wages paid to each employee during the taxable year. Form 940 is due by January 31 following the end of the calendar year. However, if timely deposits were made in full payment of the tax due, then the employer has until February 10 to file Form 940.

Preparing Form 940.

Use Form 940 on page 145 to file the employer's annual federal unemployment tax return for the current year based on the work completed for Solarheat Systems Inc. In preparing this return, refer to Form 940 (Illustration 34) which was filed for the previous year and to the instructions below. Before you begin, complete the top part of this form.

1. Columns 1 to 9 are used by an employer who has been granted an *experience rate* lower than 2.7% by a state for the whole or part of the taxable calendar year. A business without an experience rate should use only Columns 1, 2, 3, and 9. Since Solarheat Systems Inc. has not been granted an experience rate, the 2.7% rate applies. Therefore, use only Columns 1, 2, 3, and 9.

   NOTE: A business may be granted an experience rate that is lower than 2.7% based on its employment experience.

   a. In Column 1, enter the name of the state to which the employer is required to pay contributions. Here, enter *Calif.* for "California."

(continued)

Preparing Form 940 (continued)

   b. In Column 2, enter *178-4621*, the reporting number assigned to Solarheat Systems Inc. by the state.

   c. In Column 3, enter the taxable payroll on which Solarheat must pay contributions to the unemployment fund of California. In California, only the first $6,000 that is paid to an employee is subject to the federal unemployment tax. To aid you in obtaining the taxable payroll amount for Column 3, use page 143. Look at the YEARLY TOTALS line of each Employee's Earnings Record to determine the total taxable wages that were paid to all employees based on this $6,000 maximum for each employee.

   d. Omit Columns 4, 5, 6, 7, and 8.

   e. In Column 9, enter the amount of contributions actually paid into the state fund. This amount is 2.7% times the amount in Column 3. Total Columns 3 and 9.

2. On Line 10, enter the same amount for the total tentative credit that was entered in Column 9.
3. On Line 11, enter the total amount for salaries and wages which was paid to all Solarheat employees during the calendar year. To aid you, use page 143.
4. Omit Line 12 which refers to exempt salaries or wages for agricultural labor, benefit payments for sickness or injury under a workmen's compensation law, etc. Omit Column (a) since Solarheat Systems Inc. is not eligible to claim the new jobs tax credit.
5. On Line 13, enter the total amount of wages paid to each employee in excess of $6,000. The $6,000 wage limitation is for FUTA purposes only. (Do not use the state wage limitation for this entry.)
6. On Line 14, enter the same amount that was entered on Line 13 (Line 12 + Line 13).
7. On Line 15, omit the lines for **a** and **b**. Then, on the line for **c**, enter the total taxable FUTA wages (Line 14, Column (b) − Line 11) which is the amount based on the first $6,000 paid to each employee during the calendar year.
8. On Line 16, enter the amount for the gross federal tax which is figured by multiplying Line 15c by 0.034.

(continued on page 38)

Form **940**
Department of the Treasury
Internal Revenue Service

Employer's Annual Federal Unemployment Tax Return

19--

T	
FF	
FD	
FP	
I	
T	

If incorrect, make any necessary change ▶

Name (as distinguished from trade name): Solarheat Systems Inc.
Calendar Year: 19--
Trade name, if any
Employer identification number: 94-186438
Address and ZIP code: 901 Arcade Street; Clovis, CA 93612

Name of State 1	State reporting number as shown on employer's State contribution returns 2	Taxable payroll (as defined in State act) 3	Experience rate period 4 From—	To—	Experience rate 5	Contributions had rate been 2.7% (col. 3 × 2.7%) 6	Contributions payable at experience rate (col. 3 × col. 5) 7	Additional credit (col. 6 minus col. 7) 8	Contributions actually paid to State 9
Calif.	178-4621	65,872.50							1,778.56
	Totals ▶	65,872.50							1,778.56

Line		(a) New jobs credit wages	(b) Amount paid	Amount
10	Total tentative credit (column 8 plus column 9—see instructions on page 4)			1,778 56
11	Total remuneration (including exempt remuneration) paid during the calendar year for services of employees			133,285 89
	Exempt Remuneration (See Instructions on Page 4)			
12	Exempt remuneration. (Explain each exemption shown, attaching additional sheet if necessary) ▶	-0-	-0-	
13	Remuneration in excess of the first $4,200 in column (a), and the first $6,000 in column (b), paid to individual employees exclusive of exempt amounts entered on line 12. Do not use State wage limitation	-0-	67,413.39	
14	Total exempt remuneration (line 12 plus line 13)	-0-	67,413.39	
15 a	New jobs credit total wages (subtract line 12, column (a) from line 11)	-0-		
b	New jobs credit wages (subtract line 14, column (a) from line 11)	-0-		
c	Total taxable FUTA wages (subtract line 14, column (b) from line 11)			65,872 50
16	Gross Federal tax (multiply line 15c by .034)			2,239 67
17	Maximum credit (multiply line 15c by .027)		1,778.56	
18	Line 10 or line 17 whichever is smaller		1,778.56	
19	Amount, if any, of wages on line 15c attributable to Rhode Island $........ × .003		-0-	
20	Credit allowable (subtract line 19 from line 18)			1,778 56
21	Net Federal tax (subtract line 20 from line 16)			461 11

Record of Federal Tax Deposits for Unemployment Tax (Form 508)

Quarter	Liability by period	Date of deposit	Amount of deposit
First	235.17	4/3/--	235.17
Second	129.11	7/2/--	129.11
Third	-0-		-0-
Fourth	96.83	1/15/--	96.83

Line		Amount
22	Total Federal tax deposited	461 11
23	**Balance due** (subtract line 22 from line 21—this should not exceed $100). Pay to Internal Revenue Service ▶	-0-
24	**Overpayment** (subtract line 21 from line 22) ▶	-0-
25	If no longer in business at end of year, write "Final" here ▶	

Under penalties of perjury, I declare that I have examined this return, including accompanying schedules and statements, and to the best of my knowledge and belief, it is true, correct and complete, and that no part of any payment made to a State unemployment fund claimed as a credit was or is to be deducted from the remuneration of employees.

Date ▶ January 15, 19-- Signature ▶ *Jesse Flores* Title (Owner, etc.) ▶ General Manager

Form 940

Illustration 34 Form 940—Employer's Annual Federal Unemployment Tax Return

Preparing Form 940 (concluded)

9. On Line 17, center the amount for the maximum credit. Multiply Line 15c by 0.027.
10. On Line 18, enter the amount on Line 10 or Line 17, whichever is smaller.
11. Omit Line 19.
12. On Line 20, enter the amount for the credit allowable. This is the same amount shown on Line 18.
13. On Line 21, enter the amount for the net federal unemployment tax (Line 20 – Line 16) which is to be paid to the Internal Revenue Service.
14. The tax deposits that were made during the calendar year were already entered above Line 22 under the space labeled *Record of Federal Tax Deposits for Unemployment Tax (Form 508).* The total of these deposits is entered on Line 22.
15. On Line 23, enter the balance due (Line 21 – Line 22) which should not exceed $100. If there is an overpayment (Line 22 – Line 21), enter this amount on Line 24.
16. Omit Line 25. Then on the next line, enter the date on which Form 940 is to be signed by Jesse Flores, the General Manager. Also enter his title on the same line.

After preparing Form 940, give it to Mr. Flores for his signature. Form 940 is filed along with a check in payment of the tax liability and with Form 508 (described below).

Form 508. The form that is used for reporting and paying the federal unemployment tax is *Form 508–Federal Tax Deposit*. This tax is figured on a quarterly basis and is deposited in an authorized commercial bank or a Federal Reserve Bank. To determine if a deposit should be made for any of the first three quarters in a calendar year, figure the total tax by multiplying by 0.007 that part of the first $6,000 of each employee's annual wages that were paid during the quarter. If the amount is more than $100, deposit it during the first month following the quarter. If the amount is $100 or less, it need not be deposited. However, this amount must be added to the next quarter's tax deposit.

EXAMPLE: If the FUTA tax for the first quarter was $75, it would not have to be deposited. If the tax for the second quarter was $80, a deposit is required because the FUTA tax liability for the two quarters ($75 + $80 = $155) is more than $100.

At the end of the year, if the tax reported on Form 940 less the amounts deposited for the year is more than $100, the entire amount must be deposited by January 31. If the tax for the year less any deposits is $100 or less, the amount must be either deposited or paid along with Form 940 by January 31. If the proper amounts have been deposited, the balance due will not exceed $100.

Form 508 (Illustration 35) shows the payment of the final deposit that was sent along with Form 940 (Illustration 34) and a check for the amount of $96.83 on January 15, 19—.

Preparing Form 508.

Use Form 508 on page 144 for the payment of the last federal unemployment tax deposit for the final fourth quarter of the taxable year. Form 508 is to be mailed together with Form 940 (which you have just completed) and with a Solarheat voucher check written for the proper amount of the tax deposit. Under the space labeled NAME OF BANK, enter *CALIFORNIA NATIONAL BANK.* Under the space labeled AMOUNT OF DEPOSIT, enter the amount already recorded on Form 940 as the final deposit for the fourth quarter.

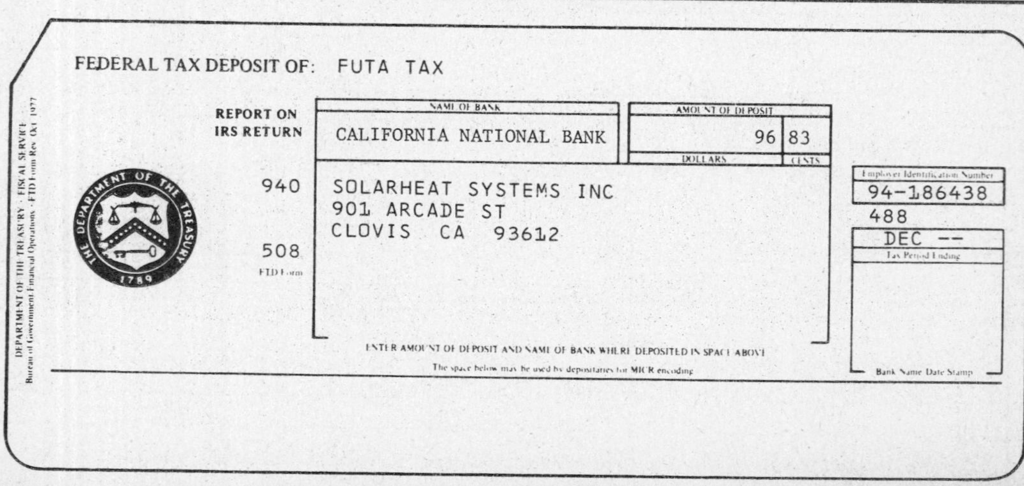
FEDERAL TAX DEPOSIT OF: FUTA TAX

DEPARTMENT OF THE TREASURY · FISCAL SERVICE
Bureau of Government Financial Operations · FTD Form Rev. Oct. 1977

REPORT ON IRS RETURN: 940

NAME OF BANK: CALIFORNIA NATIONAL BANK

AMOUNT OF DEPOSIT: 96 (DOLLARS) 83 (CENTS)

508
FTD Form

SOLARHEAT SYSTEMS INC
901 ARCADE ST
CLOVIS CA 93612

Employer Identification Number: 94-186438
488
DEC --
Tax Period Ending

ENTER AMOUNT OF DEPOSIT AND NAME OF BANK WHERE DEPOSITED IN SPACE ABOVE

The space below may be used by depositaries for MICR encoding

Bank Name Date Stamp

Illustration 35
Form 508—Federal Tax Deposit

10

PAYROLL SYSTEMS

The forms used for the Payroll Register and the Employee's Earnings Record to complete the project are like those that are found in many businesses. Of course, these forms will vary according to the length of the pay period, the number of employees, and the number of deductions that are made from earnings. Basically, however, most businesses keep a payroll register, a cash journal, and employee's earnings records to provide the information needed in preparing monthly, quarterly, and annual reports that are required by the various laws. This section will acquaint you with the other forms that are available which are used in businesses to simplify and speed up the preparation of payrolls.

STANDARD FORMS

Although many large businesses design their own payroll records, some firms can adapt their payroll records to the standard forms obtained from stationery stores. If a business has no unusual problems, it is usually more economical to purchase the standard forms than to have special forms printed. Basically, the standard forms contain the same information that was included in the forms used in this project. Any business that is planning to set up new payroll records or to make changes in existing records should investigate the standard forms that are available before becoming involved in the expense of designing and printing its own forms.

HANDWRITTEN PAYROLL SYSTEMS

In completing this project, the three basic steps involved in preparing the payroll after computing the time worked for each employee were the:

1. Recording of the information for each employee in the Payroll Register for each of the four pay periods.

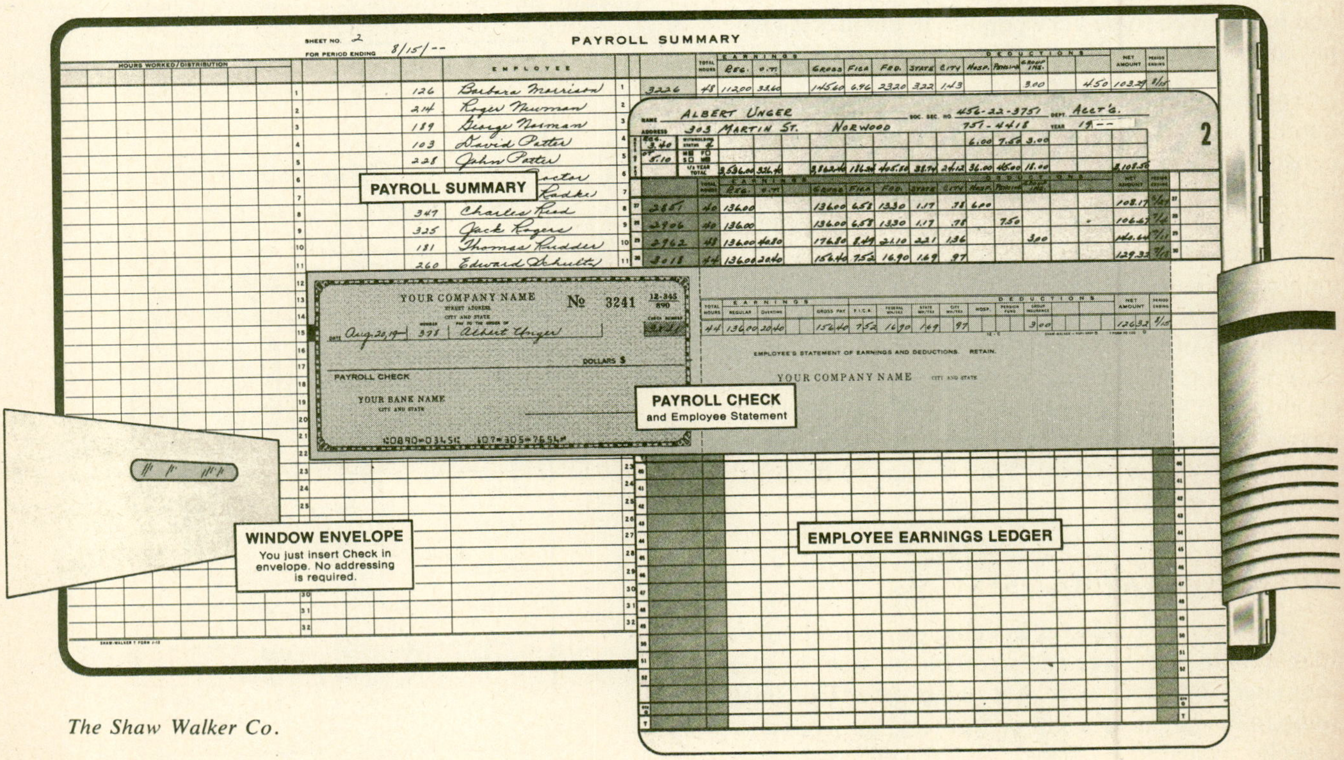

The Shaw Walker Co.

Illustration 36 Pegboard Payroll System

2. Preparing the pay envelopes or writing the payroll checks to pay the employees.
3. Posting the payroll data from the Payroll Register for each pay period to each Employee's Earnings Record.

Some payroll records are designed so that all the data can be prepared at one time. Illustration 36 on page 39 shows a payroll system that completes all three steps in one writing. This system consists of a plastic, wood, or metal board on which are placed the various payroll forms. A sheet from the payroll register is inserted first. On top of this form is placed a sheet of carbon paper and the employee's earnings record for an employee. On top of the employee's earnings record is placed a carbon-paper sheet and another form that may be either a receipt or a check depending on whether the salary or wages are paid by cash or by check. The columns for the earnings and the deductions on all three forms are the same. On the right side of the board are pegs or notches that are spaced the same width as the lines on the payroll register. The employee's earnings record and the combination receipt and check are placed on the proper pegs so that a carbon copy of the information is recorded on a line in the payroll register. As each employee's earnings record and each check are placed on the board, they are moved down one notch so that each entry is made on a separate line in the payroll register. This payroll system has proved to be very popular in businesses where payroll records are handwritten.

Another handwritten payroll system that is frequently used is shown in Illustration 37. This system consists of a combination payroll envelope and receipt that is used to pay employees with cash. When a payroll is paid by cash, a separate receipt is prepared. The employee receives a copy for a record while the employer keeps the original copy to be used later for preparing the federal quarterly tax returns. When the stub is torn off for the employer's records, a duplicate copy remains on the pay envelope as a record for the employee. The information for the receipt is from the payroll register. Some companies require the employee to sign the receipt. This is done to help insure the control of cash.

AUTOMATED PAYROLL SYSTEMS

Automated systems for keeping payroll records are adaptable to both large and small businesses. The large companies either own or rent computers. The smaller companies may rent small computers, may have their payrolls prepared by banks or data processing companies, or may rent time on a large, time-sharing computer.

Most manufacturers of accounting or posting machines can adapt them to payroll work. Illustration 38 shows one type of payroll form that is prepared by automation. Here the check and the receipt, the employee's earnings record, and the payroll journal are completed in one operation.

It is obvious that the preparation of the payrolls in any business is repetitious. Today, more and more businesses reduce the time needed for preparing payrolls by the use of efficient automated machines that provide almost instantly data to be used for a report or for any other purpose. The following paragraphs briefly explain how such a system works.

Punched-Card Payroll System. Under this system, vital payroll data for each employee is punched into a master card like the one in Illustration 39. Other cards showing earnings for the pay period and deductions for various purposes are prepared by punching holes in cards that are properly coded. These cards are "read" into a card reader that prints the payroll register and accumulates figures for the employee's earnings records and reports. Illustration 40 shows a payroll register that was prepared from punched cards.

Electronic Computers. Many large businesses use electronic computers for their payroll operations. Smaller businesses can rent time on an electronic computer on a time-sharing basis. These computers operate at fantastic speeds, make calculations almost

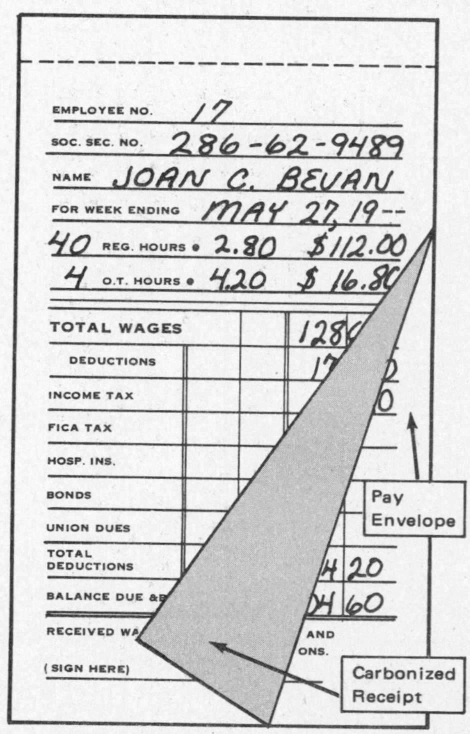

Illustration 37 Combination Payroll Envelope and Receipt

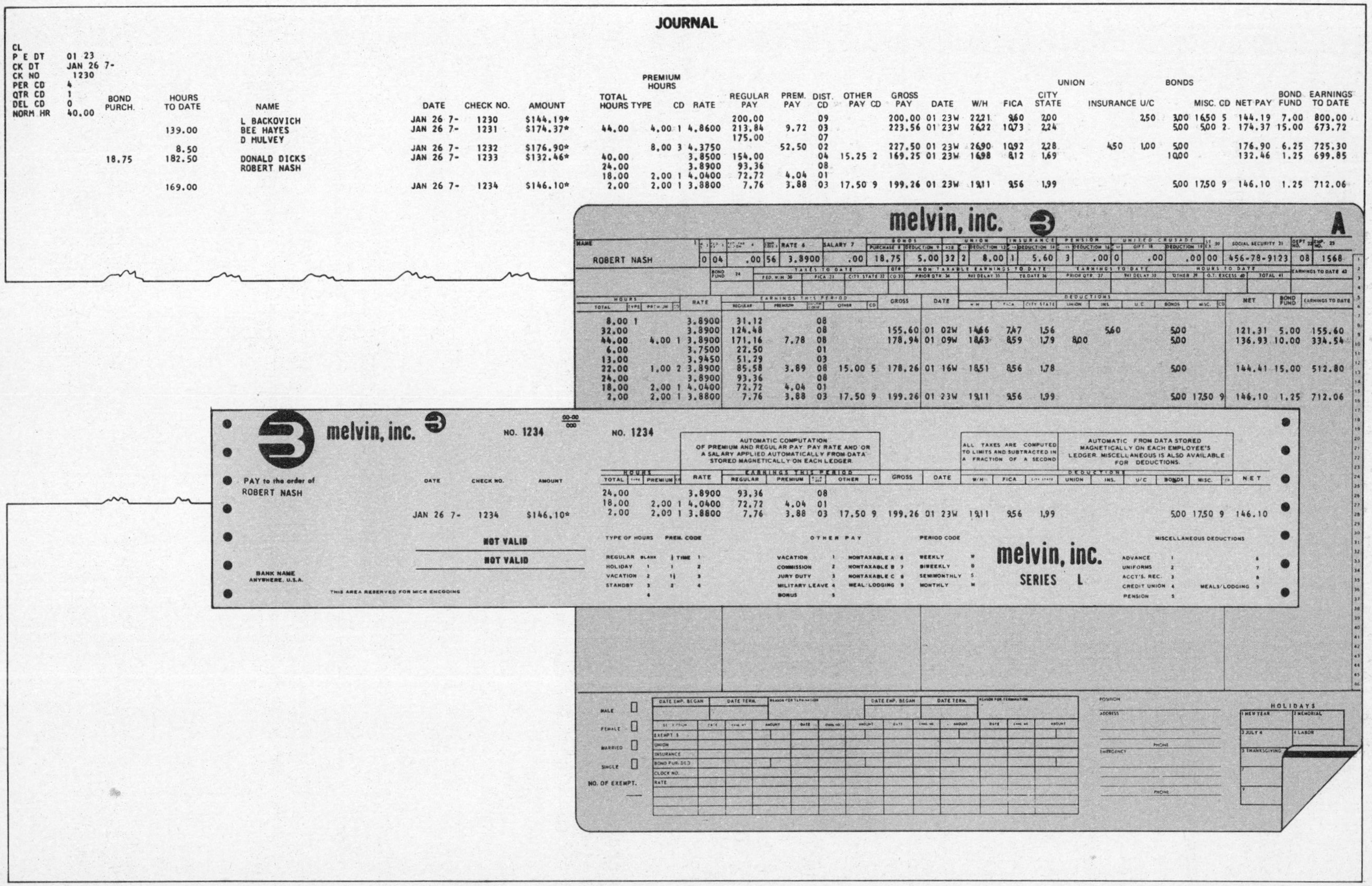

Illustration 38 Automated Payroll System

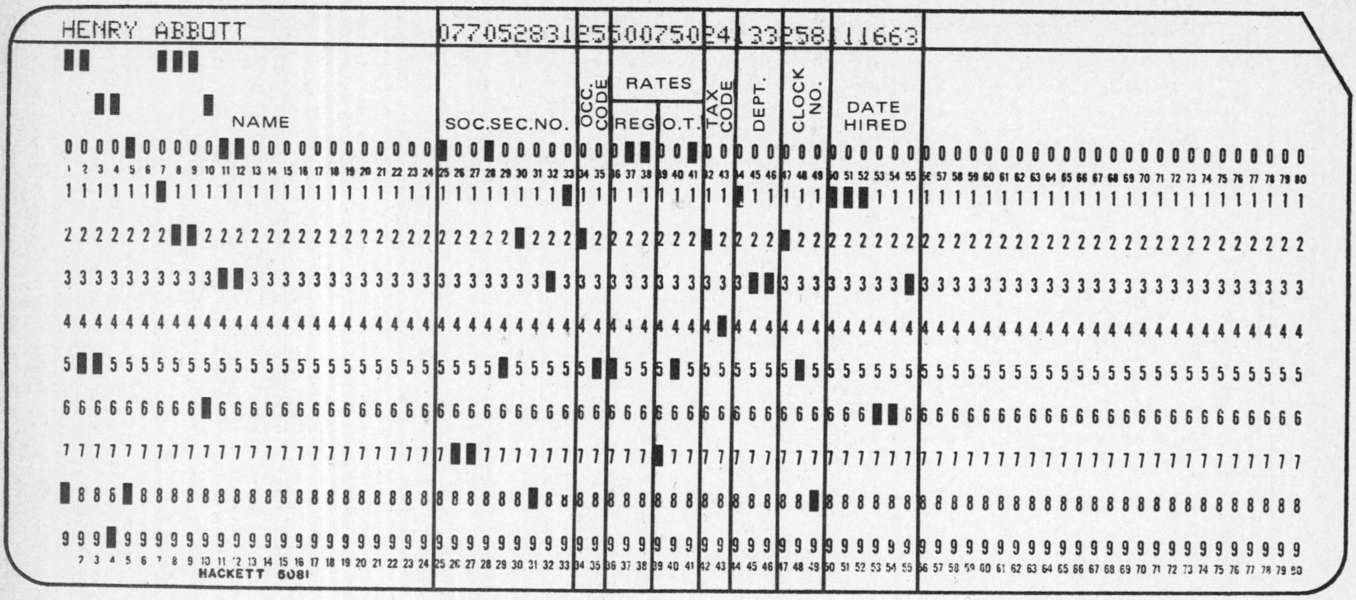

Illustration 39 Payroll Master Card

instantly, read data from an "input" device such as a punched card or magnetic tape, store data in a memory unit, and transfer data to a printer that prints it at a high speed. While many of the operations in such a complex system are automated, the basic principles covered here are followed even in this type of payroll system.

Other Electronic Aids. New electronic technology products assist all businesses in the computation of payrolls as well as in other business and accounting applications. A programmable electronic calculator can be programmed to automatically perform some of the functions involved in the computation of payrolls. This type of calculator is programmed by a cartridge that may be inserted into the machine to provide automatic instructions and constants such as for the FICA tax. This calculator does not change the payroll procedure but makes it easier, faster, and more accurate.

The minicomputer is less costly in price where more businesses can afford to buy them. This electronic product can also be programmed to prepare a payroll as well as many other services.

SHEET 1 OF 6 | DATE JANUARY 7 19--

C.W. TOLAND, inc.

PAYROLL REGISTER

NAME / DESCRIPTION	EMPL. NO.		TAX CODE	DAYS	BASE RATE	HOURS		CURRENT GROSS EARNINGS	DEDUCTIONS			CURRENT NET PAY	YEAR TO DATE		
	DEPT.	CLOCK				REGULAR	OVERTIME		WITH. TAX	F.I.C.A.	OTHER		EARNINGS	WITH. TAX	F.I.C.A.
JANE CONDORODIS	233	258	24		5:00										
SAVINGS BOND											5:00				
				5		40:0		200:00	14:30	12:26	5:00	168:44	200:00	14:30	12:26
VICKI CONTRERAS	231	100	23		3:80										
SAVINGS											7:50				
				5		40:0	2:0	163:40	23:80	10:02	7:50	122:08	163:40	23:80	10:02
SANDRA SHRUM	231	145	24		4:15										
SAVINGS											5:50				
SAVINGS BOND											5:00				
				5		40:0	2:0	178:45	19:30	10:94	10:50	137:71	178:45	19:30	10:94

Illustration 40 Payroll Register Automatically Prepared from Punched Cards

11 ACCOUNTING ENTRIES FOR THE PAYROLL

Up to now, you have only been concerned with the clerical work involved in the preparation of the weekly payrolls, the payroll records, and the federal returns and deposit forms. No knowledge of accounting was required. In many small businesses, the payrolls are prepared by an employee who also does part or all of the bookkeeping. If you have studied accounting, you will find that the additional practice involved in recording the entries for each payroll is helpful. Solarheat Systems Inc. uses a journal with many columns in which all the transactions can be entered. A multicolumn journal that combines all journals into one book of original entry is called a *combination journal*.

Use the forms of the combination journal on pages 147-149 to record only the beginning payroll entries for the weekly payrolls in this textbook. You will not have to record the payment of the payroll liabilities. The account titles that are used by Solarheat are:

- Cash
- Payroll Cash
- Employees Income Tax Payable
- FICA Tax Payable
- Federal Unemployment Tax Payable
- Group Insurance Payable
- Medical Insurance Payable
- State Unemployment Tax Payable
- Union Dues Payable
- Payroll Taxes Expense
- Salary Expense

RECORDING THE DECEMBER 3-9 PAYROLL

As you follow the explanation below, look at the two payroll entries of December 12 as they were recorded in the Combination Journal (Illustration 41).

Debit. The total amount earned by all employees represents the salary expense for the week of December 3-9. On December 12, *Salary Expense* was debited for the total of the TOTAL EARNINGS column in the Payroll Register.

Credit. For the week of December 3-9, the employees are paid in cash. This means that a decrease will occur in the asset Cash. Therefore, to record the amount paid to the employees, credit *Cash* for the total of the NET PAY column in the Payroll Register.

All amounts that are withheld from each employee's weekly earnings represent increases in the liabilities of the company. These amounts are considered as liabilities because they are a part of what the employees earned but are still unpaid. Credit these liability accounts: *Employees Income Tax Payable* for the total of the FEDERAL INCOME TAX column in the Payroll Register, *FICA Tax Payable* for the total of the FICA TAX column, and *Union Dues Payable* for the total of the OTHER column.

Recording the Employer's Payroll Tax Liabilities. For each pay period, an employer must pay certain payroll taxes. The employer must match the same amount that was withheld for FICA taxes

COMBINATION JOURNAL — PAGE

	1 Cash Debit	2 Cash Credit	Date	Account Title	Doc. No.	Post. Ref.	3 General Debit	4 General Credit	
3		2,839 28	Dec. 12	Salary Expense			3,558 63		3
4				Employees Income Tax Pay.				456 20	4
5				FICA Tax Payable				218 15	5
6				Union Dues Payable				45 00	6
7			12	Payroll Taxes Expense			241 39		7
8				FICA Tax Payable				218 15	8
9				Fed. Unempl. Tax Pay.				4 78	9
10				State Unempl. Tax Pay.				18 46	10

Illustration 41
Payroll Entries of December 12 As Recorded in the Combination Journal

from the employees' earnings by paying 6.13% (0.0613)—the same rate contributed by each employee. An employer also pays federal and state unemployment taxes at a limit of $6,000 on each employee's earnings in a calendar year. These taxes are paid only by the employer. Most of Solarheat's employees (except for the new ones) have exceeded the taxable limit of $6,000 for the federal unemployment tax and the taxable limit of $6,000 for the state unemployment tax.

The employer's payroll tax liabilities are based on these rates: 6.13% (0.0613) for FICA tax (the same rate as for each employee's contribution), 0.7% (0.007) for federal unemployment tax, and 2.7% (0.027) for state unemployment tax. The limits above which these taxes do not apply are explained below.

1. Only earnings up to $22,900 for each employee are subject to the FICA tax. Earnings over $22,900 are tax exempt.
2. Earnings up to $6,000 for each employee are subject to the federal unemployment tax. Earnings over this amount are tax exempt.
3. In California, the earnings up to $6,000 for each employee are subject to the state unemployment tax. No tax is paid on earnings over $6,000.

The amounts for the accumulated taxable earnings for each employee are shown in the last column on the Employee's Earnings Record. Each Record must be checked to determine the amount of earnings subject to the above limits before the payroll entries for the employer's tax liabilities can be recorded for each week.

To record the entries for the employer's payroll tax liabilities in the Combination Journal, debit *Payroll Taxes Expense* for the total of the three tax liabilities. Then credit these accounts: *FICA Tax Payable* for the employer's "match" of the same amount that was withheld for FICA taxes from the employees' earnings, *Fed. Unempl. Tax Payable* for 0.7% (0.007) of those earnings subject to the federal unemployment tax, and *State Unempl. Tax Payable* for 2.7% (0.027) of those earnings subject to the state unemployment tax.

RECORDING THE DECEMBER 10-16 PAYROLL

Use the same procedure given for the previous week with the exception that *Medical Insurance Payable* will also be credited for the total of the MEDICAL INSURANCE column in the Payroll Register. Note that Jesse Flores' earnings reached $22,900 this week. Only those earnings up to $22,900 are subject to the withholding of FICA tax. The amount above $22,900 is exempt. Determine the amount that is taxable before recording the payroll entries for this week.

RECORDING THE DECEMBER 17-23 PAYROLL

Since Solarheat changes over to paying its employees by check this week, it is necessary to establish a balance in the new Payroll Cash account. In this way, the company can transfer money from the Cash account to pay its Payroll Cash account each week. In addition to the NET PAY that must be placed in this special bank account, Solarheat is adding a reserve of $500. The entry to be made for the December 17-23 payroll is: debit *Payroll Cash* for the NET PAY amount + $500; credit *Cash* for the NET PAY amount + $500. After the NET PAY amount plus the $500 is transferred, the payroll checks are written against the Payroll Cash account.

The entry for recording the employer's payroll tax liabilities is made in the same manner as the previous week except that the new account, Payroll Cash, will be used instead of Cash.

RECORDING THE DECEMBER 24-30 PAYROLL

Use the same procedure given for the week of December 17-23 to record this week's payroll except that *Group Insurance Payable* must be credited for the total of the GROUP INSURANCE column in the Payroll Register.

ACTIVITIES 1-7

NAME ____________________

PERIOD ____________ DATE ____________

ACTIVITY 1

For this activity, you are to fill out Form SS-5, Application for a Social Security Number, shown below.

ID: CN: DO:

DO NOT WRITE IN THE ABOVE SPACE

APPLICATION FOR A SOCIAL SECURITY NUMBER

See Instructions on Back. Print in Black or Dark Blue Ink or Use Typewriter.

1 Print FULL NAME YOU WILL USE IN WORK OR BUSINESS (First Name) (Middle Name or Initial—if none, draw line ____) (Last Name)

2 Print FULL NAME GIVEN YOU AT BIRTH

6 YOUR DATE OF BIRTH (Month) (Day) (Year)

3 PLACE OF BIRTH (City) (County if known) (State)

7 YOUR PRESENT AGE (Age on last birthday)

4 MOTHER'S FULL NAME AT HER BIRTH (Her maiden name)

8 YOUR SEX MALE ☐ FEMALE ☐

5 FATHER'S FULL NAME (Regardless of whether living or dead)

9 YOUR COLOR OR RACE WHITE ☐ NEGRO ☐ OTHER ☐

10 HAVE YOU EVER BEFORE APPLIED FOR OR HAD A UNITED STATES SOCIAL SECURITY, RAILROAD, OR TAX ACCOUNT NUMBER? NO ☐ DON'T KNOW ☐ YES ☐ → (If "Yes" Print State in which you applied and Date you applied and Social Security Number if known)

11 YOUR MAILING ADDRESS (Number and Street, Apt. No., P.O. Box, or Rural Route) (City) (State) (Zip Code)

12 TODAY'S DATE

14 NOTICE: Whoever, with intent to falsify his or someone else's true identity, willfully furnishes or causes to be furnished false information in applying for a social security number, is subject to a fine of not more than $1,000 or imprisonment for up to 1 year, or both.

13 TELEPHONE NUMBER

Sign YOUR NAME HERE (Do Not Print)

DHEW, Social Security Administration
Form SS-5

☐ RESCREEN ☐ ASSIGN ☐ DUP ISSUED

Return completed application to nearest SOCIAL SECURITY ADMINISTRATION OFFICE

ACTIVITY 2

For this activity, you are to complete Form W-4. The front of this form appears below.

Form **W-4**

Department of the Treasury
Internal Revenue Service

Employee's Withholding Allowance Certificate

(Use for Wages Paid After December 31, 19--)

This certificate is for income tax withholding purposes only. It will remain in effect until you change it. If you claim exemption from withholding, you will have to file a new certificate on or before April 30 of next year.

Type or print your full name | Your social security number

Home address (number and street or rural route)

City or town, State, and ZIP code

Marital Status: ☐ Single ☐ Married ☐ Married, but withhold at higher Single rate

Note: *If married, but legally separated, or spouse is a nonresident alien, check the single block.*

1 Total number of allowances you are claiming . . . .

2 Additional amount, if any, you want deducted from each pay (if your employer agrees) . . . . $

3 I claim exemption from withholding (see instructions). Enter "Exempt" . . . .

Under the penalties of perjury, I certify that the number of withholding allowances claimed on this certificate does not exceed the number to which I am entitled. If claiming exemption from withholding, I certify that I incurred no liability for Federal income tax for last year and I anticipate that I will incur no liability for Federal income tax for this year.

Signature ►.. Date ►.., 19........

.... Detach along this line ....

Figure Your Total Withholding Allowances Below

(a) Allowance(s) for exemption(s)—Enter 1 for each personal exemption you can claim on your Federal income tax return* . . .

(b) Special withholding allowance—Enter 1 if single with 1 employer, or married with 1 employer and spouse not employed** . . .

(c) Allowance(s) for credit(s) and/or deduction(s)—Enter number from tables on page 2 . . . .

(d) Total (add lines (a) through (c) above)—Enter here and on line 1, Form W-4, above . . . .

*If you are in doubt as to whom you may claim as a dependent, see the instructions that came with your last Federal income tax return or call your local Internal Revenue Service office.

**This allowance is used solely for purposes of figuring your withholding tax, and cannot be claimed when you file your tax return.

NAME ____________________

PERIOD ____________ DATE ____________

ACTIVITY 3

Study Guide—SECTION 1: LAWS AND REGULATIONS AFFECTING A PAYROLL

1. What are some of the laws that affect payroll procedures in business?

   a.

   b.

   c.

   d.

   e.

2. Under the provisions of the Social Security Act that refer to old-age, survivor, and disabled worker benefits, what information must the payroll records show?

   a.

   b.

   c.

   d.

   e.

3. What is the current rate of tax on employer and employee under the Federal Insurance Contributions Act?

4. How is the FICA tax on the employee collected from the employee?

(continued)

ACTIVITY 3 (concluded)

Study Guide—SECTION 1: LAWS AND REGULATIONS AFFECTING A PAYROLL

5. What is the rate of tax on employers under the Federal Unemployment Tax Act?

6. What is meant by a work week under the Fair Labor Standards Act?

7. What records must the employer keep under the Internal Revenue Code to provide information about the withholding of income tax?

   a.

   b.

   c.

8. Explain some of the other reasons why businesses must keep certain information about payrolls.

   a.

   b.

   c.

NAME________________________________

PERIOD ______________________ DATE__________

ACTIVITY 4

Study Guide—SECTION 2: BASES FOR SALARY AND WAGE PAYMENTS

1. Explain what is meant by "time wages." Give four examples.

2. Under the Fair Labor Standards Act, what is the minimum hourly rate of pay and the overtime rate of pay?

3. Explain what is meant by the piece-rate basis for paying wages.

4. How is the regular hourly rate of pay determined for piece-rate workers under the Fair Labors Standards Act?

5. a. If an employee earned $140.40 for 45 hours of work on a piece-rate basis, what is the hourly rate?

   b. In addition to the regular earnings paid this week, how much overtime pay is this employee paid?

   c. If an employee earned $114 for 40 hours of work on a piece-rate basis, what is the hourly rate?

   d. How much would the employee in *c.* be paid? Why?

(*continued*)

ACTIVITY 4 (concluded)

Study Guide—SECTION 2: BASES FOR SALARY AND WAGE PAYMENTS

6. Explain what is meant by a *commission*. Is a commission considered as a part of a regular salary or wage payment in preparing a payroll?

7. Explain what is meant by a *bonus payment*. Is a bonus payment included in earnings to determine the overtime rate of pay? Explain your answer.

8. Weekly wage payments for a 40-hour week are given below. Figure the regular hourly rate of pay and the overtime rate of pay at 1½ times the regular hourly rate.

Weekly Wages	*Hourly Rate*	*Overtime Rate*	*Weekly Wages*	*Hourly Rate*	*Overtime Rate*
$118	$______	$______	$150	$______	$______
136	______	______	180	______	______

9. Various monthly wage payments are given below. Complete the table showing the yearly, weekly, hourly, and overtime rates. Figure the overtime rate at 1½ times the regular hourly rate. Assume that the work week is 35 hours and that the overtime rate applies after 35 hours. (The hourly rate should be figured to the third decimal place if this makes a difference in the overtime rate.)

Monthly Wages	*Yearly Rate*	*Weekly Rate*	*Hourly Rate*	*Overtime Rate*
$477.75	$______	$______	$______	$______
523.25	______	______	______	______
637.00	______	______	______	______
682.50	______	______	______	______
796.25	______	______	______	______

10. During a 37½-hour week, Jane Hoff earns $120. Under the Fair Labor Standards Act, figure her wages when she works these hours:

a. 40 hours .... $____________ b. 45 hours .... $____________

11. During a certain week, Brigit Rehn worked 44 hours and produced 770 units. The regular piece-rate is 20¢ per unit. Figure Brigit's total earnings for the week, assuming that she received the regular overtime rate for work over 40 hours.

NAME ______ PERIOD ______ DATE ______

ACTIVITY 5

For this activity, you are to fill out your own personnel record on the form below.

PERSONAL AND EMPLOYMENT DATA

Solarheat Systems Inc.

NAME Martin (Last) Linda (First) V. (Middle) SOC. SEC. NO. 025-52-5558

ADDRESS 359 Park Street (Street Address) New Bedford Mass. #02740 (City, State, ZIP Code) TELEPHONE NO. 996-2946

PERSON NOTIFIED IN CASE OF EMERGENCY Mrs. Eccleston (Name) 162 Cottage St. (Address) 995-2435 (Telephone Number)

LAST EMPLOYER Mister Donut 2065 Acushnet Ave (Company Name and Address) ______ (Telephone Number) Waitress (Your Job Description)

REASON FOR LEAVING unsatisfied with work

PHYSICAL DESCRIPTION 5'1" (Height) 120 (Weight) ______ (Other Description)
(Complete only if work related)

DATE EMPLOYED ______

JOB DESCRIPTION ______

DEPARTMENT ______

EMPLOYEE CLOCK NO. ______

INCOME TAX WITHHOLDING ALLOWANCES ______

MARITAL STATUS ______

HIRED AS: ☐ Full Time ☐ Part Time ☐ Temporary

SALARY/WAGES PER WEEK $ ______

Hourly Rate $ ______ Overtime Rate $ ______

DEDUCTIONS: Credit Union .... $ ______

Group Insurance ..... $ ______

Medical Insurance .... $ ______

Union Dues .... $ ______

U.S. Savings Bond .... $ ______

Other .... $ ______

DATE OF BIRTH ______

DATE LEFT EMPLOYMENT ______

Remarks: ______

ACTIVITY 6

The Employee's Earnings Record that you are to use for this activity appears in the forms section of this textbook. Please refer to page 15 for instructions.

NAME Linda Martin

PERIOD ______________ DATE 11/10/80

ACTIVITY 7

Study Guide—SECTION 3: BASIC PAYROLL RECORDS AND REQUIRED DATA

1. What basic information must payroll records contain?

   a. Title of the form

   b. The department or branch indicated

   c. The name of each employee

2. How long must records of wage-and-hour computations be kept? ~~A~~ Upon which wage-and hour computations are based they must be kept for 3 years.

3. List several forms that may be used as employees' time records.

   a. employee's earnings record

   b. Payroll Register

   c. ~~Payroll check~~ A personnel record

4. What information must hourly records show? It must show the time of day and the day of the week when the work begins, the hours worked each day, and the total hours worked each work week.

(continued)

ACTIVITY 7 (concluded)

Study Guide—SECTION 3: BASIC PAYROLL RECORDS AND REQUIRED DATA

5. What information must be included in salary-and-wage records?

a. the basis on which wages are paid (hourly, weekly, piecework ect.)

b. hourly pay rate for any week when overtime is worked.

c. total daily or weekly straightime earnings

d. total overtime earnings

e. additions or deductions from the employee's wages for each pay period

f. total wages paid each pay period

g. dates of payment and of the pay period covered by the payment

6. What are the three basic records in which payroll information is normally kept?

a. Personnel record

b. Payroll register

c. Employee's earning's record

WEEKLY TIME RECORD — Solarheat Systems Inc.

For week ending December 9 19--

Name Jackson, Paula

Dept. Office   Employee No. 2

DAY WORKED	REGULAR HOURS	OVERTIME HOURS	TOTAL HOURS WORKED
Monday	8.0		8.0
Tuesday	8.0		8.0
Wednesday	8.0		8.0
Thursday	8.0		8.0
Friday	8.0		8.0
Saturday			
Sunday			
		TOTAL HOURS ...	40.0

$135.00

WEEKLY TIME RECORD — Solarheat Systems Inc.

For week ending December 9 19--

Name ~~Linda Martin~~ Martin, Linda

Dept. Office   Employee No. 3

DAY WORKED	REGULAR HOURS	OVERTIME HOURS	TOTAL HOURS WORKED
Monday	8.0		8.0
Tuesday	8.0		8.0
Wednesday	8.0		8.0
Thursday	8.0		8.0
Friday	8.0		8.0
Saturday			
Sunday			
		TOTAL HOURS ...	40.0

$135.00

WEEKLY SALES REPORT — Solarheat Systems Inc.

For week ending December 9 19--

NO.	SALESPERSON	SALES	X 8 % RATE	= COMMISSION EARNED
12	Klaus, Elsie	$4,876.48	8%	$390.12
13	Hirasuna, James	4,632.40	8%	370.59

TOTAL SALES $9,508.88   TOTAL COMMISSIONS $760.71

WEEK OF DECEMBER 3-9

NAME RUBEN SALAZAR

CLOCK NO. 22

SOC. SEC. NO. 341 42 5608

PERIOD WEEK ENDING DECEMBER 9, 19--

	MORNING		AFTERNOON		NIGHT		REGULAR HOURS	OVERTIME HOURS
	In	Out	In	Out	In	Out		
M	7:56	12:03	12:58	2:35			5.5	
T	7:59	12:01	12:57	5:06			8.0	
W	7:54	12:05	12:59	5:04			8.0	
T	7:59	12:03	12:56	6:03			8.0	1.0
F	7:57	12:06	12:58	5:05			8.0	
S								
S								
						TOTAL HOURS	37.5	1.0

TYPE	RATE	HOURS	EARNINGS
Regular	$ 6.90	37.5	$ 258.75
Overtime	10.35	1.0	10.35
Special			
TOTAL		38.5	$ 269.10

FOR PAYROLL USE ONLY

NAME LEROY BROWN

CLOCK NO. 23

SOC. SEC. NO. 263 23 3724

PERIOD WEEK ENDING DECEMBER 9, 19--

	MORNING		AFTERNOON		NIGHT		REGULAR HOURS	OVERTIME HOURS
	In	Out	In	Out	In	Out		
M	7:59	12:00	12:56	5:06			8.0	
T	7:57	12:01	12:59	5:02			8.0	
W	7:56	12:01	12:58	5:04			8.0	
T	7:58	12:03	12:59	5:05			8.0	
F	7:55	12:05	12:54	5:03			8.0	
S	9:00	12:02						3.0
S								
						TOTAL HOURS	40.0	3.0

TYPE	RATE	HOURS	EARNINGS
Regular	$ 4.40	40.0	$ 176.00
Overtime	6.60	3.0	19.80
Special			
TOTAL		42.0	$ 195.80

FOR PAYROLL USE ONLY

NAME DARLENE MCLAUGHLIN

CLOCK NO. 24

SOC. SEC. NO. 147 62 6118

PERIOD WEEK ENDING DECEMBER 9, 19--

	MORNING		AFTERNOON		NIGHT		REGULAR HOURS	OVERTIME HOURS
	In	Out	In	Out	In	Out		
M	7:53	12:04	12:59	5:34			8.0	0.5
T	7:56	12:01	12:57	3:32			6.5	
W	8:09	12:03	12:59	5:35			7.8	0.5
T								
F	7:59	12:01	12:57	5:34			8.0	0.5
S								
S								
						TOTAL HOURS	30.3	1.5

TYPE	RATE	HOURS	EARNINGS
Regular	$ 5.00	30.3	$ 151.50
Overtime	7.50	1.5	11.25
Special			
TOTAL		31.8	$ 162.75

FOR PAYROLL USE ONLY

NAME DIANE VUKOVICH

CLOCK NO. 25

SOC. SEC. NO. 342 15 1394

PERIOD WEEK ENDING DECEMBER 9, 19--

	MORNING		AFTERNOON		NIGHT		REGULAR HOURS	OVERTIME HOURS
	In	Out	In	Out	In	Out		
M								
T	7:57	12:01	12:59	5:02			8.0	
W	7:56	12:01	12:58	5:04	5:55	7:35	8.0	1.5
T	7:58	12:03	12:59	5:05			8.0	
F	7:55	12:05	12:54	5:03	5:59	7:33	8.0	1.5
S	9:00	12:02						3.0
S								
						TOTAL HOURS	32.0	6.0

TYPE	RATE	HOURS	EARNINGS
Regular	$ 5.40	32.0	$ 172.80
Overtime	8.10	6.0	48.60
Special			
TOTAL		38.2	$ 221.40

FOR PAYROLL USE ONLY

NAME SAM RILEY

CLOCK NO. 26

SOC. SEC. NO. 247 27 1279

PERIOD WEEK ENDING DECEMBER 9, 19--

	MORNING In	MORNING Out	AFTERNOON In	AFTERNOON Out	NIGHT In	NIGHT Out	REGULAR HOURS	OVERTIME HOURS
M	7:59	12:00	12:56	5:06			8.0	
T	7:57	12:01	12:59	5:02			8.0	
W	7:56	12:01	12:58	5:04	5:55	7:35	8.0	1.5
T	7:58	12:03	12:59	5:05			8.0	
F	7:55	12:05	12:54	5:03			8.0	
S								
S								
TOTAL HOURS							40.0	1.5

TYPE	RATE	HOURS	EARNINGS
Regular	$5.90	40.0	$236.00
Overtime	8.85	1.5	13.28
Special			
TOTAL		41.5	$249.28

FOR PAYROLL USE ONLY

NAME SARA NEUFELD

CLOCK NO. 27

SOC. SEC. NO. 143 62 4762

PERIOD WEEK ENDING DECEMBER 9, 19--

	MORNING In	MORNING Out	AFTERNOON In	AFTERNOON Out	NIGHT In	NIGHT Out	REGULAR HOURS	OVERTIME HOURS
M	7:56	12:03	12:58	2:35			5.5	
T	7:59	12:01	12:57	5:06	5:58	8:33	8.0	2.5
W	7:54	12:05	12:59	5:04			8.0	
T	7:59	12:03	12:56	6:03			8.0	1.0
F	7:57	12:06	12:58	5:05	5:58	7:32	8.0	1.5
S	9:00	11:34	12:57	3:32				5.0
S								
TOTAL HOURS							37.5	10.0

TYPE	RATE	HOURS	EARNINGS
Regular	$5.70	37.5	$213.75
Overtime	8.55	10.0	85.50
Special			
TOTAL		47.5	$299.25

FOR PAYROLL USE ONLY

1-6 = 1/10
7-12 = 2/10
13-18 = 3/10
19-24 = 4/10
25-30 = 5/10

NAME MIKE LEONARDO

CLOCK NO. 28

SOC. SEC. NO. 147 15 4321

PERIOD WEEK ENDING DECEMBER 9, 19--

	MORNING In	MORNING Out	AFTERNOON In	AFTERNOON Out	NIGHT In	NIGHT Out	REGULAR HOURS	OVERTIME HOURS
M	7:56	12:03	12:58	2:35			5.5	
T	7:59	12:01	12:57	5:06			8.0	
W	7:54	12:05	12:59	5:04			8.0	
T	7:59	12:03	12:56	6:03			8.0	1.0
F	7:57	12:06	12:58	5:05			8.0	
S	9:00	11:34						2.05
S								
TOTAL HOURS							37.5	3.5

TYPE	RATE	HOURS	EARNINGS
Regular	$4.50	37.5	$168.75
Overtime	6.75	3.5	23.63
Special			
TOTAL		41.0	$192.38

FOR PAYROLL USE ONLY

PIECE-RATE PRODUCTION REPORT

Solarheat Systems Inc.

For week ending *December 9* 19--

NO.	NAME	MON.	TU.	WED.	THU.	FRI.	TOTAL PRODUCTION	X RATE	= GROSS PAY
42	Baker, Edna	316	328	312	310	324	1590	$.14¢	$222.60
43	Svenson, Karl	361	352	343	356	341	1753	.12¢	$210.36

P. R - piece rate
If edna worked 44 hrs
40 hrs
4 hrs overtime
5.06
44) 222.60

NAME EDNA BAKER

CLOCK NO. 42

SOC. SEC. NO. 372 37 2843

PERIOD WEEK ENDING DECEMBER 9, 19--

	MORNING In	MORNING Out	AFTERNOON In	AFTERNOON Out	NIGHT In	NIGHT Out	REGULAR HOURS	OVERTIME HOURS
M	7:59	12:00	12:56	5:06			8.0	
T	7:57	12:01	12:59	5:02			8.0	
W	7:56	12:01	12:58	5:04			8.0	
T	7:58	12:03	12:59	5:05			8.0	4.0
F	7:55	12:05	12:54	5:03			8.0	
S								
S								
TOTAL HOURS							40.0	4.0

If working overtime ex.

TYPE	RATE	HOURS	EARNINGS
Regular	$ P.R (5.06)	40.0	$ 222.60
Overtime	2.53	4.0	10.12
Special			
TOTAL		44.0	$ 232.72

FOR PAYROLL USE ONLY

NAME KARL SVENSON

CLOCK NO. 43

SOC. SEC. NO. 163 19 1968

PERIOD WEEK ENDING DECEMBER 9, 19--

	MORNING In	MORNING Out	AFTERNOON In	AFTERNOON Out	NIGHT In	NIGHT Out	REGULAR HOURS	OVERTIME HOURS
M	7:56	12:03	12:58	2:35			5.5	
T	7:59	12:01	12:57	5:06			8.0	
W	7:54	12:05	12:59	5:04			8.0	
T	7:59	12:03	12:56	5:03			8.0	
F	7:57	12:06	12:58	5:05			8.0	
S								
S								
TOTAL HOURS							37.5	

TYPE	RATE	HOURS	EARNINGS
Regular	$ 5.6096	37.5	$ 210.36
Overtime			
Special			
TOTAL		37.5	$ 210.36

FOR PAYROLL USE ONLY

PAYROLL REGISTER

WEEK ENDED December 9, 19--

DATE OF PAYMENT December 9, 19--

	EMPL. NO.	EMPLOYEE'S NAME	MARITAL STATUS	ALLOW-ANCES	TOTAL HOURS	EARNINGS REGULAR	EARNINGS OVERTIME	EARNINGS TOTAL	DEDUCTIONS FEDERAL INC. TAX	DEDUCTIONS FICA TAX	DEDUCTIONS GROUP INSURANCE	DEDUCTIONS MEDICAL INSURANCE	DEDUCTIONS OTHER	DEDUCTIONS TOTAL	PAID NET PAY	PAID CK. NO.	
1	1	Flores, Jesse	M	4	40	460.00		460.00	73.90	28.20				102.10	357.90		1
2	2	Jackson, [illegible]	M	0	40	180.00		180.00	21.10	11.03				32.13	147.87		2
3	3	Martin, Linda	S	1	40	135.00		135.00	15.40	8.28				23.68	111.32		3
4	12	Long, Elsie	M	2		390.12		390.12	62.40	23.91				86.31	303.81		4
5	13	Lizangna, James	M	4		370.59		370.59	49.90	22.72				72.62	297.97		5
6	22	Salazar, Ruben	M	2	38.5	[illegible]	10.35	269.10	30.80	16.50			U 5.00	52.30	216.80		6
7	23	Brown, Leroy	M	5	43	176.00	19.80	195.80	[illegible]	12.00			U 5.00	26.90	168.90		7
8	24	McLaughlin, [illegible]	S	1	31.8	151.50	11.25	162.25	20.60	9.48			U 5.00	35.58	127.17		8
9	25	[illegible], Diane	M	2	38.2	172.80	48.60	221.40	22.10	13.57			U 5.00	41.67	179.73		9
10	26	Riley, Sam	M	2	40	236.00	13.28	249.28	26.70	15.28			U 5.00	46.98	202.30		10
11	27	[illegible], Sara	M	0	47.5	213.75	85.50	299.25	44.30	18.34			U 5.00	67.64	231.61		11
12	28	Leonardo, Mike	M	2	41	168.75	23.63	192.38	17.70	11.79			U 5.00	34.49	157.89		12
13	42	Baker, Edna	M	0	40	222.60		222.60	28.40	13.65			U 5.00	47.05	175.55		13
14	43	Swenson, Karl	S	1		210.36		210.36	32.00	12.90			U 5.00	49.90	160.46		14
15																	15
16																	16
17																	17
18		TOTAL				3,346.22	212.41	3,558.63	456.20	218.15			45.00	719.35	2,839.28		18

Other Deductions: B—U.S. Savings Bonds; C—Credit Union; U—Union Dues; UF—United Fund

CURRENCY ANALYSIS

For week ending ______________________ 19______

Solarheat Systems Inc.

EMPLOYEE'S NAME	AMOUNT TO BE PAID		BILLS				COINS				
			$20	$10	$5	$1	50¢	25¢	10¢	5¢	1¢
Flores, Jesse	357	90	17	1	1	2	1	1	1	1	
Jackson, Paula	147	87	7		1	2	1	1	1		2
Martin, Linda	111	32	5	1		1		1		1	2
Khans, Elsie	303	81	15			3	1	1		1	1
Hirasuna, James	297.	97	14	1	1	2	1	1	2		2
Salazar, Ruben	216.	80	10	1	1	1	1	1		1	
Brown, Leroy	168.	90	8		1	3	1	1	1	1	
McLaughlin, Darlene	127.	17	6		1	2			1	1	2
Vukovich, Diane	129.	23	8	1	1	4	1		2		3
Riley, Sam	202	30	10			2		1		1	
Penfield, Sara	231	61	11	1		1	1		1		1
Leonardo, Mike	157	89	7	1	1	2	1	1	1		4
Baker, Edna	175	55	8	1	1		1			1	
Svenson, Karl	160	46	8					1	2	2	1
TOTAL →	2839	28	134	80	45	25	10	10	12	8	18

PAYROLL CHANGE REQUISITION

CALIFORNIA NATIONAL BANK
of Clovis, CA 93612

FIRM ______________ 19____

	NO.	AMOUNT
BILLS: $20	134	$2680.00
$10	8	80.00
$5	9	45.00
$1	25	25.00
COINS: 50¢	10	5.00
25¢	10	2.50
10¢	12	1.20
5¢	8	.40
1¢	18	.18
TOTAL		$2839.28

Solarheat Systems Inc.

901 Arcade Street
Clovis, CA 93612

NO. 93169

90–085
1211

DATE Dec. 12, 19

Cash

AMOUNT
$ 2839.28

PAY Two Thousand eight-hundred thirty-nine 28/100 DOLLARS

CALIFORNIA NATIONAL BANK
of Clovis, CA 93612

⑆121100858⑆ 2381⑈4576⑈346

Solarheat Systems Inc.

Jesse Flores
AUTHORIZED SIGNATURE

Solarheat Systems Inc. 901 Arcade Street Clovis, CA 93612 NO. 93169

DETACH BEFORE DEPOSITING CHECK

DATE	DESCRIPTION	AMOUNT	DISCOUNT %	DISCOUNT AMOUNT	OTHER DEDUCTIONS	NET AMOUNT

NO. 1 FOR WEEK ENDING 12/9 19

NAME Flores, Jesse DEPT. Administrative

EXPLANATION	HOURS	RATE	AMOUNT
Regular Hours	[illegible]	$ [illegible]	$ 460.00
Overtime Hours			

LESS TOTAL DEDUCTIONS: TOTAL EARNINGS $ 460.00

Income Tax	73.90	
FICA Tax	28.20	
____		
____		
____		102.10

NET PAY DUE $ 357.90

APPROVED ____

RECEIVED IN FULL FOR SERVICES TO DATE

NO. 2 FOR WEEK ENDING 12/9 19

NAME Jackson, Paula DEPT. Office

EXPLANATION	HOURS	RATE	AMOUNT
Regular Hours	[illegible]	$ [illegible]	$ 180.00
Overtime Hours			

LESS TOTAL DEDUCTIONS: TOTAL EARNINGS $ 180.00

Income Tax	21.10	
FICA Tax	11.03	
____		
____		
____		32.13

NET PAY DUE $ 147.87

APPROVED ____

RECEIVED IN FULL FOR SERVICES TO DATE

NO. 3 FOR WEEK ENDING 12/4 19

NAME Martin, Linda DEPT. Office

EXPLANATION	HOURS	RATE	AMOUNT
Regular Hours	40.0	$ [illegible]	$ 135.00
Overtime Hours			

LESS TOTAL DEDUCTIONS: TOTAL EARNINGS $ 135.00

Income Tax	15.40	
FICA Tax	8.28	
____		
____		
____		23.68

NET PAY DUE $ 111.32

APPROVED ____

RECEIVED IN FULL FOR SERVICES TO DATE

NO. 42 FOR WEEK ENDING 12/9 19

NAME Klaus, Elsie DEPT. Salesperson

EXPLANATION	HOURS	RATE	AMOUNT
Regular Hours	[illegible]	$ [illegible]	$ 390.12
Overtime Hours			

LESS TOTAL DEDUCTIONS: TOTAL EARNINGS $ 390.12

Income Tax	62.40	
FICA Tax	23.91	
____		
____		
____		86.31

NET PAY DUE $ 303.81

APPROVED ____

RECEIVED IN FULL FOR SERVICES TO DATE

NO. 13 FOR WEEK ENDING 12/9 19____

NAME Hirvonen, Jane DEPT. Salesperson

EXPLANATION	HOURS	RATE	AMOUNT
Regular Hours	37.05	$ 8.90	$ 370.59
Overtime Hours			

LESS TOTAL DEDUCTIONS: TOTAL EARNINGS $ 370.59

Income Tax	49.90	
FICA Tax	22.72	
____________		
____________		
____________		72.62

NET PAY DUE $ 297.97

APPROVED ____________

RECEIVED IN FULL FOR SERVICES TO DATE

NO. 22 FOR WEEK ENDING 12/9 19____

NAME Salazar, Ruben DEPT. Prod. Worker

EXPLANATION	HOURS	RATE	AMOUNT
Regular Hours	25.875	$ 6.90	$ 258.25
Overtime Hours	1.05	10.35	10.35

LESS TOTAL DEDUCTIONS: TOTAL EARNINGS $ 269.10

Income Tax	30.80	
FICA Tax	16.50	
____________	5.00	
____________		
____________		52.30

NET PAY DUE $ 216.80

APPROVED ____________

RECEIVED IN FULL FOR SERVICES TO DATE

NO. 23 FOR WEEK ENDING 12/9 19____

NAME Brown Leroy DEPT. Prod. Worker

EXPLANATION	HOURS	RATE	AMOUNT
Regular Hours	40.0	$ 4.40	$ 176.00
Overtime Hours	3.0	6.60	19.80

LESS TOTAL DEDUCTIONS: TOTAL EARNINGS $ 195.80

Income Tax	9.90	
FICA Tax	12.00	
____________	5.00	
____________		
____________		26.90

NET PAY DUE $ 168.90

APPROVED ____________

RECEIVED IN FULL FOR SERVICES TO DATE

NO. 24 FOR WEEK ENDING 12/9 19____

NAME McLaughlin, Darlene DEPT. Prod. Worker

EXPLANATION	HOURS	RATE	AMOUNT
Regular Hours	38.3	$ 5.00	$ 151.00
Overtime Hours	1.5	7.50	11.25

LESS TOTAL DEDUCTIONS: TOTAL EARNINGS $ 162.25

Income Tax	20.60	
FICA Tax	9.98	
____________	5.00	
____________		
____________		35.58

NET PAY DUE $ 126.42

APPROVED ____________

RECEIVED IN FULL FOR SERVICES TO DATE

NO. 25 FOR WEEK ENDING 12/9 19 ____

NAME Vukovich, Diane DEPT. Prod. Worker

EXPLANATION	HOURS	RATE	AMOUNT
Regular Hours	32.0	$ 5.40	$ 172.80
Overtime Hours	6.0	8.10	48.60

LESS TOTAL DEDUCTIONS: TOTAL EARNINGS $ 221.40

Income Tax 23.10

FICA Tax 12.57

____________ 5.00

____________ ....

____________ 41.67

NET PAY DUE $ 179.73

APPROVED ____________ RECEIVED IN FULL FOR SERVICES TO DATE

NO. 26 FOR WEEK ENDING 12/9 19 ____

NAME Riley, Sam DEPT. Prod. Worker

EXPLANATION	HOURS	RATE	AMOUNT
Regular Hours	40.0	$ 5.90	$ 236.00
Overtime Hours	1.5	8.85	13.28

LESS TOTAL DEDUCTIONS: TOTAL EARNINGS $ 249.28

Income Tax 26.70

FICA Tax 15.28

____________ 5.00

____________ ....

____________ 46.98

NET PAY DUE $ 202.30

APPROVED ____________ RECEIVED IN FULL FOR SERVICES TO DATE

NO. 27 FOR WEEK ENDING 12/9 19 ____

NAME Neufield, Sara DEPT. Prod. Worker

EXPLANATION	HOURS	RATE	AMOUNT
Regular Hours	37.5	$ 5.70	$ 213.75
Overtime Hours	10.0	8.55	85.50

LESS TOTAL DEDUCTIONS: TOTAL EARNINGS $ 299.25

Income Tax 44.30

FICA Tax 18.34

____________ 5.00

____________ ....

____________ 67.64

NET PAY DUE $ 231.61

APPROVED ____________ RECEIVED IN FULL FOR SERVICES TO DATE

NO. 28 FOR WEEK ENDING 12/9 19 ____

NAME Leonardo, Mike DEPT. Prod. Worker

EXPLANATION	HOURS	RATE	AMOUNT
Regular Hours	37.5	$ 4.50	$ 168.75
Overtime Hours	3.5	6.75	23.63

LESS TOTAL DEDUCTIONS: TOTAL EARNINGS $ 192.38

Income Tax 17.20

FICA Tax 11.79

____________ 5.00

____________ ....

____________ 34.49

NET PAY DUE $ 157.89

APPROVED ____________ RECEIVED IN FULL FOR SERVICES TO DATE

NO. 42 FOR WEEK ENDING 12/9 19____

NAME Baker, Edna DEPT. Prod. Worker

EXPLANATION	HOURS	RATE	AMOUNT
Regular Hours	40.0	$ 5.56	$ 222.60
Overtime Hours	4.0	2.53	10.12

LESS TOTAL DEDUCTIONS: TOTAL EARNINGS $ 232.72

Income Tax	28.40	
FICA Tax	13.65	
______	5.00	
______		
______		47.05

NET PAY DUE $ 175.55

APPROVED ______

RECEIVED IN FULL FOR SERVICES TO DATE

NO. 43 FOR WEEK ENDING 12/9 19____

NAME Svenson, Karl DEPT. Prod. Worker

EXPLANATION	HOURS	RATE	AMOUNT
Regular Hours	37.5	$ 5.6096	$ 210.36
Overtime Hours			

LESS TOTAL DEDUCTIONS: TOTAL EARNINGS $ 210.36

Income Tax	32.00	
FICA Tax	12.90	
______	5.00	
______		
______		49.90

NET PAY DUE $ 160.46

APPROVED ______

RECEIVED IN FULL FOR SERVICES TO DATE

NO. ______ FOR WEEK ENDING ______ 19____

NAME ______ DEPT. ______

EXPLANATION	HOURS	RATE	AMOUNT
Regular Hours		$	$
Overtime Hours			

LESS TOTAL DEDUCTIONS: TOTAL EARNINGS $ ______

Income Tax		
FICA Tax		
______		
______		
______		

NET PAY DUE $ ______

APPROVED ______

RECEIVED IN FULL FOR SERVICES TO DATE

NO. ______ FOR WEEK ENDING ______ 19____

NAME ______ DEPT. ______

EXPLANATION	HOURS	RATE	AMOUNT
Regular Hours		$	$
Overtime Hours			

LESS TOTAL DEDUCTIONS: TOTAL EARNINGS $ ______

Income Tax		
FICA Tax		
______		
______		
______		

NET PAY DUE $ ______

APPROVED ______

RECEIVED IN FULL FOR SERVICES TO DATE

WEEKLY TIME RECORD — Solarheat Systems Inc.

For week ending December 16 19--

Name Jackson, Paula

Dept. Office Employee No. 2

DAY WORKED	REGULAR HOURS	OVERTIME HOURS	TOTAL HOURS WORKED
Monday	8.0		
Tuesday	8.0		
Wednesday	8.0		
Thursday	8.0		
Friday	8.0		
Saturday			
Sunday			
		TOTAL HOURS ...	40.0

WEEKLY TIME RECORD — Solarheat Systems Inc.

For week ending December 16 19--

Name Linda Martin

Dept. Office Employee No. 3

DAY WORKED	REGULAR HOURS	OVERTIME HOURS	TOTAL HOURS WORKED
Monday	8.0		
Tuesday	8.0		
Wednesday	8.0		
Thursday	8.0		
Friday	8.0		
Saturday			
Sunday			
		TOTAL HOURS ...	40.0

WEEK OF DECEMBER 10-16

WEEKLY SALES REPORT — Solarheat Systems Inc.

For week ending December 16 19--

NO.	SALESPERSON	SALES	X	% RATE	=	COMMISSION EARNED
12	Klaus, Elsie	$4,782.80		8%		$ ~~385~~ 382.62
13	Hirasuna, James	4,597.40		8%		367.79

TOTAL SALES $ 9,380.20 TOTAL COMMISSIONS $ 750.41

NAME RUBEN SALAZAR

CLOCK NO. 22

SOC. SEC. NO. 341 42 5608

PERIOD WEEK ENDING DECEMBER 16, 19--

	MORNING		AFTERNOON		NIGHT		REGULAR HOURS	OVERTIME HOURS
	In	Out	In	Out	In	Out		
M	7:57	12:02	1:04	5:05			7.9 ~~8.0~~	
T	8:00	12:01					4.0	
W	7:54	12:04	12:58	6:01			8.0	1.0
T	7:57	12:02	12:59	5:02			8.0	
F	7:56	12:01	12:57	6:03			8.0	1.0
S								
S								
TOTAL HOURS							35.9 ~~36.0~~	2.0

TYPE	RATE	HOURS	EARNINGS
Regular	$ 6.90	35.9 ~~36.0~~	$ 247.71 ~~248.40~~
Overtime	10.35	2.0	20.70
Special			
TOTAL		37.9 ~~38.0~~	$ 268.41 ~~269.10~~

FOR PAYROLL USE ONLY

NAME LEROY BROWN

CLOCK NO. 23

SOC. SEC. NO. 263 23 3724

PERIOD WEEK ENDING DECEMBER 16, 19--

	MORNING		AFTERNOON		NIGHT		REGULAR HOURS	OVERTIME HOURS
	In	Out	In	Out	In	Out		
M	7:54	12:03	12:57	5:04	6:00	8:34	8.0	2.5
T	8:00	12:04	12:57	5:06			8.0	
W	7:58	12:01	12:59	5:02			8.0	
T	7:57	12:03	12:56	5:04			8.0	
F	8:00	12:02	12:58	5:02			8.0	
S								
S								
TOTAL HOURS							40.0	2.5

TYPE	RATE	HOURS	EARNINGS
Regular	$ 4.40	40.0	$ 176.00
Overtime	6.60	2.5	16.50
Special			
TOTAL		42.5	$ 192.50

FOR PAYROLL USE ONLY

NAME DARLENE MCLAUGHLIN

CLOCK NO. 24

SOC. SEC. NO. 147 62 6118

PERIOD WEEK ENDING DECEMBER 16, 19--

	MORNING		AFTERNOON		NIGHT		REGULAR HOURS	OVERTIME HOURS
	In	Out	In	Out	In	Out		
M	8:03	12:02	12:56	5:02			7.9	
T	7:53	12:04	12:57	5:06			8.0	
W	7:58	12:00					4.0	
T	8:00	12:02	1:00	5:03			8.0	
F	7:56	12:01	12:56	6:04			8.0	1.0
S								
S								
TOTAL HOURS							35.9	1.0

TYPE	RATE	HOURS	EARNINGS
Regular	$ 5.00	35.9	$ 179.50
Overtime	7.50	1.0	7.50
Special			
TOTAL		36.9	$ 187.00

FOR PAYROLL USE ONLY

NAME DIANE VUKOVICH

CLOCK NO. 25

SOC. SEC. NO. 342 15 1394

PERIOD WEEK ENDING DECEMBER 16, 19--

	MORNING		AFTERNOON		NIGHT		REGULAR HOURS	OVERTIME HOURS
	In	Out	In	Out	In	Out		
M	7:54	12:03	12:57	5:04	6:00	8:34	8.0	2.5
T	8:00	12:04	12:57	5:06			8.0	
W	7:58	12:01	12:59	5:02	5:54	9:04	8.0	3.0
T	7:57	12:03	12:56	5:04			8.0	
F	8:00	12:02	12:58	5:02	5:57	7:34	8.0	1.5
S								
S								
TOTAL HOURS							40.0	7.0

TYPE	RATE	HOURS	EARNINGS
Regular	$ 5.40	40.0	$ 216.00
Overtime	8.10	7.0	56.70
Special			
TOTAL		47.0	$ 272.70

FOR PAYROLL USE ONLY

NAME SAM RILEY

CLOCK NO. 26

SOC. SEC. NO. 247 27 1279

PERIOD WEEK ENDING DECEMBER 16, 19--

	MORNING		AFTERNOON		NIGHT		REGULAR HOURS	OVERTIME HOURS
	In	Out	In	Out	In	Out		
M	7:54	12:03	12:57	5:04			8.0	
T	8:00	12:04	12:57	5:06	5:57	9:02	8.0	3.0
W	7:58	12:01	12:59	5:02			8.0	
T	7:57	12:03	12:56	5:04			8.0	
F	8:00	12:02	12:58	5:02	5:57	7:34	8.0	1.5
S								
S								
TOTAL HOURS							40.0	4.5

TYPE	RATE	HOURS	EARNINGS
Regular	$5.90	40.0	$236.00
Overtime	8.85	4.5	39.83
Special			
TOTAL		44.5	$275.83

FOR PAYROLL USE ONLY

NAME SARA NEUFELD

CLOCK NO. 27

SOC. SEC. NO. 143 62 4762

PERIOD WEEK ENDING DECEMBER 16, 19--

	MORNING		AFTERNOON		NIGHT		REGULAR HOURS	OVERTIME HOURS
	In	Out	In	Out	In	Out		
M	7:57	12:02	1:04	5:05			7.9	
T	8:00	12:01	1:00	5:02			8.0	
W	7:54	12:04	12:58	6:01			8.0	1.0
T	7:57	12:02	12:59	5:02	6:00	8:34	8.0	2.5
F	7:56	12:01	12:57	6:03			8.0	1.0
S	8:29	11:33						3.0
S								
TOTAL HOURS							39.9	7.5

TYPE	RATE	HOURS	EARNINGS
Regular	$5.70	39.9	$227.43
Overtime	8.55	7.5	64.13
Special			
TOTAL		47.4	$291.56

FOR PAYROLL USE ONLY

NAME MIKE LEONARDO

CLOCK NO. 28

SOC. SEC. NO. 147 15 4321

PERIOD WEEK ENDING DECEMBER 16, 19--

	MORNING		AFTERNOON		NIGHT		REGULAR HOURS	OVERTIME HOURS
	In	Out	In	Out	In	Out		
M	7:57	12:02	1:04	5:05			7.9	
T	8:00	12:01	1:00	5:02			8.0	
W	7:54	12:04	12:58	6:01			8.0	1.0
T	7:57	12:02	12:59	5:02			8.0	
F	7:56	12:01	12:57	6:03			8.0	1.0
S	8:29	11:33						3.0
S								
TOTAL HOURS							39.9	5.0

TYPE	RATE	HOURS	EARNINGS
Regular	$4.50	39.9	$179.55
Overtime	6.75	5.0	33.75
Special			
TOTAL		44.9	$213.30

FOR PAYROLL USE ONLY

PIECE-RATE PRODUCTION REPORT

Solarheat Systems Inc.

For week ending *December 16* 19 --

NO.	NAME	MON.	TU.	WED.	THU.	FRI.	TOTAL PRODUCTION	X RATE	= GROSS PAY
42	Baker, Edna	263	241	118	256	247	1,125	$ 14¢	$ 157.50
43	Svenson, Karl	324	352	396	365	393	1830	12¢	219.60

NAME EDNA BAKER

CLOCK NO. 42

SOC. SEC. NO. 372 37 2843

PERIOD WEEK ENDING DECEMBER 16, 19--

	MORNING In	MORNING Out	AFTERNOON In	AFTERNOON Out	NIGHT In	NIGHT Out	REGULAR HOURS	OVERTIME HOURS
M	7:54	12:03	12:57	5:04			8.0	
T	8:00	12:04	12:57	5:06			8.0	
W	7:58	12:01					4.0	
T	7:57	12:03	12:56	5:04			8.0	
F	8:00	12:02	12:58	5:02			8.0	
S								
S								
TOTAL HOURS							36.0	

TYPE	RATE	HOURS	EARNINGS
Regular	$ 5.06	36.0	$ 157.50
Overtime			
Special			
TOTAL		36.0	$ 157.50

FOR PAYROLL USE ONLY

NAME KARL SVENSON

CLOCK NO. 43

SOC. SEC. NO. 163 19 1968

PERIOD WEEK ENDING DECEMBER 16, 19--

	MORNING In	MORNING Out	AFTERNOON In	AFTERNOON Out	NIGHT In	NIGHT Out	REGULAR HOURS	OVERTIME HOURS
M	7:57	12:02	1:04	5:05			7.9	
T	8:00	12:01	1:00	5:02			8.0	
W	7:54	12:04	12:58	6:01			8.0	1.0
T	7:57	12:02	12:59	5:02			8.0	
F	7:56	12:01	12:57	6:03			8.0	1.0
S								
S								
TOTAL HOURS							39.9	2.0

TYPE	RATE	HOURS	EARNINGS
Regular	$ 5.241	39.9	$ 219.60
Overtime	2.62	2.0	5.24
Special			
TOTAL		41.9	$ 224.84

FOR PAYROLL USE ONLY

PAYROLL REGISTER

WEEK ENDED ____________ DATE OF PAYMENT December 15, 1980

	EMPL. NO.	EMPLOYEE'S NAME	MARITAL STATUS	ALLOW-ANCES	TOTAL HOURS	EARNINGS: REGULAR	EARNINGS: OVERTIME	EARNINGS: TOTAL	DEDUCTIONS: FEDERAL INC. TAX	DEDUCTIONS: FICA TAX	DEDUCTIONS: GROUP INSURANCE	DEDUCTIONS: MEDICAL INSURANCE	DEDUCTIONS: OTHER	DEDUCTIONS: TOTAL	PAID: NET PAY	PAID: CK. NO.	
1	1	Flores, Jesse	M	4		460 00		460 00	23 90	22 07	10 00	22 00		122 97	337 03		1
2	2	Jackson, Paula	M	0	40	180 00		180 00	21 10	11 03							2
3	3	Martinez, Linda	S	1	40	135 00		135 00	15 40	8 28							3
4	12	Nans, Elsie	M	2	37.1	382 62		382 62	59 60	23 45							4
5	13	Arasuna, Jane	M	4		367 79		367 79	47 40	22 55							5
6	22	Salazar, Ruben	M	2	37.9	247 71	20 70	268 41									6
7	23	Brown, Leroy	M	5	40	176 00	16 50	192 50									7
8	24	McLaughlin, Darlene	S	1	35.9	179 50	7 50	187 00									8
9	25	Ogkovich, Diane	M	2	42	216 00	56 70	272 70									9
10	26	Riley, Sam	M	2	44.5	236 00	39 83	275 83									10
11	27	Newfield, Sara	M	0	47.4	227 43	60 13	291 56									11
12	28	Leonardo, Mike	M	2	44.4	179 55	33 75	213 30									12
13	42	Baker, Edna	M	0	36.6	157 50		157 50									13
14	43	Svenson, Karl	S	1	44.4	219 60	5 24	224 84									14
15																	15
16																	16
17																	17
18		TOTAL															18

Other Deductions: B—U.S. Savings Bonds; C—Credit Union; U—Union Dues; UF—United Fund

CURRENCY ANALYSIS

Solarheat Systems Inc.

For week ending ______________________ 19______

EMPLOYEE'S NAME	AMOUNT TO BE PAID		BILLS				COINS				
			$20	$10	$5	$1	50¢	25¢	10¢	5¢	1¢
TOTAL ➡											

PAYROLL CHANGE REQUISITION

CALIFORNIA NATIONAL BANK
of Clovis, CA 93612

FIRM ______________________ 19______

	NO.	AMOUNT
BILLS: $20		$
$10		
$5		
$1		
COINS: 50¢		
25¢		
10¢		
5¢		
1¢		
TOTAL		$

Solarheat Systems Inc.

901 Arcade Street
Clovis, CA 93612

NO. 93195

90–085
1211

DATE ______________________ 19 ____

AMOUNT
$

PAY ____ DOLLARS

CALIFORNIA NATIONAL BANK
of Clovis, CA 93612

⑆121100858O⑆ 2381⑈4576⑈346

Solarheat Systems Inc.

____
AUTHORIZED SIGNATURE

Solarheat Systems Inc. 901 Arcade Street Clovis, CA 93612 NO. 93195 DETACH BEFORE DEPOSITING CHECK

DATE	DESCRIPTION	AMOUNT	DISCOUNT		OTHER DEDUCTIONS	NET AMOUNT
			%	AMOUNT		

WEEKLY TIME RECORD

Solarheat Systems Inc.

For week ending December 23 19--

Name Jackson, Paula

Dept. Office Employee No. 2

DAY WORKED	REGULAR HOURS	OVERTIME HOURS	TOTAL HOURS WORKED
Monday	8.0		
Tuesday	8.0		
Wednesday	8.0		
Thursday	8.0		
Friday	8.0		
Saturday			
Sunday			
		TOTAL HOURS ...	

WEEKLY TIME RECORD

Solarheat Systems Inc.

For week ending December 23 19--

Name

Dept. Office Employee No. 3

DAY WORKED	REGULAR HOURS	OVERTIME HOURS	TOTAL HOURS WORKED
Monday	8.0		
Tuesday	8.0		
Wednesday	8.0		
Thursday	8.0		
Friday	8.0		
Saturday			
Sunday			
		TOTAL HOURS ...	

WEEK OF DECEMBER 17-23

WEEKLY SALES REPORT

Solarheat Systems Inc.

For week ending December 23 19--

NO.	SALESPERSON	SALES	X % RATE	= COMMISSION EARNED
12	Klaus, Elsie	$4,814.42		$
13	Hirasuna, James	4,864.32		

TOTAL SALES $ ______ TOTAL COMMISSIONS $ ______

NAME RUBEN SALAZAR

CLOCK NO. 22

SOC. SEC. NO. 341 42 5608

PERIOD WEEK ENDING DECEMBER 23, 19--

	MORNING In	MORNING Out	AFTERNOON In	AFTERNOON Out	NIGHT In	NIGHT Out	REGULAR HOURS	OVERTIME HOURS
M	7:53	12:04	12:59	5:34				
T	7:56	12:01	12:57	3:32				
W	8:09	12:03	12:59	5:35				
T	7:57	12:02	1:02	5:01				
F	7:59	12:01	12:57	5:34				
S								
S								
TOTAL HOURS								

TYPE	RATE	HOURS	EARNINGS
Regular	$		$
Overtime			
Special			
TOTAL			$

FOR PAYROLL USE ONLY

NAME LEROY BROWN

CLOCK NO. 23

SOC. SEC. NO. 263 23 3724

PERIOD WEEK ENDING DECEMBER 23, 19--

	MORNING In	MORNING Out	AFTERNOON In	AFTERNOON Out	NIGHT In	NIGHT Out	REGULAR HOURS	OVERTIME HOURS
M	8:00	12:00	1:00	5:00				
T	8:00	12:00	1:00	5:00				
W	7:59	12:03	12:58	5:04	6:00	8:00		
T	7:56	12:01	12:59	5:01				
F	8:00	12:04	12:57	5:05				
S	8:00	12:02						
S								
TOTAL HOURS								

TYPE	RATE	HOURS	EARNINGS
Regular	$		$
Overtime			
Special			
TOTAL			$

FOR PAYROLL USE ONLY

NAME DIANE VUKOVICH

CLOCK NO. 25

SOC. SEC. NO. 342 15 1394

PERIOD WEEK ENDING DECEMBER 23, 19--

	MORNING In	MORNING Out	AFTERNOON In	AFTERNOON Out	NIGHT In	NIGHT Out	REGULAR HOURS	OVERTIME HOURS
M	8:00	12:00	1:00	5:00				
T	8:00	12:00	1:00	5:00				
W	7:59	12:00	12:58	5:04				
T	7:56	12:01	12:59	5:01				
F	8:00	12:04	12:57	5:05				
S	8:00	12:02						
S								
TOTAL HOURS								

TYPE	RATE	HOURS	EARNINGS
Regular	$		$
Overtime			
Special			
TOTAL			$

FOR PAYROLL USE ONLY

NAME SAM RILEY

CLOCK NO. 26

SOC. SEC. NO. 247 27 1279

PERIOD WEEK ENDING DECEMBER 23, 19--

	MORNING In	MORNING Out	AFTERNOON In	AFTERNOON Out	NIGHT In	NIGHT Out	REGULAR HOURS	OVERTIME HOURS
M	8:00	12:00	1:00	5:00				
T	8:00	12:00	1:00	5:00				
W	7:59	12:03	12:58	5:04				
T	7:56	12:01	12:59	5:01	6:00	8:00		
F	8:00	12:04	12:57	5:05				
S								
S								
TOTAL HOURS								

TYPE	RATE	HOURS	EARNINGS
Regular	$		$
Overtime			
Special			
TOTAL			$

FOR PAYROLL USE ONLY

NAME SARA NEUFELD

CLOCK NO. 27

SOC. SEC. NO. 143 62 4762

PERIOD WEEK ENDING DECEMBER 23, 19--

	MORNING		AFTERNOON		NIGHT		REGULAR HOURS	OVERTIME HOURS
	In	Out	In	Out	In	Out		
M	7:53	12:04	12:59	5:34				
T	7:56	12:01	12:57	3:32				
W	8:09	12:03	12:59	5:35				
T	7:57	12:02	1:02	5:01				
F	7:59	12:01	12:57	5:34				
S	8:57	11:34						
S								
TOTAL HOURS								

TYPE	RATE	HOURS	EARNINGS
Regular	$		$
Overtime			
Special			
TOTAL			$

FOR PAYROLL USE ONLY

NAME MIKE LEONARDO

CLOCK NO. 28

SOC. SEC. NO. 147 15 4321

PERIOD WEEK ENDING DECEMBER 23, 19--

	MORNING		AFTERNOON		NIGHT		REGULAR HOURS	OVERTIME HOURS
	In	Out	In	Out	In	Out		
M	7:53	12:04	12:59	5:34				
T	7:56	12:01	12:57	3:32				
W	8:09	12:03	12:59	5:35				
T	7:57	12:02						
F	7:59	12:01	12:57	5:34				
S	8:57	11:34						
S								
TOTAL HOURS								

TYPE	RATE	HOURS	EARNINGS
Regular	$		$
Overtime			
Special			
TOTAL			$

FOR PAYROLL USE ONLY

NAME GLORIA LESHEN

CLOCK NO. 29

SOC. SEC. NO. 473 28 6925

PERIOD WEEK ENDING DECEMBER 23, 19--

	MORNING		AFTERNOON		NIGHT		REGULAR HOURS	OVERTIME HOURS
	In	Out	In	Out	In	Out		
M	7:56	12:03	12:58	2:35				
T	7:59	12:01	12:57	5:06	5:58	8:33		
W	7:54	12:05	12:59	5:04				
T	7:59	12:03	12:56	6:03				
F	7:57	12:06	12:58	5:05	5:58	7:32		
S								
S								
TOTAL HOURS								

TYPE	RATE	HOURS	EARNINGS
Regular	$		$
Overtime			
Special			
TOTAL			$

FOR PAYROLL USE ONLY

PIECE-RATE PRODUCTION REPORT

Solarheat Systems Inc.

For week ending *December 23* 19 *--*

NO.	NAME	MON.	TU.	WED.	THU.	FRI.	TOTAL PRODUCTION X RATE = GROSS PAY
42	*Baker, Edna*	332	320	328	341	334	______ $ ______ $ ______
43	*Svenson, Karl*	342	348	339	328	337	

NAME EDNA BAKER

CLOCK NO. 42

SOC. SEC. NO. 372 37 2843

PERIOD WEEK ENDING DECEMBER 23, 19--

	MORNING In	MORNING Out	AFTERNOON In	AFTERNOON Out	NIGHT In	NIGHT Out	REGULAR HOURS	OVERTIME HOURS
M	8:00	12:00	1:00	5:00				
T	8:00	12:00	1:00	5:00				
W	7:59	12:03	12:58	5:04				
T	7:56	12:01	12:59	5:01				
F	8:00	12:04	12:57	5:05				
S								
S								
TOTAL HOURS								

TYPE	RATE	HOURS	EARNINGS
Regular	$		$
Overtime			
Special			
TOTAL			$

FOR PAYROLL USE ONLY

NAME KARL SVENSON

CLOCK NO. 43

SOC. SEC. NO. 163 19 1968

PERIOD WEEK ENDING DECEMBER 23, 19--

	MORNING In	MORNING Out	AFTERNOON In	AFTERNOON Out	NIGHT In	NIGHT Out	REGULAR HOURS	OVERTIME HOURS
M	7:53	12:04	12:59	5:34				
T	7:56	12:01	12:57	3:32				
W	8:09	12:03	12:59	5:35				
T	7:57	12:02	1:02	5:01				
F	7:59	12:01	12:57	5:34				
S								
S								
TOTAL HOURS								

TYPE	RATE	HOURS	EARNINGS
Regular	$		$
Overtime			
Special			
TOTAL			$

FOR PAYROLL USE ONLY

PAYROLL REGISTER

WEEK ENDED ______________ DATE OF PAYMENT ______________

	EMPL. NO.	EMPLOYEE'S NAME	MARITAL STATUS	ALLOW-ANCES	TOTAL HOURS	EARNINGS			DEDUCTIONS						PAID		
						REGULAR	OVERTIME	TOTAL	FEDERAL INC. TAX	FICA TAX	GROUP INSURANCE	MEDICAL INSURANCE	OTHER	TOTAL	NET PAY	CK. NO.	
1																	1
2																	2
3																	3
4																	4
5																	5
6																	6
7																	7
8																	8
9																	9
10																	10
11																	11
12																	12
13																	13
14																	14
15																	15
16																	16
17																	17
18		TOTAL															18

Other Deductions: B—U.S. Savings Bonds; C—Credit Union; U—Union Dues; UF—United Fund

Solarheat Systems Inc.

901 Arcade Street
Clovis, CA 93612

NO. 93220

90–085 / 1211

DATE ______________________ 19____

AMOUNT
$

PAY ____ DOLLARS

CALIFORNIA NATIONAL BANK
of Clovis, CA 93612

⑆121100858⑆ 2381⑈4576⑈346

Solarheat Systems Inc.

____
AUTHORIZED SIGNATURE

Solarheat Systems Inc. 901 Arcade Street Clovis, CA 93612 NO. 93220

DETACH BEFORE DEPOSITING CHECK

DATE	DESCRIPTION	AMOUNT	DISCOUNT		OTHER DEDUCTIONS	NET AMOUNT
			%	AMOUNT		

	DOLLARS	CENTS
BALANCE BROUGHT FORWARD		
DEPOSIT ____ (DATE)		
TOTAL		
NO. 1		
DATE ____ 19__		
TO ____		
FOR ____		
AMOUNT THIS CHECK		
BALANCE CARRIED FORWARD		

Solarheat Systems Inc.

901 Arcade Street
Clovis, CA 93612

NO. 1

90-085
1211

DATE ______ 19__

PAY TO THE ORDER OF ______ $______

______ DOLLARS

SOLARHEAT SYSTEMS INC. — PAYROLL ACCOUNT

CALIFORNIA NATIONAL BANK
of Clovis, CA 93612

______ AUTHORIZED SIGNATURE

⑆121100858O⑆ 4276⑈3391⑈721

Solarheat Systems Inc. STATEMENT OF EMPLOYEE EARNINGS AND PAYROLL DEDUCTIONS

WEEK ENDED	EARNINGS			DEDUCTIONS						PAID	
	REGULAR	OVERTIME	TOTAL	FEDERAL INC. TAX	FICA TAX	GROUP INSURANCE	MEDICAL INSURANCE	OTHER	TOTAL	NET PAY	CK. NO

	DOLLARS	CENTS
BALANCE BROUGHT FORWARD		
DEPOSIT ____ (DATE)		
TOTAL		
NO. 2		
DATE ____ 19__		
TO ____		
FOR ____		
AMOUNT THIS CHECK		
BALANCE CARRIED FORWARD		

Solarheat Systems Inc.

901 Arcade Street
Clovis, CA 93612

NO. 2

90-085
1211

DATE ______ 19__

PAY TO THE ORDER OF ______ $______

______ DOLLARS

SOLARHEAT SYSTEMS INC. — PAYROLL ACCOUNT

CALIFORNIA NATIONAL BANK
of Clovis, CA 93612

______ AUTHORIZED SIGNATURE

⑆121100858O⑆ 4276⑈3391⑈721

Solarheat Systems Inc. STATEMENT OF EMPLOYEE EARNINGS AND PAYROLL DEDUCTIONS

WEEK ENDED	EARNINGS			DEDUCTIONS						PAID	
	REGULAR	OVERTIME	TOTAL	FEDERAL INC. TAX	FICA TAX	GROUP INSURANCE	MEDICAL INSURANCE	OTHER	TOTAL	NET PAY	CK. NO

BALANCE BROUGHT FORWARD	DOLLARS	CENTS
DEPOSIT ______ (DATE)		
TOTAL		
NO. 3		
DATE ______ 19__		
TO ______		
FOR ______		
AMOUNT THIS CHECK		
BALANCE CARRIED FORWARD		

Solarheat Systems Inc.

901 Arcade Street
Clovis, CA 93612

NO. 3

90-085
1211

DATE ______ 19__

PAY TO THE ORDER OF ______ $______

______ DOLLARS

CALIFORNIA NATIONAL BANK
of Clovis, CA 93612

SOLARHEAT SYSTEMS INC. — PAYROLL ACCOUNT

AUTHORIZED SIGNATURE

⑆121100858O⑆ 4276⑈3391⑈721

Solarheat Systems Inc.

STATEMENT OF EMPLOYEE EARNINGS AND PAYROLL DEDUCTIONS

WEEK ENDED	EARNINGS			DEDUCTIONS						PAID	
	REGULAR	OVERTIME	TOTAL	FEDERAL INC. TAX	FICA TAX	GROUP INSURANCE	MEDICAL INSURANCE	OTHER	TOTAL	NET PAY	CK. NO

BALANCE BROUGHT FORWARD	DOLLARS	CENTS
DEPOSIT ______ (DATE)		
TOTAL		
NO. 4		
DATE ______ 19__		
TO ______		
FOR ______		
AMOUNT THIS CHECK		
BALANCE CARRIED FORWARD		

Solarheat Systems Inc.

901 Arcade Street
Clovis, CA 93612

NO. 4

90-085
1211

DATE ______ 19__

PAY TO THE ORDER OF ______ $______

______ DOLLARS

CALIFORNIA NATIONAL BANK
of Clovis, CA 93612

SOLARHEAT SYSTEMS INC. — PAYROLL ACCOUNT

AUTHORIZED SIGNATURE

⑆121100858O⑆ 4276⑈3391⑈721

Solarheat Systems Inc.

STATEMENT OF EMPLOYEE EARNINGS AND PAYROLL DEDUCTIONS

WEEK ENDED	EARNINGS			DEDUCTIONS						PAID	
	REGULAR	OVERTIME	TOTAL	FEDERAL INC. TAX	FICA TAX	GROUP INSURANCE	MEDICAL INSURANCE	OTHER	TOTAL	NET PAY	CK. NO

	DOLLARS	CENTS
BALANCE BROUGHT FORWARD		
DEPOSIT ________ (DATE)		
TOTAL		
NO. 5		
DATE ________ 19___		
TO ________		
FOR ________		
AMOUNT THIS CHECK		
BALANCE CARRIED FORWARD		

Solarheat Systems Inc.

901 Arcade Street
Clovis, CA 93612

NO. 5

90-085
1211

DATE ________ 19___

PAY TO THE ORDER OF ________ $________

________ DOLLARS

CALIFORNIA NATIONAL BANK
of Clovis, CA 93612

SOLARHEAT SYSTEMS INC. — PAYROLL ACCOUNT

____
AUTHORIZED SIGNATURE

⑆121100858O⑆ 4276⑈3391⑈721

Solarheat Systems Inc. STATEMENT OF EMPLOYEE EARNINGS AND PAYROLL DEDUCTIONS

WEEK ENDED	EARNINGS			DEDUCTIONS						PAID	
	REGULAR	OVERTIME	TOTAL	FEDERAL INC. TAX	FICA TAX	GROUP INSURANCE	MEDICAL INSURANCE	OTHER	TOTAL	NET PAY	CK. NO

	DOLLARS	CENTS
BALANCE BROUGHT FORWARD		
DEPOSIT ________ (DATE)		
TOTAL		
NO. 6		
DATE ________ 19___		
TO ________		
FOR ________		
AMOUNT THIS CHECK		
BALANCE CARRIED FORWARD		

Solarheat Systems Inc.

901 Arcade Street
Clovis, CA 93612

NO. 6

90-085
1211

DATE ________ 19___

PAY TO THE ORDER OF ________ $________

________ DOLLARS

CALIFORNIA NATIONAL BANK
of Clovis, CA 93612

SOLARHEAT SYSTEMS INC. — PAYROLL ACCOUNT

____
AUTHORIZED SIGNATURE

⑆121100858O⑆ 4276⑈3391⑈721

Solarheat Systems Inc. STATEMENT OF EMPLOYEE EARNINGS AND PAYROLL DEDUCTIONS

WEEK ENDED	EARNINGS			DEDUCTIONS						PAID	
	REGULAR	OVERTIME	TOTAL	FEDERAL INC. TAX	FICA TAX	GROUP INSURANCE	MEDICAL INSURANCE	OTHER	TOTAL	NET PAY	CK. NO

	DOLLARS	CENTS
BALANCE BROUGHT FORWARD		
DEPOSIT ________ (DATE)		
TOTAL		
NO. 7		
DATE ________ 19___		
TO ________		
FOR ________		
AMOUNT THIS CHECK		
BALANCE CARRIED FORWARD		

Solarheat Systems Inc.

901 Arcade Street
Clovis, CA 93612

NO. 7

90-085
1211

DATE ________ 19___

PAY TO THE ORDER OF ________ $________

________ DOLLARS

CALIFORNIA NATIONAL BANK
of Clovis, CA 93612

SOLARHEAT SYSTEMS INC. — PAYROLL ACCOUNT

____
AUTHORIZED SIGNATURE

⑆121100858O⑆ 4276⑈3391⑈721

Solarheat Systems Inc.

STATEMENT OF EMPLOYEE EARNINGS AND PAYROLL DEDUCTIONS

WEEK ENDED	EARNINGS			DEDUCTIONS						PAID	
	REGULAR	OVERTIME	TOTAL	FEDERAL INC. TAX	FICA TAX	GROUP INSURANCE	MEDICAL INSURANCE	OTHER	TOTAL	NET PAY	CK. NO

	DOLLARS	CENTS
BALANCE BROUGHT FORWARD		
DEPOSIT ________ (DATE)		
TOTAL		
NO. 8		
DATE ________ 19___		
TO ________		
FOR ________		
AMOUNT THIS CHECK		
BALANCE CARRIED FORWARD		

Solarheat Systems Inc.

901 Arcade Street
Clovis, CA 93612

NO. 8

90-085
1211

DATE ________ 19___

PAY TO THE ORDER OF ________ $________

________ DOLLARS

CALIFORNIA NATIONAL BANK
of Clovis, CA 93612

SOLARHEAT SYSTEMS INC. — PAYROLL ACCOUNT

____
AUTHORIZED SIGNATURE

⑆121100858O⑆ 4276⑈3391⑈721

Solarheat Systems Inc.

STATEMENT OF EMPLOYEE EARNINGS AND PAYROLL DEDUCTIONS

WEEK ENDED	EARNINGS			DEDUCTIONS						PAID	
	REGULAR	OVERTIME	TOTAL	FEDERAL INC. TAX	FICA TAX	GROUP INSURANCE	MEDICAL INSURANCE	OTHER	TOTAL	NET PAY	CK. NO

	DOLLARS	CENTS
BALANCE BROUGHT FORWARD		
DEPOSIT ______ (DATE)		
TOTAL		

NO. 9

DATE ______________ 19____

TO ______________________

FOR _____________________

	DOLLARS	CENTS
AMOUNT THIS CHECK		
BALANCE CARRIED FORWARD		

Solarheat Systems Inc.
901 Arcade Street
Clovis, CA 93612

NO. 9

$\frac{90\text{-}085}{1211}$

DATE ______________________ 19____

PAY TO THE ORDER OF ______________________________________ $__________

____ DOLLARS

CALIFORNIA NATIONAL BANK
of Clovis, CA 93612

SOLARHEAT SYSTEMS INC. — PAYROLL ACCOUNT

____
AUTHORIZED SIGNATURE

⑆121100858O⑆ 4276⑈3391⑈721

Solarheat Systems Inc.

STATEMENT OF EMPLOYEE EARNINGS AND PAYROLL DEDUCTIONS

WEEK ENDED	EARNINGS			DEDUCTIONS						PAID	
	REGULAR	OVERTIME	TOTAL	FEDERAL INC. TAX	FICA TAX	GROUP INSURANCE	MEDICAL INSURANCE	OTHER	TOTAL	NET PAY	CK. NO

	DOLLARS	CENTS
BALANCE BROUGHT FORWARD		
DEPOSIT ______ (DATE)		
TOTAL		

NO. 10

DATE ______________ 19____

TO ______________________

FOR _____________________

	DOLLARS	CENTS
AMOUNT THIS CHECK		
BALANCE CARRIED FORWARD		

Solarheat Systems Inc.
901 Arcade Street
Clovis, CA 93612

NO. 10

$\frac{90\text{-}085}{1211}$

DATE ______________________ 19____

PAY TO THE ORDER OF ______________________________________ $__________

____ DOLLARS

CALIFORNIA NATIONAL BANK
of Clovis, CA 93612

SOLARHEAT SYSTEMS INC. — PAYROLL ACCOUNT

____
AUTHORIZED SIGNATURE

⑆121100858O⑆ 4276⑈3391⑈721

Solarheat Systems Inc.

STATEMENT OF EMPLOYEE EARNINGS AND PAYROLL DEDUCTIONS

WEEK ENDED	EARNINGS			DEDUCTIONS						PAID	
	REGULAR	OVERTIME	TOTAL	FEDERAL INC. TAX	FICA TAX	GROUP INSURANCE	MEDICAL INSURANCE	OTHER	TOTAL	NET PAY	CK. NO

	DOLLARS	CENTS
BALANCE BROUGHT FORWARD		
DEPOSIT ______ (DATE)		
TOTAL		
NO. 11		
DATE ______ 19__		
TO ______		
FOR ______		
AMOUNT THIS CHECK		
BALANCE CARRIED FORWARD		

Solarheat Systems Inc.
901 Arcade Street
Clovis, CA 93612

NO. 11

90-085
1211

DATE ______________ 19____

PAY TO THE ORDER OF ______________________________ $ ________

______________________________ DOLLARS

SOLARHEAT SYSTEMS INC. — PAYROLL ACCOUNT

CALIFORNIA NATIONAL BANK
of Clovis, CA 93612

______________ AUTHORIZED SIGNATURE

⑆121100858O⑆ 4276⑈3391⑈721

Solarheat Systems Inc.

STATEMENT OF EMPLOYEE EARNINGS AND PAYROLL DEDUCTIONS

WEEK ENDED	EARNINGS			DEDUCTIONS						PAID	
	REGULAR	OVERTIME	TOTAL	FEDERAL INC. TAX	FICA TAX	GROUP INSURANCE	MEDICAL INSURANCE	OTHER	TOTAL	NET PAY	CK. NO

	DOLLARS	CENTS
BALANCE BROUGHT FORWARD		
DEPOSIT ______ (DATE)		
TOTAL		
NO. 12		
DATE ______ 19__		
TO ______		
FOR ______		
AMOUNT THIS CHECK		
BALANCE CARRIED FORWARD		

Solarheat Systems Inc.
901 Arcade Street
Clovis, CA 93612

NO. 12

90-085
1211

DATE ______________ 19____

PAY TO THE ORDER OF ______________________________ $ ________

______________________________ DOLLARS

SOLARHEAT SYSTEMS INC. — PAYROLL ACCOUNT

CALIFORNIA NATIONAL BANK
of Clovis, CA 93612

______________ AUTHORIZED SIGNATURE

⑆121100858O⑆ 4276⑈3391⑈721

Solarheat Systems Inc.

STATEMENT OF EMPLOYEE EARNINGS AND PAYROLL DEDUCTIONS

WEEK ENDED	EARNINGS			DEDUCTIONS						PAID	
	REGULAR	OVERTIME	TOTAL	FEDERAL INC. TAX	FICA TAX	GROUP INSURANCE	MEDICAL INSURANCE	OTHER	TOTAL	NET PAY	CK. NO

	DOLLARS	CENTS
BALANCE BROUGHT FORWARD		
DEPOSIT ____ (DATE)		
TOTAL		
AMOUNT THIS CHECK		
BALANCE CARRIED FORWARD		

NO. 13

DATE ________ 19 ____

TO ________

FOR ________

Solarheat Systems Inc.
901 Arcade Street
Clovis, CA 93612

NO. 13

90-085 / 1211

DATE ________ 19 ____

PAY TO THE ORDER OF ________ $ ________

________ DOLLARS

CALIFORNIA NATIONAL BANK
of Clovis, CA 93612

SOLARHEAT SYSTEMS INC. — PAYROLL ACCOUNT

________ AUTHORIZED SIGNATURE

⑆121100858O⑆ 4276⑈3391⑈721

Solarheat Systems Inc.

STATEMENT OF EMPLOYEE EARNINGS AND PAYROLL DEDUCTIONS

WEEK ENDED	EARNINGS			DEDUCTIONS						PAID	
	REGULAR	OVERTIME	TOTAL	FEDERAL INC. TAX	FICA TAX	GROUP INSURANCE	MEDICAL INSURANCE	OTHER	TOTAL	NET PAY	CK. NO

	DOLLARS	CENTS
BALANCE BROUGHT FORWARD		
DEPOSIT ____ (DATE)		
TOTAL		
AMOUNT THIS CHECK		
BALANCE CARRIED FORWARD		

NO. 14

DATE ________ 19 ____

TO ________

FOR ________

Solarheat Systems Inc.
901 Arcade Street
Clovis, CA 93612

NO. 14

90-085 / 1211

DATE ________ 19 ____

PAY TO THE ORDER OF ________ $ ________

________ DOLLARS

CALIFORNIA NATIONAL BANK
of Clovis, CA 93612

SOLARHEAT SYSTEMS INC. — PAYROLL ACCOUNT

________ AUTHORIZED SIGNATURE

⑆121100858O⑆ 4276⑈3391⑈721

Solarheat Systems Inc.

STATEMENT OF EMPLOYEE EARNINGS AND PAYROLL DEDUCTIONS

WEEK ENDED	EARNINGS			DEDUCTIONS						PAID	
	REGULAR	OVERTIME	TOTAL	FEDERAL INC. TAX	FICA TAX	GROUP INSURANCE	MEDICAL INSURANCE	OTHER	TOTAL	NET PAY	CK. NO

WEEKLY TIME RECORD

Solarheat Systems Inc.

For week ending *December 30* 19*--*

Name *Jackson, Paula*

Dept. *Office* Employee No. *2*

DAY WORKED	REGULAR HOURS	OVERTIME HOURS	TOTAL HOURS WORKED
Monday			
Tuesday	8.0		
Wednesday	8.0		
Thursday	8.0		
Friday	8.0		
Saturday		6.0	
Sunday			
		TOTAL HOURS . . .	

WEEKLY TIME RECORD

Solarheat Systems Inc.

For week ending *December 30* 19*--*

Name

Dept. *Office* Employee No. *3*

DAY WORKED	REGULAR HOURS	OVERTIME HOURS	TOTAL HOURS WORKED
Monday			
Tuesday	8.0		
Wednesday	8.0		
Thursday	8.0		
Friday	8.0		
Saturday		6.0	
Sunday			
		TOTAL HOURS . . .	

WEEK OF DECEMBER 24-30

WEEKLY SALES REPORT

Solarheat Systems Inc.

For week ending *December 30* 19*--*

NO.	SALESPERSON	SALES	X	% RATE	=	COMMISSION EARNED
12	Klaus, Elsie	$ 4,249.08				$
13	Hirasuna, James	4,127.23				

TOTAL SALES $ ______ TOTAL COMMISSIONS $ ______

NAME RUBEN SALAZAR

CLOCK NO. 22

SOC. SEC. NO. 341 42 5068

PERIOD WEEK ENDING DECEMBER 30, 19--

	MORNING		AFTERNOON		NIGHT		REGULAR HOURS	OVERTIME HOURS
	In	Out	In	Out	In	Out		
M								
T	7:53	12:04	12:57	5:06				
W	7:58	12:00	12:59	5:04				
T	8:00	12:02	1:00	5:03				
F	7:56	12:01	12:56	6:04				
S								
S								
TOTAL HOURS								

TYPE	RATE	HOURS	EARNINGS
Regular	$		$
Overtime			
Special			
TOTAL			$

FOR PAYROLL USE ONLY

NAME LEROY BROWN

CLOCK NO. 23

SOC. SEC. NO. 263 23 3724

PERIOD WEEK ENDING DECEMBER 30, 19--

	MORNING		AFTERNOON		NIGHT		REGULAR HOURS	OVERTIME HOURS
	In	Out	In	Out	In	Out		
M								
T	8:00	12:03	12:57	5:04				
W	7:57	12:01	12:59	5:02				
T	7:58	12:02	12:55	5:03				
F	8:00	12:01	12:57	5:06				
S	7:57	12:04	12:58	5:02				
S								
TOTAL HOURS								

TYPE	RATE	HOURS	EARNINGS
Regular	$		$
Overtime			
Special			
TOTAL			$

FOR PAYROLL USE ONLY

NAME DIANE VUKOVICH

CLOCK NO. 25

SOC. SEC. NO. 342 15 1394

PERIOD WEEK ENDING DECEMBER 30, 19--

	MORNING		AFTERNOON		NIGHT		REGULAR HOURS	OVERTIME HOURS
	In	Out	In	Out	In	Out		
M								
T	8:00	12:03	12:57	5:04	5:58	8:32		
W	7:57	12:01	12:59	5:02				
T	7:58	12:02	12:55	5:03				
F	8:00	12:01	12:57	5:06				
S	7:57	12:04	12:58	5:05				
S								
TOTAL HOURS								

TYPE	RATE	HOURS	EARNINGS
Regular	$		$
Overtime			
Special			
TOTAL			$

FOR PAYROLL USE ONLY

NAME SAM RILEY

CLOCK NO. 26

SOC. SEC. NO. 247 27 1279

PERIOD WEEK ENDING DECEMBER 30, 19--

	MORNING		AFTERNOON		NIGHT		REGULAR HOURS	OVERTIME HOURS
	In	Out	In	Out	In	Out		
M								
T	8:00	12:03	12:57	5:04				
W	7:57	12:01	12:59	5:02				
T	7:58	12:02	12:55	5:03				
F	8:00	12:01	12:57	5:06				
S	7:57	12:04	12:59	5:04				
S								
TOTAL HOURS								

TYPE	RATE	HOURS	EARNINGS
Regular	$		$
Overtime			
Special			
TOTAL			$

FOR PAYROLL USE ONLY

NAME SARA NEUFELD

CLOCK NO. 27

SOC. SEC. NO. 143 62 4762

PERIOD WEEK ENDING DECEMBER 30, 19--

	MORNING In	MORNING Out	AFTERNOON In	AFTERNOON Out	NIGHT In	NIGHT Out	REGULAR HOURS	OVERTIME HOURS
M								
T	7:53	12:04	12:57	5:06				
W	7:58	12:00	12:59	5:04				
T	8:00	12:02	1:00	5:03				
F	7:56	12:01	12:56	6:04				
S	9:29	12:04						
S								
TOTAL HOURS								

TYPE	RATE	HOURS	EARNINGS
Regular	$		$
Overtime			
Special			
TOTAL			$

FOR PAYROLL USE ONLY

NAME MIKE LEONARDO

CLOCK NO. 28

SOC. SEC. NO. 147 15 4321

PERIOD WEEK ENDING DECEMBER 30, 19--

	MORNING In	MORNING Out	AFTERNOON In	AFTERNOON Out	NIGHT In	NIGHT Out	REGULAR HOURS	OVERTIME HOURS
M								
T	7:53	12:04	12:57	5:06				
W	7:58	12:00	12:59	5:04				
T	8:00	12:02	1:00	5:03				
F	7:56	12:01	12:56	6:04				
S	9:29	12:04						
S								
TOTAL HOURS								

TYPE	RATE	HOURS	EARNINGS
Regular	$		$
Overtime			
Special			
TOTAL			$

FOR PAYROLL USE ONLY

NAME GLORIA LESHEN

CLOCK NO. 29

SOC. SEC. NO. 473 28 6925

PERIOD WEEK ENDING DECEMBER 30, 19--

	MORNING In	MORNING Out	AFTERNOON In	AFTERNOON Out	NIGHT In	NIGHT Out	REGULAR HOURS	OVERTIME HOURS
M								
T	8:00	12:01	1:00	5:02				
W	7:54	12:04	12:58	6:01				
T	7:57	12:02	12:59	5:02	6:00	8:34		
F	7:56	12:01						
S								
S								
TOTAL HOURS								

TYPE	RATE	HOURS	EARNINGS
Regular	$		$
Overtime			
Special			
TOTAL			$

FOR PAYROLL USE ONLY

PIECE-RATE PRODUCTION REPORT

Solarheat Systems Inc.

For week ending December 30 19 – –

NO.	NAME	MON.	TU.	WED.	THU.	FRI.	TOTAL PRODUCTION	X RATE	= GROSS PAY
42	Baker, Edna	—	332	341	324	334		$	$
43	Svenson, Karl	—	353	348	344	356			

NAME EDNA BAKER

CLOCK NO. 42

SOC. SEC. NO. 372 37 2843

PERIOD WEEK ENDING DECEMBER 30, 19--

	MORNING In	MORNING Out	AFTERNOON In	AFTERNOON Out	NIGHT In	NIGHT Out	REGULAR HOURS	OVERTIME HOURS
M								
T	8:00	12:03	12:57	5:04				
W	7:57	12:01	12:59	5:02				
T	7:58	12:02	12:55	5:03				
F	8:00	12:01	12:57	5:06				
S								
S								
TOTAL HOURS								

TYPE	RATE	HOURS	EARNINGS
Regular	$		$
Overtime			
Special			
TOTAL			$

FOR PAYROLL USE ONLY

NAME KARL SVENSON

CLOCK NO. 43

SOC. SEC. NO. 163 19 1968

PERIOD WEEK ENDING DECEMBER 30, 19--

	MORNING In	MORNING Out	AFTERNOON In	AFTERNOON Out	NIGHT In	NIGHT Out	REGULAR HOURS	OVERTIME HOURS
M								
T	7:53	12:04	12:57	5:06				
W	7:58	12:00	12:59	5:04				
T	8:00	12:02	1:00	5:03				
F	7:56	12:01	12:56	6:04				
S								
S								
TOTAL HOURS								

TYPE	RATE	HOURS	EARNINGS
Regular	$		$
Overtime			
Special			
TOTAL			$

FOR PAYROLL USE ONLY

PAYROLL REGISTER

WEEK ENDED ________________ DATE OF PAYMENT ________________

	EMPL. NO.	EMPLOYEE'S NAME	MARITAL STATUS	ALLOW-ANCES	TOTAL HOURS	EARNINGS			DEDUCTIONS						PAID		
						REGULAR	OVERTIME	TOTAL	FEDERAL INC. TAX	FICA TAX	GROUP INSURANCE	MEDICAL INSURANCE	OTHER	TOTAL	NET PAY	CK. NO.	
1																	1
2																	2
3																	3
4																	4
5																	5
6																	6
7																	7
8																	8
9																	9
10																	10
11																	11
12																	12
13																	13
14																	14
15																	15
16																	16
17																	17
18		TOTAL															18

Other Deductions: B—U.S. Savings Bonds; C—Credit Union; U—Union Dues; UF—United Fund

Solarheat Systems Inc.

901 Arcade Street
Clovis, CA 93612

NO. 93415

90–085
1211

DATE ______________________ 19 ______

AMOUNT
$

PAY ____ DOLLARS

Solarheat Systems Inc.

CALIFORNIA NATIONAL BANK
of Clovis, CA 93612

⑆1211008580⑆ 2381⑈4576⑈346

____
AUTHORIZED SIGNATURE

Solarheat Systems Inc. 901 Arcade Street Clovis, CA 93612 NO. 93415 DETACH BEFORE DEPOSITING CHECK

DATE	DESCRIPTION	AMOUNT	DISCOUNT		OTHER DEDUCTIONS	NET AMOUNT
			o/o	AMOUNT		

EMPLOYEE'S EARNINGS RECORD

NAME Flores, Jesse EMPL. NO. 1

ADDRESS 912 Elm Street; Clovis, CA 93612

SOC. SEC. NO. 123-16-7048 ALLOWANCES 4 MARRIED X SINGLE ____

DEPARTMENT Administration

OCCUPATION General Manager

DATE EMPLOYED January 3, 1977 DATE TERMINATED ____

DEDUCTIONS:
- Credit Union ____
- Group Insurance $10 per mo.
- Medical Insurance $27 per mo.
- U.S. Savings Bond ____
- Union Dues ____
- United Fund ____
- Other ____

EARNINGS:
- Yearly $23,920
- Monthly ____
- Weekly $460
- Hourly ____
- Commission ____
- Piece Rate Per Unit ____

PAY PERIOD		EARNINGS			DEDUCTIONS						NET PAY	ACCUMULATED TAXABLE EARNINGS	WEEK
WEEK	WEEK ENDED	REGULAR	OVERTIME	TOTAL	FEDERAL INC. TAX	FICA TAX	GROUP INSURANCE	MEDICAL INSURANCE	OTHER	TOTAL			
TOTALS 3 QUAR.		17,940 00		17,940 00	2,882 10	1,099 80	90 00	243 00		4,314 90	13,625 10	17,940 00	
1	10/7	460 00		460 00	73 90	28 20				102 10	357 90	18,400 00	1
2	10/14	460 00		460 00	73 90	28 20		27 00		129 10	330 90	18,860 00	2
3	10/21	460 00		460 00	73 90	28 20				102 10	357 90	19,320 00	3
4	10/28	460 00		460 00	73 90	28 20	10 00			112 10	347 90	19,780 00	4
5	11/4	460 00		460 00	73 90	28 20				102 10	357 90	20,240 00	5
6	11/11	460 00		460 00	73 90	28 20		27 00		129 10	330 90	20,700 00	6
7	11/18	460 00		460 00	73 90	28 20				102 10	357 90	21,160 00	7
8	11/25	460 00		460 00	73 90	28 20	10 00			112 10	347 90	21,620 00	8
9	12/2	460 00		460 00	73 90	28 20				102 10	357 90	22,080 00	9
10	12/9	460 00		460 00	73 90	28 20				102 10	357 90	22,540 00	10
11													11
12													12
13													13
QUARTER TOTALS													
YEARLY TOTALS													

EMPLOYEES' EARNINGS RECORDS

EMPLOYEE'S EARNINGS RECORD

NAME Jackson, Paula EMPL. NO. 2

ADDRESS 39 Baron Street; Clovis, CA 93612

SOC. SEC. NO. 185-18-4701 ALLOWANCES 0 MARRIED X SINGLE ____

DEPARTMENT Office

OCCUPATION Secretary

DATE EMPLOYED July 5, 1976 DATE TERMINATED ____

DEDUCTIONS:
- Credit Union ____
- Group Insurance ____
- Medical Insurance $17 per mo.
- U.S. Savings Bond ____
- Union Dues ____
- United Fund ____
- Other ____

EARNINGS:
- Yearly ____
- Monthly ____
- Weekly $180
- Hourly $4.50
- Commission ____
- Piece Rate Per Unit ____

PAY PERIOD		EARNINGS			DEDUCTIONS						NET PAY	ACCUMULATED TAXABLE EARNINGS	WEEK
WEEK	WEEK ENDED	REGULAR	OVERTIME	TOTAL	FEDERAL INC. TAX	FICA TAX	GROUP INSURANCE	MEDICAL INSURANCE	OTHER	TOTAL			
TOTALS 3 QUAR.		7,020 00		7,020 00	822 90	430 17		153 00		1,406 07	5,613 93	7,020 00	
1	10/7	180 00		180 00	21 10	11 03				32 13	147 87	7,200 00	1
2	10/14	180 00		180 00	21 10	11 03		17 00		49 13	130 87	7,380 00	2
3	10/21	180 00		180 00	21 10	11 03				32 13	147 87	7,560 00	3
4	10/28	180 00		180 00	21 10	11 03				32 13	147 87	7,740 00	4
5	11/4	180 00		180 00	21 10	11 03		17 00		49 13	130 87	7,920 00	5
6	11/11	180 00		180 00	21 10	11 03				32 13	147 87	8,100 00	6
7	11/18	180 00		180 00	21 10	11 03				32 13	147 87	8,280 00	7
8	11/25	180 00		180 00	21 10	11 03				32 13	147 87	8,460 00	8
9	12/2	180 00		180 00	21 10	11 03				32 13	147 87	8,640 00	9
10	12/9	180 00		180 00	21 10	11 03			5 00	32 13	147 87	8,820 00	10
11													11
12													12
13													13
QUARTER TOTALS													
YEARLY TOTALS													

TO THE STUDENT: Use this form for your Employee's Earnings Record (see Activity 6, page 15).

EMPLOYEE'S EARNINGS RECORD

NAME Martin, Linda EMPL. NO. ________

ADDRESS 359 Park Street

SOC. SEC. NO. 127-55-5558 ALLOWANCES 1 MARRIED ____ SINGLE ✓

DEPARTMENT ________

OCCUPATION ________

DATE EMPLOYED ________ DATE TERMINATED ________

DEDUCTIONS:
- Credit Union ________
- Group Insurance ________
- Medical Insurance ________
- U.S. Savings Bond ________
- Union Dues ________
- United Fund ________
- Other ________

EARNINGS:
- Yearly ________
- Monthly ________
- Weekly ________
- Hourly ________
- Commission ________
- Piece Rate Per Unit ________

PAY PERIOD		EARNINGS			DEDUCTIONS								
WEEK	WEEK ENDED	REGULAR	OVERTIME	TOTAL	FEDERAL INC. TAX	FICA TAX	GROUP INSURANCE	MEDICAL INSURANCE	OTHER	TOTAL	NET PAY	ACCUMULATED TAXABLE EARNINGS	WEEK
TOTALS 3 QUAR.													
1													1
2													2
3													3
4													4
5													5
6													6
7													7
8													8
9													9
10	12/9	135.00		135.00	15.40	8.28				23.68	111.32	135.00	10
11													11
12													12
13													13
QUARTER TOTALS													
YEARLY TOTALS													

EMPLOYEE'S EARNINGS RECORD

NAME Klaus, Elsie — EMPL. NO. 12

ADDRESS 6784 Eden Avenue; Clovis; CA 93612

SOC. SEC. NO. 164-63-6059 — ALLOWANCES 2 — MARRIED X — SINGLE

DEPARTMENT Sales

OCCUPATION Salesperson

DATE EMPLOYED July 1, 1975 — DATE TERMINATED

DEDUCTIONS:
- Credit Union
- Group Insurance #10 per mo.
- Medical Insurance $17 per mo.
- U.S. Savings Bond
- Union Dues
- United Fund
- Other

EARNINGS:
- Yearly
- Monthly
- Weekly
- Hourly
- Commission 8%
- Piece Rate Per Unit

PAY PERIOD		EARNINGS			DEDUCTIONS						NET PAY	ACCUMULATED TAXABLE EARNINGS	WEEK
WEEK	WEEK ENDED	REGULAR	OVERTIME	TOTAL	FEDERAL INC. TAX	FICA TAX	GROUP INSURANCE	MEDICAL INSURANCE	OTHER	TOTAL			
TOTALS 3 QUAR.		15,200 48		15,200 48	2,324 40	931 79	90 00	153 00		3,499 19	11,701 29	15,200 48	
1	10/7	395 78		395 78	62 40	24 26				86 66	309 12	15,596 26	1
2	10/14	383 12		383 12	59 60	23 49		17 00		100 09	283 03	15,979 38	2
3	10/21	409 89		409 89	65 20	25 13				90 33	319 56	16,389 27	3
4	10/28	401 95		401 95	65 20	24 64	10 00			99 84	302 11	16,791 22	4
5	11/4	375 41		375 41	57 10	23 01				80 11	295 30	17,166 63	5
6	11/11	363 02		363 02	54 60	22 25		17 00		93 85	269 17	17,529 65	6
7	11/18	396 67		396 67	62 40	24 32				86 72	309 95	17,926 32	7
8	11/25	404 93		404 93	65 20	24 82	10 00			100 02	304 91	18,331 25	8
9	12/2	381 39		381 39	59 60	23 38				82 98	298 41	18,712 64	9
10	12/9	390 12		390 12	62 40	23 91				86 31	303 81	19,102 76	10
11													11
12													12
13													13
QUARTER TOTALS													
YEARLY TOTALS													

EMPLOYEE'S EARNINGS RECORD

NAME *Hirasuna, James* EMPL. NO. *13*

ADDRESS *437 Diana Drive, Clovis, CA 93612*

SOC. SEC. NO. *234-56-3429* ALLOWANCES *4* MARRIED *X* SINGLE ____

DEPARTMENT *Sales*

OCCUPATION *Salesperson*

DATE EMPLOYED *May 1, 1975* DATE TERMINATED ____

DEDUCTIONS:
- Credit Union ____
- Group Insurance *$10 per mo.*
- Medical Insurance *$27 per mo.*
- U.S. Savings Bond ____
- Union Dues ____
- United Fund ____
- Other ____

EARNINGS:
- Yearly ____
- Monthly ____
- Weekly ____
- Hourly ____
- Commission *8%*
- Piece Rate Per Unit ____

Week	Week Ended	Earnings: Regular	Earnings: Overtime	Earnings: Total	Deductions: Federal Inc. Tax	Deductions: FICA Tax	Deductions: Group Insurance	Deductions: Medical Insurance	Deductions: Other	Deductions: Total	Net Pay	Accumulated Taxable Earnings	Week
Totals 3 Quar.		14,727.26		14,727.26	1,946.10	902.78	90.00	243.00		3,181.88	11,545.38	14,727.26	
1	10/7	397.78		397.78	54.90	24.38				79.28	318.50	15,125.04	1
2	10/14	410.78		410.78	59.90	25.18		27.00		112.08	298.70	15,535.82	2
3	10/21	402.35		402.35	57.40	24.66				82.06	320.29	15,938.17	3
4	10/28	383.17		383.17	52.40	23.49	10.00			85.89	297.28	16,321.34	4
5	11/4	372.14		372.14	49.90	22.81				72.71	299.43	16,693.48	5
6	11/11	395.66		395.66	54.90	24.25		27.00		106.15	289.51	17,089.14	6
7	11/18	407.57		407.57	57.40	24.98				82.38	325.19	17,496.71	7
8	11/25	362.10		362.10	47.40	22.20	10.00			79.60	282.50	17,858.81	8
9	12/2	398.69		398.69	54.90	24.44				79.34	319.35	18,257.50	9
10	12/9	370.59		370.59	49.90	22.72				72.63	297.97	18,628.09	10
11													11
12													12
13													13
Quarter Totals													
Yearly Totals													

EMPLOYEE'S EARNINGS RECORD

NAME Salazar, Ruben EMPL. NO. 22

ADDRESS 660 Apache Circle; Clovis; CA 93612

SOC. SEC. NO. 341-42-5608 ALLOW-ANCES 2 MARRIED X SINGLE ____

DEPARTMENT Production

OCCUPATION Production Worker – Hourly Basis

DATE EMPLOYED October 15, 1977 DATE TERMINATED ____

DEDUCTIONS:
- Credit Union ____
- Group Insurance $10 per mo.
- Medical Insurance $17 per mo.
- U.S. Savings Bond ____
- Union Dues $5 per wk.
- United Fund ____
- Other ____

EARNINGS:
- Yearly ____
- Monthly ____
- Weekly ____
- Hourly $6.90
- Commission ____
- Piece Rate Per Unit ____

PAY PERIOD		EARNINGS			DEDUCTIONS						NET PAY	ACCUMULATED TAXABLE EARNINGS	WEEK
WEEK	WEEK ENDED	REGULAR	OVERTIME	TOTAL	FEDERAL INC. TAX	FICA TAX	GROUP INSURANCE	MEDICAL INSURANCE	OTHER	TOTAL			
TOTALS 3 QUAR.		10,216.14	186.30	10,402.44	1,201.20	637.67	90.00	153.00	U 195.00	2,276.87	8,125.57	10,402.44	
1	10/7	276.00		276.00	33.00	16.92			U 5.00	54.92	221.08	10,678.44	1
2	10/14	269.10		269.10	30.80	16.50		17.00	U 5.00	69.30	199.80	10,947.54	2
3	10/21	276.00	10.35	286.35	35.20	17.55			U 5.00	57.75	228.60	11,233.89	3
4	10/28	276.00		276.00	33.00	16.92	10.00		U 5.00	64.92	211.08	11,509.89	4
5	11/4	276.00	15.53	291.53	37.40	17.87			U 5.00	60.27	231.26	11,801.42	5
6	11/11	272.55		272.55	33.00	16.71		17.00	U 5.00	71.71	200.84	12,073.97	6
7	11/18	275.31		275.31	33.00	16.88			U 5.00	54.88	220.43	12,349.28	7
8	11/25	276.00	20.70	296.70	37.40	18.19	10.00		U 5.00	70.59	226.11	12,645.98	8
9	12/2	276.00	25.88	301.88	39.60	18.51			U 5.00	63.11	238.77	12,947.86	9
10	12/9	258.75	10.35	269.10	30.80	16.50			U 5.00	53.30	216.80	13,216.96	10
11													11
12													12
13													13
QUARTER TOTALS													
YEARLY TOTALS													

EMPLOYEE'S EARNINGS RECORD

NAME Brown, Leroy EMPL. NO. 23

ADDRESS 610 Beech Road; Clovis; CA 93612

SOC. SEC. NO. 263-23-3724 ALLOWANCES 5 MARRIED X SINGLE

DEPARTMENT Production

OCCUPATION Production Worker-Hourly Basis

DATE EMPLOYED August 15, 1977 DATE TERMINATED

DEDUCTIONS:
- Credit Union
- Group Insurance #10 per mo.
- Medical Insurance #27 per mo.
- U.S. Savings Bond
- Union Dues #5 per wk.
- United Fund
- Other

EARNINGS:
- Yearly
- Monthly
- Weekly
- Hourly #4.40
- Commission
- Piece Rate Per Unit

PAY PERIOD		EARNINGS			DEDUCTIONS						NET PAY	ACCUMULATED TAXABLE EARNINGS	WEEK
WEEK	WEEK ENDED	REGULAR	OVERTIME	TOTAL	FEDERAL INC. TAX	FICA TAX	GROUP INSURANCE	MEDICAL INSURANCE	OTHER	TOTAL			
TOTALS 3 QUAR.		6,859 60	79 20	6,938 80	245 70	425 35	90 00	243 00	U 195 00	1,199 05	5,739 75	6,938 80	
1	10/7	176 00	6 60	182 60	8 10	11 19			U 5 00	24 29	158 31	7,121 40	1
2	10/14	171 60		171 60	6 30	10 52		27 00	U 5 00	48 82	122 78	7,293 00	2
3	10/21	175 12		175 12	6 30	10 73			U 5 00	22 03	153 09	7,468 12	3
4	10/28	176 00		176 00	6 30	10 79	10 00		U 5 00	32 09	143 91	7,644 12	4
5	11/4	176 00	13 20	189 20	8 10	11 60			U 5 00	24 70	164 50	7,833 32	5
6	11/11	176 00		176 00	6 30	10 79		27 00	U 5 00	49 09	126 91	8,009 32	6
7	11/18	175 56		175 56	6 30	10 76			U 5 00	22 06	153 50	8,184 88	7
8	11/25	176 00	13 20	189 20	8 10	11 60	10 00		U 5 00	34 70	154 50	8,374 08	8
9	12/2	174 68	26 40	201 08	11 70	12 33			U 5 00	29 03	172 05	8,575 16	9
10	12/9	176 00	19 80	195 80	9 90	12 00			U 5 00	26 90	168 90	8,770 96	10
11													11
12													12
13													13
QUARTER TOTALS													
YEARLY TOTALS													

EMPLOYEE'S EARNINGS RECORD

NAME McLaughlin, Darlene EMPL. NO. 24

ADDRESS 511 Delhi Pike; Clovis, CA 93612

SOC. SEC. NO. 147-62-6118 ALLOWANCES 1 MARRIED ___ SINGLE X

DEPARTMENT Production

OCCUPATION Production Worker-Hourly Basis

DATE EMPLOYED July 3, 1976 DATE TERMINATED ___

DEDUCTIONS:
- Credit Union ___
- Group Insurance #10 per mo.
- Medical Insurance #17 per mo.
- U.S. Savings Bond ___
- Union Dues #5 per wk.
- United Fund ___
- Other ___

EARNINGS:
- Yearly ___
- Monthly ___
- Weekly ___
- Hourly #5
- Commission ___
- Piece Rate Per Unit ___

PAY PERIOD		EARNINGS			DEDUCTIONS						NET PAY	ACCUMULATED TAXABLE EARNINGS	WEEK
WEEK	WEEK ENDED	REGULAR	OVERTIME	TOTAL	FEDERAL INC. TAX	FICA TAX	GROUP INSURANCE	MEDICAL INSURANCE	OTHER	TOTAL			
TOTALS 3 QUAR.		7,800.00	135.00	7,935.00	1,154.40	486.42	90.00	153.00	U 195.00	2,078.82	5,856.18	7,935.00	
1	10/7	200.00	7.50	207.50	29.60	12.72			U 5.00	47.32	160.18	8,142.50	1
2	10/14	200.00		200.00	29.60	12.26		17.00	U 5.00	63.86	136.14	8,342.50	2
3	10/21	199.50		199.50	27.20	12.23			U 5.00	44.43	155.07	8,542.00	3
4	10/28	200.00	15.00	215.00	32.00	13.18	10.00		U 5.00	60.18	154.82	8,757.00	4
5	11/4	200.00		200.00	29.60	12.26			U 5.00	46.86	153.14	8,957.00	5
6	11/11	199.00		199.00	27.20	12.20		17.00	U 5.00	61.40	137.60	9,156.00	6
7	11/18	200.00	7.50	207.50	29.60	12.72			U 5.00	47.32	160.18	9,363.50	7
8	11/25	200.00		200.00	29.60	12.26	10.00		U 5.00	56.86	143.14	9,563.50	8
9	12/2	195.00		195.00	27.20	11.95			U 5.00	44.15	150.85	9,758.50	9
10	12/9	151.50	11.25	162.75	20.60	9.98			U 5.00	35.58	127.17	9921.25	10
11													11
12													12
13													13
QUARTER TOTALS													
YEARLY TOTALS													

EMPLOYEE'S EARNINGS RECORD

NAME Riley, Sam EMPL. NO. 26

ADDRESS 695 Dina Lane; Clovis, CA 93612

SOC. SEC. NO. 742-72-7912 ALLOWANCES 2 MARRIED X SINGLE

DEPARTMENT Production

OCCUPATION Production Worker-Hourly Basis

DATE EMPLOYED November 6, 19-- DATE TERMINATED

DEDUCTIONS:
- Credit Union
- Group Insurance #10 per mo.
- Medical Insurance #17 per mo.
- U.S. Savings Bond
- Union Dues #5 per wk.
- United Fund
- Other

EARNINGS:
- Yearly
- Monthly
- Weekly
- Hourly #5.90
- Commission
- Piece Rate Per Unit

PAY PERIOD		EARNINGS			DEDUCTIONS						NET PAY	ACCUMULATED TAXABLE EARNINGS	
WEEK	WEEK ENDED	REGULAR	OVERTIME	TOTAL	FEDERAL INC. TAX	FICA TAX	GROUP INSURANCE	MEDICAL INSURANCE	OTHER	TOTAL			WEEK
TOTALS 3 QUAR.													
1													1
2													2
3													3
4													4
5													5
6	11/11	236 00	44 25	280 25	35 20	17 18		17 00	U 5 00	74 38	205 87	280 25	6
7	11/18	236 00		236 00	24 90	14 47			U 5 00	44 37	191 63	516 25	7
8	11/25	230 10		230 10	24 90	14 11	10 00		U 5 00	54 01	176 09	746 35	8
9	12/2	236 00	17 70	253 70	28 60	15 55			U 5 00	49 15	204 55	1,000 05	9
10	12/9	236 00	13 28	249 28	26 70	15 28			U 5 00	46 98	202 30	1249 33	10
11													11
12													12
13													13
QUARTER TOTALS													
YEARLY TOTALS													

EMPLOYEE'S EARNINGS RECORD

NAME Neufeld, Sara EMPL. NO. 27

ADDRESS 808 Alvin Lane; Clovis, CA 93612

SOC. SEC. NO. 341-26-6247 ALLOWANCES 0 MARRIED X SINGLE

DEPARTMENT Production

OCCUPATION Production Worker - Hourly Basis

DATE EMPLOYED September 11, 19-- DATE TERMINATED

DEDUCTIONS:
- Credit Union
- Group Insurance $10 per mo.
- Medical Insurance $17 per mo.
- U.S. Savings Bond
- Union Dues $5 per wk.
- United Fund
- Other

EARNINGS:
- Yearly
- Monthly
- Weekly
- Hourly $5.70
- Commission
- Piece Rate
- Per Unit

WEEK	PAY PERIOD WEEK ENDED	EARNINGS REGULAR	EARNINGS OVERTIME	EARNINGS TOTAL	DEDUCTIONS FEDERAL INC. TAX	FICA TAX	GROUP INSURANCE	MEDICAL INSURANCE	OTHER	DEDUCTIONS TOTAL	NET PAY	ACCUMULATED TAXABLE EARNINGS	WEEK
	TOTALS 3 QUAR.	684 00		684 00	85 20	41 93	10 00	17 00	U 15 00	169 13	514 87	684 00	
1	10/7	228 00		228 00	28 40	13 98			U 5 00	47 38	180 62	912 00	1
2	10/14	227 43		227 43	28 40	13 94		17 00	U 5 00	64 34	163 09	1,139 43	2
3	10/21	228 00	4 28	232 28	30 60	14 24			U 5 00	49 84	182 44	1,371 71	3
4	10/28	228 00		228 00	28 40	13 98	10 00		U 5 00	57 38	170 62	1,599 71	4
5	11/4	222 30		222 30	28 40	13 63			U 5 00	47 03	175 27	1,822 01	5
6	11/11	182 40		182 40	21 10	11 18		17 00	U 5 00	54 28	128 12	2,004 41	6
7	11/18	228 00	8 55	236 55	30 60	14 50			U 5 00	50 10	186 45	2,240 96	7
8	11/25	228 00	12 83	240 83	32 80	14 76	10 00		U 5 00	62 56	178 27	2,481 79	8
9	12/2	226 86	17 10	243 96	32 80	14 95			U 5 00	52 75	191 21	2,725 75	9
10	12/9	213 75	85 50	299 25	44 30	18 34			U 5 00	67 64	231 61	3025 00	10
11													11
12													12
13													13
	QUARTER TOTALS												
	YEARLY TOTALS												

EMPLOYEE'S EARNINGS RECORD

NAME Leonardo, Mike EMPL. NO. 28

ADDRESS 581 Summit Road; Clovis, CA 93612

SOC. SEC. NO. 471-51-2341 ALLOWANCES 2 MARRIED X SINGLE

DEPARTMENT Production

OCCUPATION Production Worker - Hourly Basis

DATE EMPLOYED August 1, 1977 DATE TERMINATED

DEDUCTIONS:
- Credit Union
- Group Insurance #10 per mo.
- Medical Insurance #17 per mo.
- U.S. Savings Bond
- Union Dues $5 per wk.
- United Fund
- Other

EARNINGS:
- Yearly
- Monthly
- Weekly
- Hourly $4.50
- Commission
- Piece Rate
- Per Unit

WEEK	WEEK ENDED	EARNINGS: REGULAR	EARNINGS: OVERTIME	EARNINGS: TOTAL	DEDUCTIONS: FEDERAL INC. TAX	FICA TAX	GROUP INSURANCE	MEDICAL INSURANCE	OTHER	TOTAL	NET PAY	ACCUMULATED TAXABLE EARNINGS	WEEK
TOTALS 3 QUAR.		7,020.00		7,020.00	620.10	430.33	90.00	153.00	U 195.00	1,488.43	5,531.57	7,020.00	
1	10/7	179.55		179.55	14.10	11.01			U 5.00	30.11	149.44	7,199.55	1
2	10/14	180.00		180.00	15.90	11.03		17.00	U 5.00	48.93	131.07	7,379.55	2
3	10/21	180.00	10.13	190.13	17.70	11.65			U 5.00	34.35	155.78	7,569.68	3
4	10/28	175.50		175.50	14.10	10.76	10.00		U 5.00	39.86	135.64	7,745.18	4
5	11/4	180.00		180.00	15.90	11.03			U 5.00	31.93	148.07	7,925.18	5
6	11/11	162.00		162.00	12.30	9.93		17.00	U 5.00	44.23	117.77	8,087.18	6
7	11/18	180.00	13.50	193.50	17.70	11.86			U 5.00	34.56	158.94	8,280.68	7
8	11/25	179.10	6.75	185.85	15.90	11.39	10.00		U 5.00	42.29	143.56	8,466.53	8
9	12/2	180.00	3.38	183.38	15.90	11.24			U 5.00	32.14	151.24	8,649.91	9
10	12/9	168.75	23.63	192.38	17.70	11.79			U 5.00	34.49	157.89	8,818.66	10
11													11
12													12
13													13
QUARTER TOTALS													
YEARLY TOTALS													

EMPLOYEE'S EARNINGS RECORD

NAME Baker, Edna EMPL. NO. 42

ADDRESS 277 Minot Avenue; Clovis, CA 93612

SOC. SEC. NO. 273-73-3482 ALLOWANCES 0 MARRIED X SINGLE

DEPARTMENT Production

OCCUPATION Production Worker—Piece-Rate Basis

DATE EMPLOYED July 3, 1977 DATE TERMINATED

DEDUCTIONS:
- Credit Union
- Group Insurance
- Medical Insurance $17 per mo.
- U.S. Savings Bond
- Union Dues $5 per wk.
- United Fund
- Other

EARNINGS:
- Yearly
- Monthly
- Weekly
- Hourly
- Commission
- Piece Rate Per Unit $0.14

PAY PERIOD		EARNINGS			DEDUCTIONS						NET PAY	ACCUMULATED TAXABLE EARNINGS	WEEK
WEEK	WEEK ENDED	REGULAR	OVERTIME	TOTAL	FEDERAL INC. TAX	FICA TAX	GROUP INSURANCE	MEDICAL INSURANCE	OTHER	TOTAL			
TOTALS 3 QUAR.		8,865.92	51.19	8,917.11	1,107.60	546.62		153.00	U 195.00	2,002.22	6,914.89	8,917.11	
1	10/7	223.72		223.72	28.40	13.71			U 5.00	47.11	176.61	9,140.83	1
2	10/14	286.44	4.55	290.99	44.30	17.84		17.00	U 5.00	84.14	206.85	9,431.82	2
3	10/21	227.92		227.92	28.40	13.97			U 5.00	47.37	180.55	9,659.74	3
4	10/28	228.34		228.34	28.40	14.00			U 5.00	47.40	180.94	9,888.08	4
5	11/4	224.28	1.92	226.20	28.40	13.87			U 5.00	47.27	178.93	10,114.28	5
6	11/11	229.32		229.32	28.40	14.06		17.00	U 5.00	64.46	164.86	10,343.60	6
7	11/18	239.68	3.80	243.48	32.80	14.93			U 5.00	52.73	190.75	10,587.08	7
8	11/25	228.48		228.48	28.40	14.01			U 5.00	47.41	181.07	10,815.56	8
9	12/2	230.02		230.02	30.60	14.10			U 5.00	49.70	180.32	11,045.58	9
10	12/9	222.60		222.60	28.40	13.65			U 5.00	47.05	175.55	11,268.18	10
11													11
12													12
13													13
QUARTER TOTALS													
YEARLY TOTALS													

EMPLOYEE'S EARNINGS RECORD

NAME Svenson, Karl EMPL. NO. 43

ADDRESS 670 Delta Avenue; Clovis, CA 93612

SOC. SEC. NO. 869-91-2032 ALLOWANCES 1 MARRIED ___ SINGLE X

DEPARTMENT Production

OCCUPATION Production Worker-Piece-Rate Basis

DATE EMPLOYED January 2, 1977 DATE TERMINATED ___

DEDUCTIONS:
- Credit Union ___
- Group Insurance $10 per mo.
- Medical Insurance $17 per mo.
- U.S. Savings Bond ___
- Union Dues $5 per wk.
- United Fund ___
- Other ___

EARNINGS:
- Yearly ___
- Monthly ___
- Weekly ___
- Hourly ___
- Commission ___
- Piece Rate Per Unit $0.12

PAY PERIOD		EARNINGS			DEDUCTIONS						NET PAY	ACCUMULATED TAXABLE EARNINGS	WEEK
WEEK	WEEK ENDED	REGULAR	OVERTIME	TOTAL	FEDERAL INC. TAX	FICA TAX	GROUP INSURANCE	MEDICAL INSURANCE	OTHER	TOTAL			
TOTALS 3 QUAR.		8,116 92	83 16	8,200 08	1,156 80	502 66	90 00	153 00	U 195 00	2,097 46	6,102 62	8,200 08	
1	10/7	208 08		208 08	29 60	12 76			U 5 00	47 36	160 72	8,408 16	1
2	10/14	210 24		210 24	32 00	12 89		17 00	U 5 00	66 89	143 35	8,618 40	2
3	10/21	214 08		214 08	32 00	13 12			U 5 00	50 12	163 96	8,832 48	3
4	10/28	216 12		216 12	32 00	13 25	10 00		U 5 00	60 25	155 87	9,048 60	4
5	11/4	280 08	20 86	300 94	56 40	18 45			U 5 00	79 85	221 09	9,349 54	5
6	11/11	203 76		203 76	29 60	12 49		17 00	U 5 00	64 09	139 67	9,553 30	6
7	11/18	205 56		205 56	29 60	12 60			U 5 00	47 20	158 36	9,758 86	7
8	11/25	238 08	5 66	243 74	39 60	14 94	10 00		U 5 00	69 54	174 20	10,002 60	8
9	12/2	208 20		208 20	29 60	12 76			U 5 00	47 36	160 84	10,210 80	9
10	12/9	210 36		210 36	32 00	12 90			U 5 00	49 90	160 46	10421 16	10
11													11
12													12
13													13
QUARTER TOTALS													
YEARLY TOTALS													

TO THE STUDENT: Use this form for Gloria Leshen's Employee's Earnings Record.

EMPLOYEE'S EARNINGS RECORD

NAME ______________________ EMPL. NO. ________

ADDRESS ______________________

SOC. SEC. NO. ____________ ALLOW-ANCES ______ MARRIED ______ SINGLE ______

DEPARTMENT ______________________

OCCUPATION ______________________

DATE EMPLOYED ____________ DATE TERMINATED ____________

DEDUCTIONS:
- Credit Union ________
- Group Insurance ________
- Medical Insurance ________
- U.S. Savings Bond ________
- Union Dues ________
- United Fund ________
- Other ________

EARNINGS:
- Yearly ________
- Monthly ________
- Weekly ________
- Hourly ________
- Commission ________
- Piece Rate Per Unit ________

PAY PERIOD		EARNINGS			DEDUCTIONS						NET PAY	ACCUMULATED TAXABLE EARNINGS	WEEK
WEEK	WEEK ENDED	REGULAR	OVERTIME	TOTAL	FEDERAL INC. TAX	FICA TAX	GROUP INSURANCE	MEDICAL INSURANCE	OTHER	TOTAL			
TOTALS 3 QUAR.													
1													1
2													2
3													3
4													4
5													5
6													6
7													7
8													8
9													9
10													10
11													11
12													12
13													13
QUARTER TOTALS													
YEARLY TOTALS													

INSTRUCTIONS FOR FORM 941

To complete Form 941, you must figure the amounts needed for these lines:

Lines 2, 3, and 6 (*Taxable FICA wages paid*)

Use the form below which lists the name of each Solarheat employee for your computations. Look at the QUARTER TOTALS line on each Employee's Earnings Record, and list the proper figures in the last two columns of this page. The totals of these two columns are the amounts for Lines 2 and 3 of Form 941.

Employee	*Total Wages Subject to Withholding During Last Quarter, 19–*	*Federal Income Tax Withheld*
Flores, Jesse	$	$
Jackson, Paula		
____________ . . . . . . (Student's Name)		
Klaus, Elsie		
Hirasuna, James		
Salazar, Ruben		
Brown, Leroy		
McLaughlin, Darlene		
Vukovich, Diane		
Riley, Sam		
Neufeld, Sara		
Leonardo, Mike		
Baker, Edna		
Svenson, Karl		
Leshen, Gloria		
TOTAL	$ (Line 2)	$ (Line 3)

For the amount to be entered in the middle of Line 6, look at Jesse Flores' Employee's Earnings Record. He was the only Solarheat employee who reached the $22,900 FICA tax limit on wages for this taxable year. First, subtract $22,900 from Mr. Flores' total salary for this year. Then, subtract this result from the first column's total (*Line 2*) to find the amount to be entered in the middle of Line 6 on Form 941.

1. Jesse Flores' total salary, 19—	$
Less $22,900 FICA tax limit on wages	22,900.00
Result	$

2. Line 2 total	$
Less result in 1	
Amount to enter in middle of Line 6	$

PAYROLL RETURNS

DEPARTMENT OF THE TREASURY · FISCAL SERVICE
Bureau of Government Financial Operations · FTD Form Rev. Oct. 1977

FEDERAL TAX DEPOSIT OF: WITHHELD INCOME AND FICA TAX

REPORT ON IRS RETURN

NAME OF BANK	AMOUNT OF DEPOSIT	
	DOLLARS	CENTS

941

SOLARHEAT SYSTEMS INC
901 ARCADE ST
CLOVIS CA 93612

501
FTD Form

Employer Identification Number
94-186438
488

DEC 31 --
Tax Period Ending

ENTER AMOUNT OF DEPOSIT AND NAME OF BANK WHERE DEPOSITED IN SPACE ABOVE.

The space below may be used by depositaries for MICR encoding.

Bank Name/Date Stamp

Form **941**

Department of the Treasury
Internal Revenue Service

Employer's Quarterly Federal Tax Return

T	
FF	
FD	
FP	
I	
T	

Your name, address, employer identification number, and calendar quarter of return. (If not correct, please change)

Name (as distinguished from trade name) — Date quarter ended

Trade name, if any — Employer identification number

Address and ZIP code

If address is different from prior return, check here ▶ ☐

1 Number of employees (except household) employed in the pay period that includes March 12th (complete for first quarter only) . . . .

2 Total wages and tips subject to withholding, plus other compensation . . . . →

3 Total income tax withheld from wages, tips, annuities, gambling, etc. (see instructions) . . . .

4 Adjustment of withheld income tax for preceding quarters of calendar year . . . .

5 Adjusted total of income tax withheld . . . . →

6 Taxable FICA wages paid . . . . $.................... multiplied by 12.26% = TAX . .

7 Taxable tips reported . . . . $.................... multiplied by 6.13% = TAX . .

8 Total FICA taxes (add lines 6 and 7) . . . . →

9 Adjustment of FICA taxes (see instructions) . . . .

10 Adjusted total of FICA taxes . . . . →

11 Total taxes (add lines 5 and 10) . . . .

Record of Federal Tax Deposits (See instructions on page 4)

Deposit period ending:		I. Tax liability for period	II. Date of deposit	III. Amount deposited
Overpayment from previous quarter. . . .				
First month of quarter	1st through 7th day			
	8th through 15th day			
	16th through 22d day	2,417.20	10/24/--	2,417.20
	23d through last day			
A First month total	A	2,417.20		2,417.20
Second month of quarter	1st through 7th day			
	8th through 15th day	2,444.12	11/14/--	2,444.12
	16th through 22d day			
	23d through last day			
B Second month total	B	2,444.12		2,444.12
Third month of quarter	1st through 7th day	2,606.88	12/5/--	2,606.88
	8th through 15th day			
	16th through 22d day			
	23d through last day	4,575.85	1/3/--	4,575.85
C Third month total	C	7,182.73		7,182.73
D Total for quarter (add items A, B, and C) .				
E Final deposit made for quarter. (Enter zero if the final deposit made for the quarter is included in item D)				

12 Total deposits for quarter (including final deposit made for quarter) and overpayment from previous quarter. (See instructions on page 4) . . . .

Note: *If undeposited taxes at the end of the quarter are $200 or more, deposit the full amount with an authorized financial institution or a Federal Reserve bank according to the instructions on the back of the Federal Tax Deposit Form 501. Enter this deposit in the Record of Federal Tax Deposits and include it in line 12.*

13 Undeposited taxes due (subtract line 12 from line 11—this should be less than $200). Pay to Internal Revenue Service and enter here . . . . →

14 If line 12 is more than line 11, enter overpayment here ▶ $ and check if to be: ☐ Applied to next return, or ☐ Refunded.

15 If you are not liable for returns in the future, write **"FINAL"** (See instructions) ▶ Date final wages paid ▶

Under penalties of perjury, I declare that I have examined this return, including accompanying schedules and statements, and to the best of my knowledge and belief it is true, correct, and complete.

Date ▶ Signature ▶ Title ▶

Form **941**

1 Control number
222
2 Employer's State number

For Official Use Only

3 Employer's name, address, and ZIP code

4 Subtotal ☐ Correction ☐ Void ☐

5 Employer's identification number

6 Advance EIC payment

7

8 Employee's social security number

9 Federal income tax withheld

10 Wages, tips, other compensation

11 FICA tax withheld

12 Total FICA wages

13 Employee's name (first, middle, last)

14 Pension plan coverage? Yes/No

15*

16 FICA tips

17 Employee's address and ZIP code

Copy A For Social Security Administration
*See Instructions for Forms W-2 and W-2P and back of Copy D

Form **W–2 Wage and Tax Statement 19--**

Department of the Treasury—Internal Revenue Service

---

1 Control number
222
2 Employer's State number

3 Employer's name, address, and ZIP code

4 Subtotal ☐ Correction ☐ Void ☐

5 Employer's identification number

6 Advance EIC payment

7

8 Employee's social security number

9 Federal income tax withheld

10 Wages, tips, other compensation

11 FICA tax withheld

12 Total FICA wages

13 Employee's name (first, middle, last)

14 Pension plan coverage? Yes/No

15

16 FICA tips

17 Employee's address and ZIP code

Copy A For Social Security Administration
*See Instructions for Forms W-2 and W-2P and back of Copy D

Form **W–2 Wage and Tax Statement 19--**

Department of the Treasury—Internal Revenue Service

---

1 Control number
222
2 Employer's State number

3 Employer's name, address, and ZIP code

4 Subtotal ☐ Correction ☐ Void ☐

5 Employer's identification number

6 Advance EIC payment

7

8 Employee's social security number

9 Federal income tax withheld

10 Wages, tips, other compensation

11 FICA tax withheld

12 Total FICA wages

13 Employee's name (first, middle, last)

14 Pension plan coverage? Yes/No

15

16 FICA tips

17 Employee's address and ZIP code

Copy A For Social Security Administration
*See Instructions for Forms W-2 and W-2P and back of Copy D

Form **W–2 Wage and Tax Statement 19--**

Department of the Treasury—Internal Revenue Service

INSTRUCTIONS FOR FORM 940

NOTE: Before you begin work on Form 940, first determine the data needed for Column 3 and Line 11 of this return. To help you, each employee's name at the end of the calendar year is listed below. Refer to the YEARLY TOTALS line of each Employee's Earnings Record, and list the proper figures in the last two columns on this page.

Employee	*Total Taxable Wages in Calendar Year [Limited to $6,000 Maximum for Each Employee]*	*Total Renumeration Paid During Calendar Year for Services of Employees*
Flores, Jesse	$__________	__________
Jackson, Paula	__________	__________
__________ . . . . . . (*Student's Name*)	__________	__________
Klaus, Elsie	__________	__________
Hirasuna, James	__________	__________
Salazar, Ruben	__________	__________
Brown, Leroy	__________	__________
McLaughlin, Darlene	__________	__________
Vukovich, Diane	__________	__________
Riley, Sam	__________	__________
Neufeld, Sara	__________	__________
Leonardo, Mike	__________	__________
Baker, Edna	__________	__________
Svenson, Karl	__________	__________
Leshen, Gloria	__________	__________
TOTAL	$__________ (*Column 3*)	$__________ (*Line 11*)

DEPARTMENT OF THE TREASURY · FISCAL SERVICE
Bureau of Government Financial Operations · FTD Form Rev. Oct. 1977

FEDERAL TAX DEPOSIT OF: FUTA TAX

REPORT ON IRS RETURN

NAME OF BANK	AMOUNT OF DEPOSIT	
	DOLLARS	CENTS

940

SOLARHEAT SYSTEMS INC
901 ARCADE ST
CLOVIS CA 93612

508
FTD Form

Employer Identification Number
94-186438

488

DEC --
Tax Period Ending

ENTER AMOUNT OF DEPOSIT AND NAME OF BANK WHERE DEPOSITED IN SPACE ABOVE.

The space below may be used by depositaries for MICR encoding.

Bank Name/Date Stamp

Form **940**
Department of the Treasury
Internal Revenue Service

Employer's Annual Federal Unemployment Tax Return

19--

T	
FF	
FD	
FP	
I	
T	

If incorrect, make any necessary change ▶

Name (as distinguished from trade name)

Trade name, if any

Address and ZIP code

Calendar Year
19--

Employer identification number

Name of State 1	State reporting number as shown on employer's State contribution returns 2	Taxable payroll (as defined in State act) 3	Experience rate period 4 From—	To—	Experience rate 5	Contributions had rate been 2.7% (col. 3 × 2.7%) 6	Contributions payable at experience rate (col. 3 × col. 5) 7	Additional credit (col. 6 minus col. 7) 8	Contributions actually paid to State 9
	Totals ▶								

10 Total tentative credit (column 8 plus column 9—see instructions on page 4)

11 Total remuneration (including exempt remuneration) **paid** during the calendar year for services of employees

Exempt Remuneration (See Instructions on Page 4) — (a) New jobs credit wages — (b) Amount paid

12 Exempt remuneration. (Explain each exemption shown, attaching additional sheet if necessary) ▶

13 Remuneration in excess of the first $4,200 in column (a), and the first $6,000 in column (b), paid to individual employees exclusive of exempt amounts entered on line 12. Do not use State wage limitation

14 Total exempt remuneration (line 12 plus line 13)

15 a New jobs credit total wages (subtract line 12, column (a) from line 11)

b New jobs credit wages (subtract line 14, column (a) from line 11)

c Total taxable FUTA wages (subtract line 14, column (b) from line 11)

16 Gross Federal tax (multiply line 15c by .034)

17 Maximum credit (multiply line 15c by .027)

18 Line 10 or line 17 whichever is smaller

19 Amount, if any, of wages on line 15c attributable to Rhode Island $........ × .003

20 Credit allowable (subtract line 19 from line 18)

21 Net Federal tax (subtract line 20 from line 16)

Record of Federal Tax Deposits for Unemployment Tax (Form 508)

Quarter	Liability by period	Date of deposit	Amount of deposit
First	260.56	4/12/--	260.56
Second	142.64	7/11/--	142.64
Third	-0-		-0-
Fourth	107.91	1/20/--	107.91

22 Total Federal tax deposited

23 **Balance due** (subtract line 22 from line 21—this should not exceed $100). Pay to Internal Revenue Service ▶

24 **Overpayment** (subtract line 21 from line 22) ▶

25 If no longer in business at end of year, write "**Final**" here ▶

Under penalties of perjury, I declare that I have examined this return, including accompanying schedules and statements, and to the best of my knowledge and belief, it is true, correct and complete, and that no part of any payment made to a State unemployment fund claimed as a credit was or is to be deducted from the remuneration of employees.

Date ▶ Signature ▶ Title (Owner, etc.) ▶

Form 940

COMBINATION JOURNAL

PAGE

1	2					3	4
CASH		DATE	ACCOUNT TITLE	Doc. No.	Post. Ref.	GENERAL	
DEBIT	CREDIT					DEBIT	CREDIT

PAGE

COMBINATION JOURNAL

	1	2					3	4	
	CASH		DATE	ACCOUNT TITLE	Doc. No.	Post. Ref.	GENERAL		
	DEBIT	CREDIT					DEBIT	CREDIT	
3									3
4									4
5									5
6									6
7									7
8									8
9									9
10									10
11									11
12									12
13									13
14									14
15									15
16									16
17									17
18									18
19									19
20									20
21									21
22									22
23									23

INCOME TAX WAGE-BRACKET WITHHOLDING TABLES *

WEEKLY Payroll Period—Employee MARRIED

And the wages are—		And the number of withholding allowances claimed is—										
At least	But less than	0	1	2	3	4	5	6	7	8	9	10 or more
		The amount of income tax to be withheld shall be—										
$0	$60	$0	$0	$0	$0	$0	$0	$0	$0	$0	$0	$0
60	62	.10	0	0	0	0	0	0	0	0	0	0
62	64	.40	0	0	0	0	0	0	0	0	0	0
64	66	.70	0	0	0	0	0	0	0	0	0	0
66	68	1.00	0	0	0	0	0	0	0	0	0	0
68	70	1.30	0	0	0	0	0	0	0	0	0	0
70	72	1.60	0	0	0	0	0	0	0	0	0	0
72	74	1.90	0	0	0	0	0	0	0	0	0	0
74	76	2.20	0	0	0	0	0	0	0	0	0	0
76	78	2.50	.30	0	0	0	0	0	0	0	0	0
78	80	2.80	.60	0	0	0	0	0	0	0	0	0
80	82	3.10	.90	0	0	0	0	0	0	0	0	0
82	84	3.40	1.20	0	0	0	0	0	0	0	0	0
84	86	3.70	1.50	0	0	0	0	0	0	0	0	0
86	88	4.00	1.80	0	0	0	0	0	0	0	0	0
88	90	4.30	2.10	0	0	0	0	0	0	0	0	0
90	92	4.60	2.40	.20	0	0	0	0	0	0	0	0
92	94	4.90	2.70	.50	0	0	0	0	0	0	0	0
94	96	5.20	3.00	.80	0	0	0	0	0	0	0	0
96	98	5.50	3.30	1.10	0	0	0	0	0	0	0	0
98	100	5.80	3.60	1.40	0	0	0	0	0	0	0	0
100	105	6.30	4.10	2.00	0	0	0	0	0	0	0	0
105	110	7.10	4.90	2.70	.50	0	0	0	0	0	0	0
110	115	8.00	5.60	3.50	1.30	0	0	0	0	0	0	0
115	120	8.90	6.40	4.20	2.00	0	0	0	0	0	0	0
120	125	9.80	7.20	5.00	2.80	.60	0	0	0	0	0	0
125	130	10.70	8.10	5.70	3.50	1.40	0	0	0	0	0	0
130	135	11.60	9.00	6.50	4.30	2.10	0	0	0	0	0	0
135	140	12.50	9.90	7.30	5.00	2.90	.70	0	0	0	0	0
140	145	13.40	10.80	8.20	5.80	3.60	1.50	0	0	0	0	0
At least	But less than	0	1	2	3	4	5	6	7	8	9	10 or more
145	150	14.30	11.70	9.10	6.50	4.40	2.20	.10	0	0	0	0
150	160	15.70	13.10	10.50	7.90	5.50	3.30	1.20	0	0	0	0
160	170	17.50	14.90	12.30	9.70	7.10	4.80	2.70	.50	0	0	0
170	180	19.30	16.70	14.10	11.50	8.90	6.30	4.20	2.00	0	0	0
180	190	21.10	18.50	15.90	13.30	10.70	8.10	5.70	3.50	1.40	0	0
190	200	22.90	20.30	17.70	15.10	12.50	9.90	7.30	5.00	2.90	.70	0
200	210	24.70	22.10	19.50	16.90	14.30	11.70	9.10	6.50	4.40	2.20	0
210	220	26.50	23.90	21.30	18.70	16.10	13.50	10.90	8.30	5.90	3.70	1.50
220	230	28.40	25.70	23.10	20.50	17.90	15.30	12.70	10.10	7.50	5.20	3.00
230	240	30.60	27.50	24.90	22.30	19.70	17.10	14.50	11.90	9.30	6.70	4.50
240	250	32.80	29.60	26.70	24.10	21.50	18.90	16.30	13.70	11.10	8.50	6.00
250	260	35.00	31.80	28.60	25.90	23.30	20.70	18.10	15.50	12.90	10.30	7.70
260	270	37.20	34.00	30.80	27.70	25.10	22.50	19.90	17.30	14.70	12.10	9.50
270	280	39.40	36.20	33.00	29.80	26.90	24.30	21.70	19.10	16.50	13.90	11.30
280	290	41.80	38.40	35.20	32.00	28.90	26.10	23.50	20.90	18.30	15.70	13.10
290	300	44.30	40.70	37.40	34.20	31.10	27.90	25.30	22.70	20.10	17.50	14.90
300	310	46.80	43.20	39.60	36.40	33.30	30.10	27.10	24.50	21.90	19.30	16.70
310	320	49.30	45.70	42.10	38.60	35.50	32.30	29.10	26.30	23.70	21.10	18.50
320	330	51.80	48.20	44.60	41.00	37.70	34.50	31.30	28.20	25.50	22.90	20.30
330	340	54.30	50.70	47.10	43.50	39.90	36.70	33.50	30.40	27.30	24.70	22.10
340	350	56.80	53.20	49.60	46.00	42.40	38.90	35.70	32.60	29.40	26.50	23.90
350	360	59.30	55.70	52.10	48.50	44.90	41.30	37.90	34.80	31.60	28.40	25.70
360	370	62.10	58.20	54.60	51.00	47.40	43.80	40.10	37.00	33.80	30.60	27.50
370	380	64.90	60.80	57.10	53.50	49.90	46.30	42.60	39.20	36.00	32.80	29.60
380	390	67.70	63.60	59.60	56.00	52.40	48.80	45.10	41.50	38.20	35.00	31.80
390	400	70.50	66.40	62.40	58.50	54.90	51.30	47.60	44.00	40.40	37.20	34.00
400	410	73.30	69.20	65.20	61.20	57.40	53.80	50.10	46.50	42.90	39.40	36.20
410	420	76.10	72.00	68.00	64.00	59.90	56.30	52.60	49.00	45.40	41.80	38.40
420	430	78.90	74.80	70.80	66.80	62.70	58.80	55.10	51.50	47.90	44.30	40.70
430	440	81.80	77.60	73.60	69.60	65.50	61.50	57.60	54.00	50.40	46.80	43.20

* These tables were effective at the time of publication.

WEEKLY Payroll Period—Employee MARRIED

And the wages are—		And the number of withholding allowances claimed is—										
At least	But less than	0	1	2	3	4	5	6	7	8	9	10 or more
		The amount of income tax to be withheld shall be—										
$440	$450	$85.00	$80.40	$76.40	$72.40	$68.30	$64.30	$60.30	$56.50	$52.90	$49.30	$45.70
450	460	88.20	83.60	79.20	75.20	71.10	67.10	63.10	59.00	55.40	51.80	48.20
460	470	91.40	86.80	82.20	78.00	73.90	69.90	65.90	61.80	57.90	54.30	50.70
470	480	94.60	90.00	85.40	80.80	76.70	72.70	68.70	64.60	60.60	56.80	53.20
480	490	97.80	93.20	88.60	84.00	79.50	75.50	71.50	67.40	63.40	59.30	55.70
490	500	101.00	96.40	91.80	87.20	82.60	78.30	74.30	70.20	66.20	62.10	58.20
500	510	104.20	99.60	95.00	90.40	85.80	81.10	77.10	73.00	69.00	64.90	60.90
510	520	107.70	102.80	98.20	93.60	89.00	84.30	79.90	75.80	71.80	67.70	63.70
520	530	111.30	106.10	101.40	96.80	92.20	87.50	82.90	78.60	74.60	70.50	66.50
530	540	114.90	109.70	104.60	100.00	95.40	90.70	86.10	81.50	77.40	73.30	69.30
540	550	118.50	113.30	108.10	103.20	98.60	93.90	89.30	84.70	80.20	76.10	72.10
550	560	122.10	116.90	111.70	106.50	101.80	97.10	92.50	87.90	83.30	78.90	74.90
560	570	125.70	120.50	115.30	110.10	105.00	100.30	95.70	91.10	86.50	81.90	77.70
570	580	129.30	124.10	118.90	113.70	108.50	103.50	98.90	94.30	89.70	85.10	80.50
580	590	132.90	127.70	122.50	117.30	112.10	106.90	102.10	97.50	92.90	88.30	83.70
590	600	136.50	131.30	126.10	120.90	115.70	110.50	105.30	100.70	96.10	91.50	86.90
600	610	140.10	134.90	129.70	124.50	119.30	114.10	108.90	103.90	99.30	94.70	90.10
610	620	143.70	138.50	133.30	128.10	122.90	117.70	112.50	107.30	102.50	97.90	93.30
620	630	147.30	142.10	136.90	131.70	126.50	121.30	116.10	110.90	105.70	101.10	96.50
630	640	150.90	145.70	140.50	135.30	130.10	124.90	119.70	114.50	109.30	104.30	99.70
640	650	154.50	149.30	144.10	138.90	133.70	128.50	123.30	118.10	112.90	107.70	102.90
650	660	158.10	152.90	147.70	142.50	137.30	132.10	126.90	121.70	116.50	111.30	106.10
660	670	161.70	156.50	151.30	146.10	140.90	135.70	130.50	125.30	120.10	114.90	109.70
670	680	165.30	160.10	154.90	149.70	144.50	139.30	134.10	128.90	123.70	118.50	113.30
680	690	168.90	163.70	158.50	153.30	148.10	142.90	137.70	132.50	127.30	122.10	116.90
690	700	172.50	167.30	162.10	156.90	151.70	146.50	141.30	136.10	130.90	125.70	120.50
700	710	176.10	170.90	165.70	160.50	155.30	150.10	144.90	139.70	134.50	129.30	124.10
710	720	179.70	174.50	169.30	164.10	158.90	153.70	148.50	143.30	138.10	132.90	127.70
720	730	183.30	178.10	172.90	167.70	162.50	157.30	152.10	146.90	141.70	136.50	131.30
730	740	186.90	181.70	176.50	171.30	166.10	160.90	155.70	150.50	145.30	140.10	134.90
At least	But less than	0	1	2	3	4	5	6	7	8	9	10 or more
740	750	190.50	185.30	180.10	174.90	169.70	164.50	159.30	154.10	148.90	143.70	138.50
750	760	194.10	188.90	183.70	178.50	173.30	168.10	162.90	157.70	152.50	147.30	142.10
760	770	197.70	192.50	187.30	182.10	176.90	171.70	166.50	161.30	156.10	150.90	145.70
770	780	201.30	196.10	190.90	185.70	180.50	175.30	170.10	164.90	159.70	154.50	149.30
780	790	204.90	199.70	194.50	189.30	184.10	178.90	173.70	168.50	163.30	158.10	152.90
790	800	208.50	203.30	198.10	192.90	187.70	182.50	177.30	172.10	166.90	161.70	156.50
800	810	212.10	206.90	201.70	196.50	191.30	186.10	180.90	175.70	170.50	165.30	160.10
810	820	215.70	210.50	205.30	200.10	194.90	189.70	184.50	179.30	174.10	168.90	163.70
820	830	219.30	214.10	208.90	203.70	198.50	193.30	188.10	182.90	177.70	172.50	167.30
830	840	222.90	217.70	212.50	207.30	202.10	196.90	191.70	186.50	181.30	176.10	170.90
840	850	226.50	221.30	216.10	210.90	205.70	200.50	195.30	190.10	184.90	179.70	174.50
850	860	230.10	224.90	219.70	214.50	209.30	204.10	198.90	193.70	188.50	183.30	178.10
860	870	233.70	228.50	223.30	218.10	212.90	207.70	202.50	197.30	192.10	186.90	181.70
870	880	237.30	232.10	226.90	221.70	216.50	211.30	206.10	200.90	195.70	190.50	185.30
880	890	240.90	235.70	230.50	225.30	220.10	214.90	209.70	204.50	199.30	194.10	188.90
890	900	244.50	239.30	234.10	228.90	223.70	218.50	213.30	208.10	202.90	197.70	192.50
900	910	248.10	242.90	237.70	232.50	227.30	222.10	216.90	211.70	206.50	201.30	196.10
910	920	251.70	246.50	241.30	236.10	230.90	225.70	220.50	215.30	210.10	204.90	199.70
920	930	255.30	250.10	244.90	239.70	234.50	229.30	224.10	218.90	213.70	208.50	203.30
930	940	258.90	253.70	248.50	243.30	238.10	232.90	227.70	222.50	217.30	212.10	206.90
940	950	262.50	257.30	252.10	246.90	241.70	236.50	231.30	226.10	220.90	215.70	210.50
950	960	266.10	260.90	255.70	250.50	245.30	240.10	234.90	229.70	224.50	219.30	214.10
960	970	269.70	264.50	259.30	254.10	248.90	243.70	238.50	233.30	228.10	222.90	217.70
970	980	273.30	268.10	262.90	257.70	252.50	247.30	242.10	236.90	231.70	226.50	221.30
980	990	276.90	271.70	266.50	261.30	256.10	250.90	245.70	240.50	235.30	230.10	224.90
		36 percent of the excess over $990 plus—										
$990 and over		278.70	273.50	268.30	263.10	257.90	252.70	247.50	242.30	237.10	231.90	226.70

(continued)

WEEKLY Payroll Period—Employee NOT MARRIED

And the wages are-		And the number of withholding allowances claimed is—										
At least	But less than	0	1	2	3	4	5	6	7	8	9	10 or more
		The amount of income tax to be withheld shall be—										
$0	$33	$0	$0	$0	$0	$0	$0	$0	$0	$0	$0	$0
33	34	.10	0	0	0	0	0	0	0	0	0	0
34	35	.30	0	0	0	0	0	0	0	0	0	0
35	36	.40	0	0	0	0	0	0	0	0	0	0
36	37	.60	0	0	0	0	0	0	0	0	0	0
37	38	.80	0	0	0	0	0	0	0	0	0	0
38	39	.90	0	0	0	0	0	0	0	0	0	0
39	40	1.10	0	0	0	0	0	0	0	0	0	0
40	41	1.20	0	0	0	0	0	0	0	0	0	0
41	42	1.40	0	0	0	0	0	0	0	0	0	0
42	43	1.60	0	0	0	0	0	0	0	0	0	0
43	44	1.70	0	0	0	0	0	0	0	0	0	0
44	45	1.90	0	0	0	0	0	0	0	0	0	0
45	46	2.00	0	0	0	0	0	0	0	0	0	0
46	47	2.20	0	0	0	0	0	0	0	0	0	0
47	48	2.40	.10	0	0	0	0	0	0	0	0	0
48	49	2.50	.20	0	0	0	0	0	0	0	0	0
49	50	2.70	.40	0	0	0	0	0	0	0	0	0
50	51	2.80	.50	0	0	0	0	0	0	0	0	0
51	52	3.00	.70	0	0	0	0	0	0	0	0	0
52	53	3.20	.90	0	0	0	0	0	0	0	0	0
53	54	3.30	1.00	0	0	0	0	0	0	0	0	0
54	55	3.50	1.20	0	0	0	0	0	0	0	0	0
55	56	3.60	1.30	0	0	0	0	0	0	0	0	0
56	57	3.80	1.50	0	0	0	0	0	0	0	0	0
57	58	4.00	1.70	0	0	0	0	0	0	0	0	0
58	59	4.10	1.80	0	0	0	0	0	0	0	0	0
59	60	4.30	2.00	0	0	0	0	0	0	0	0	0
60	62	4.50	2.20	0	0	0	0	0	0	0	0	0
62	64	4.80	2.50	.20	0	0	0	0	0	0	0	0
At least	But less than	0	1	2	3	4	5	6	7	8	9	10 or more
64	66	5.20	2.90	.60	0	0	0	0	0	0	0	0
66	68	5.50	3.20	.90	0	0	0	0	0	0	0	0
68	70	5.80	3.50	1.20	0	0	0	0	0	0	0	0
70	72	6.10	3.80	1.50	0	0	0	0	0	0	0	0
72	74	6.40	4.10	1.80	0	0	0	0	0	0	0	0
74	76	6.80	4.50	2.20	0	0	0	0	0	0	0	0
76	78	7.10	4.80	2.50	.20	0	0	0	0	0	0	0
78	80	7.50	5.10	2.80	.50	0	0	0	0	0	0	0
80	82	7.80	5.40	3.10	.80	0	0	0	0	0	0	0
82	84	8.20	5.70	3.40	1.10	0	0	0	0	0	0	0
84	86	8.60	6.10	3.80	1.40	0	0	0	0	0	0	0
86	88	8.90	6.40	4.10	1.80	0	0	0	0	0	0	0
88	90	9.30	6.70	4.40	2.10	0	0	0	0	0	0	0
90	92	9.60	7.00	4.70	2.40	.10	0	0	0	0	0	0
92	94	10.00	7.40	5.00	2.70	.40	0	0	0	0	0	0
94	96	10.40	7.80	5.40	3.00	.70	0	0	0	0	0	0
96	98	10.70	8.10	5.70	3.40	1.10	0	0	0	0	0	0
98	100	11.10	8.50	6.00	3.70	1.40	0	0	0	0	0	0
100	105	11.70	9.10	6.60	4.20	1.90	0	0	0	0	0	0
105	110	12.60	10.00	7.40	5.00	2.70	.40	0	0	0	0	0
110	115	13.50	10.90	8.30	5.80	3.50	1.20	0	0	0	0	0
115	120	14.40	11.80	9.20	6.60	4.30	2.00	0	0	0	0	0
120	125	15.30	12.70	10.10	7.50	5.10	2.80	.50	0	0	0	0
125	130	16.20	13.60	11.00	8.40	5.90	3.60	1.30	0	0	0	0
130	135	17.10	14.50	11.90	9.30	6.70	4.40	2.10	0	0	0	0
135	140	18.00	15.40	12.80	10.20	7.60	5.20	2.90	.60	0	0	0
140	145	18.90	16.30	13.70	11.10	8.50	6.00	3.70	1.40	0	0	0
145	150	20.00	17.20	14.60	12.00	9.40	6.80	4.50	2.20	0	0	0
150	160	21.60	18.60	16.00	13.40	10.80	8.20	5.70	3.40	1.10	0	0
160	170	23.80	20.60	17.80	15.20	12.60	10.00	7.40	5.00	2.70	.40	0

WEEKLY Payroll Period—Employee NOT MARRIED

And the wages are-		And the number of withholding allowances claimed is—										
At least	But less than	0	1	2	3	4	5	6	7	8	9	10 or more
		The amount of income tax to be withheld shall be—										
$170	$180	$26.00	$22.80	$19.70	$17.00	$14.40	$11.80	$9.20	$6.60	$4.30	$2.00	$0
180	190	28.30	25.00	21.90	18.80	16.20	13.60	11.00	8.40	5.90	3.60	1.30
190	200	30.70	27.20	24.10	20.90	18.00	15.40	12.80	10.20	7.60	5.20	2.90
200	210	33.10	29.60	26.30	23.10	19.90	17.20	14.60	12.00	9.40	6.80	4.50
210	220	35.50	32.00	28.60	25.30	22.10	19.00	16.40	13.80	11.20	8.60	6.10
220	230	38.10	34.40	31.00	27.50	24.30	21.20	18.20	15.60	13.00	10.40	7.80
230	240	40.90	36.80	33.40	29.90	26.50	23.40	20.20	17.40	14.80	12.20	9.60
240	250	43.70	39.60	35.80	32.30	28.80	25.60	22.40	19.20	16.60	14.00	11.40
250	260	46.50	42.40	38.40	34.70	31.20	27.80	24.60	21.40	18.40	15.80	13.20
260	270	49.30	45.20	41.20	37.20	33.60	30.20	26.80	23.60	20.40	17.60	15.00
270	280	52.10	48.00	44.00	40.00	36.00	32.60	29.10	25.80	22.60	19.50	16.80
280	290	54.90	50.80	46.80	42.80	38.70	35.00	31.50	28.10	24.80	21.70	18.60
290	300	57.70	53.60	49.60	45.60	41.50	37.50	33.90	30.50	27.00	23.90	20.70
300	310	60.80	56.40	52.40	48.40	44.30	40.30	36.30	32.90	29.40	26.10	22.90
310	320	64.00	59.40	55.20	51.20	47.10	43.10	39.00	35.30	31.80	28.30	25.10
320	330	67.20	62.60	58.00	54.00	49.90	45.90	41.80	37.80	34.20	30.70	27.30
330	340	70.40	65.80	61.20	56.80	52.70	48.70	44.60	40.60	36.60	33.10	29.70
340	350	73.60	69.00	64.40	59.70	55.50	51.50	47.40	43.40	39.40	35.50	32.10
350	360	76.80	72.20	67.60	62.90	58.30	54.30	50.20	46.20	42.20	38.10	34.50
360	370	80.40	75.40	70.80	66.10	61.50	57.10	53.00	49.00	45.00	40.90	36.90
370	380	84.00	78.80	74.00	69.30	64.70	60.10	55.80	51.80	47.80	43.70	39.70
380	390	87.60	82.40	77.20	72.50	67.90	63.30	58.70	54.60	50.60	46.50	42.50
390	400	91.20	86.00	80.80	75.70	71.10	66.50	61.90	57.40	53.40	49.30	45.30
400	410	94.80	89.60	84.40	79.20	74.30	69.70	65.10	60.50	56.20	52.10	48.10
410	420	98.40	93.20	88.00	82.80	77.60	72.90	68.30	63.70	59.10	54.90	50.90
420	430	102.00	96.80	91.60	86.40	81.20	76.10	71.50	66.90	62.30	57.70	53.70
430	440	105.60	100.40	95.20	90.00	84.80	79.60	74.70	70.10	65.50	60.90	56.50
440	450	109.20	104.00	98.80	93.60	88.40	83.20	78.00	73.30	68.70	64.10	59.40
450	460	112.80	107.60	102.40	97.20	92.00	86.80	81.60	76.50	71.90	67.30	62.60
460	470	116.40	111.20	106.00	100.80	95.60	90.40	85.20	80.10	75.10	70.50	65.80
At least	But less than	0	1	2	3	4	5	6	7	8	9	10 or more
470	480	120.00	114.80	109.60	104.40	99.20	94.00	88.80	83.70	78.50	73.70	69.00
480	490	123.60	118.40	113.20	108.00	102.80	97.60	92.40	87.30	82.10	76.90	72.20
490	500	127.20	122.00	116.80	111.60	106.40	101.20	96.00	90.90	85.70	80.50	75.40
500	510	130.80	125.60	120.40	115.20	110.00	104.80	99.60	94.50	89.30	84.10	78.90
510	520	134.40	129.20	124.00	118.80	113.60	108.40	103.20	98.10	92.90	87.70	82.50
520	530	138.00	132.80	127.60	122.40	117.20	112.00	106.80	101.70	96.50	91.30	86.10
530	540	141.60	136.40	131.20	126.00	120.80	115.60	110.40	105.30	100.10	94.90	89.70
540	550	145.20	140.00	134.80	129.60	124.40	119.20	114.00	108.90	103.70	98.50	93.30
550	560	148.80	143.60	138.40	133.20	128.00	122.80	117.60	112.50	107.30	102.10	96.90
560	570	152.40	147.20	142.00	136.80	131.60	126.40	121.20	116.10	110.90	105.70	100.50
570	580	156.00	150.80	145.60	140.40	135.20	130.00	124.80	119.70	114.50	109.30	104.10
580	590	159.60	154.40	149.20	144.00	138.80	133.60	128.40	123.30	118.10	112.90	107.70
590	600	163.20	158.00	152.80	147.60	142.40	137.20	132.00	126.90	121.70	116.50	111.30
600	610	166.80	161.60	156.40	151.20	146.00	140.80	135.60	130.50	125.30	120.10	114.90
610	620	170.40	165.20	160.00	154.80	149.60	144.40	139.20	134.10	128.90	123.70	118.50
620	630	174.00	168.80	163.60	158.40	153.20	148.00	142.80	137.70	132.50	127.30	122.10
630	640	177.60	172.40	167.20	162.00	156.80	151.60	146.40	141.30	136.10	130.90	125.70
640	650	181.20	176.00	170.80	165.60	160.40	155.20	150.00	144.90	139.70	134.50	129.30
650	660	184.80	179.60	174.40	169.20	164.00	158.80	153.60	148.50	143.30	138.10	132.90
660	670	188.40	183.20	178.00	172.80	167.60	162.40	157.20	152.10	146.90	141.70	136.50
670	680	192.00	186.80	181.60	176.40	171.20	166.00	160.80	155.70	150.50	145.30	140.10
680	690	195.60	190.40	185.20	180.00	174.80	169.60	164.40	159.30	154.10	148.90	143.70
690	700	199.20	194.00	188.80	183.60	178.40	173.20	168.00	162.90	157.70	152.50	147.30
700	710	202.80	197.60	192.40	187.20	182.00	176.80	171.60	166.50	161.30	156.10	150.90
710	720	206.40	201.20	196.00	190.80	185.60	180.40	175.20	170.10	164.90	159.70	154.50
		36 percent of the excess over $720 plus--										
$720 and over		208.20	203.00	197.80	192.60	187.40	182.20	177.00	171.90	166.70	161.50	156.30

FEDERAL SOCIAL SECURITY-MEDICARE TAX TABLE—6.13% Employee Tax Deduction *

NOTE: For a salary or wage payment that does not appear here, multiply the amount by 0.613%.

$ Wages less than	$ Tax	$ Wages less than	$ Tax	$ Wages less than	$ Tax	$ Wages less than	$ Tax	$ Wages less than	$ Tax	$ Wages less than	$ Tax	$ Wages less than	$ Tax	$ Wages less than	$ Tax	$ Wages less than	$ Tax	$ Wages less than	$ Tax	$ Wages less than	$ Tax
134.67	8.25	142.83	8.75	150.98	9.25	159.14	9.75	167.30	10.25	175.45	10.75	183.61	11.25	191.77	11.75	199.92	12.25	208.08	12.75	216.24	13.25
134.83	8.26	142.99	8.76	151.15	9.26	159.30	9.76	167.46	10.26	175.62	10.76	183.77	11.26	191.93	11.76	200.09	12.26	208.24	12.76	216.40	13.26
135.00	8.27	143.15	8.77	151.31	9.27	159.47	9.77	167.62	10.27	175.78	10.77	183.94	11.27	192.09	11.77	200.25	12.27	208.41	12.77	216.56	13.27
135.16	8.28	143.32	8.78	151.47	9.28	159.63	9.78	167.79	10.28	175.94	10.78	184.10	11.28	192.26	11.78	200.41	12.28	208.57	12.78	216.73	13.28
135.32	8.29	143.48	8.79	151.64	9.29	159.79	9.79	167.95	10.29	176.11	10.79	184.26	11.29	192.42	11.79	200.58	12.29	208.73	12.79	216.89	13.29
135.49	8.30	143.64	8.80	151.80	9.30	159.96	9.80	168.11	10.30	176.27	10.80	184.43	11.30	192.58	11.80	200.74	12.30	208.90	12.80	217.05	13.30
135.65	8.31	143.81	8.81	151.96	9.31	160.12	9.81	168.28	10.31	176.43	10.81	184.59	11.31	192.75	11.81	200.90	12.31	209.06	12.81	217.22	13.31
135.81	8.32	143.97	8.82	152.13	9.32	160.28	9.82	168.44	10.32	176.60	10.82	184.75	11.32	192.91	11.82	201.07	12.32	209.22	12.82	217.38	13.32
135.98	8.33	144.13	8.83	152.29	9.33	160.45	9.83	168.60	10.33	176.76	10.83	184.92	11.33	193.07	11.83	201.23	12.33	209.39	12.83	217.54	13.33
136.14	8.34	144.30	8.84	152.45	9.34	160.61	9.84	168.77	10.34	176.92	10.84	185.08	11.34	193.24	11.84	201.39	12.34	209.55	12.84	217.70	13.34
136.30	8.35	144.46	8.85	152.62	9.35	160.77	9.85	168.93	10.35	177.08	10.85	185.24	11.35	193.40	11.85	201.55	12.35	209.71	12.85	217.87	13.35
136.47	8.36	144.62	8.86	152.78	9.36	160.93	9.86	169.09	10.36	177.25	10.86	185.40	11.36	193.56	11.86	201.72	12.36	209.87	12.86	218.03	13.36
136.63	8.37	144.78	8.87	152.94	9.37	161.10	9.87	169.25	10.37	177.41	10.87	185.57	11.37	193.72	11.87	201.88	12.37	210.04	12.87	218.19	13.37
136.79	8.38	144.95	8.88	153.10	9.38	161.26	9.88	169.42	10.38	177.57	10.88	185.73	11.38	193.89	11.88	202.04	12.38	210.20	12.88	218.36	13.38
136.95	8.39	145.11	8.89	153.27	9.39	161.42	9.89	169.58	10.39	177.74	10.89	185.89	11.39	194.05	11.89	202.21	12.39	210.36	12.89	218.52	13.39
137.12	8.40	145.27	8.90	153.43	9.40	161.59	9.90	169.74	10.40	177.90	10.90	186.06	11.40	194.21	11.90	202.37	12.40	210.53	12.90	218.68	13.40
137.28	8.41	145.44	8.91	153.59	9.41	161.75	9.91	169.91	10.41	178.06	10.91	186.22	11.41	194.38	11.91	202.53	12.41	210.69	12.91	218.85	13.41
137.44	8.42	145.60	8.92	153.76	9.42	161.91	9.92	170.07	10.42	178.23	10.92	186.38	11.42	194.54	11.92	202.70	12.42	210.85	12.92	219.01	13.42
137.61	8.43	145.76	8.93	153.92	9.43	162.08	9.93	170.23	10.43	178.39	10.93	186.55	11.43	194.70	11.93	202.86	12.43	211.02	12.93	219.17	13.43
137.77	8.44	145.93	8.94	154.08	9.44	162.24	9.94	170.40	10.44	178.55	10.94	186.71	11.44	194.87	11.94	203.02	12.44	211.18	12.94	219.34	13.44
137.93	8.45	146.09	8.95	154.25	9.45	162.40	9.95	170.56	10.45	178.72	10.95	186.87	11.45	195.03	11.95	203.19	12.45	211.34	12.95	219.50	13.45
138.10	8.46	146.25	8.96	154.41	9.46	162.57	9.96	170.72	10.46	178.88	10.96	187.04	11.46	195.19	11.96	203.35	12.46	211.51	12.96	219.66	13.46
138.26	8.47	146.42	8.97	154.57	9.47	162.73	9.97	170.89	10.47	179.04	10.97	187.20	11.47	195.36	11.97	203.51	12.47	211.67	12.97	219.83	13.47
138.42	8.48	146.58	8.98	154.74	9.48	162.89	9.98	171.05	10.48	179.21	10.98	187.36	11.48	195.52	11.98	203.68	12.48	211.83	12.98	219.99	13.48
138.59	8.49	146.74	8.99	154.90	9.49	163.06	9.99	171.21	10.49	179.37	10.99	187.53	11.49	195.68	11.99	203.84	12.49	212.00	12.99	220.15	13.49
138.75	8.50	146.91	9.00	155.06	9.50	163.22	10.00	171.38	10.50	179.53	11.00	187.69	11.50	195.85	12.00	204.00	12.50	212.16	13.00	220.31	13.50
138.91	8.51	147.07	9.01	155.23	9.51	163.38	10.01	171.54	10.51	179.70	11.01	187.85	11.51	196.01	12.01	204.16	12.51	212.32	13.01	220.48	13.51
139.08	8.52	147.23	9.02	155.39	9.52	163.54	10.02	171.70	10.52	179.86	11.02	188.01	11.52	196.17	12.02	204.33	12.52	212.48	13.02	220.64	13.52
139.24	8.53	147.39	9.03	155.55	9.53	163.71	10.03	171.86	10.53	180.02	11.03	188.18	11.53	196.33	12.03	204.49	12.53	212.65	13.03	220.80	13.53
139.40	8.54	147.56	9.04	155.71	9.54	163.87	10.04	172.03	10.54	180.18	11.04	188.34	11.54	196.50	12.04	204.65	12.54	212.81	13.04	220.97	13.54
139.56	8.55	147.72	9.05	155.88	9.55	164.03	10.05	172.19	10.55	180.35	11.05	188.50	11.55	196.66	12.05	204.82	12.55	212.97	13.05	221.13	13.55
139.73	8.56	147.88	9.06	156.04	9.56	164.20	10.06	172.35	10.56	180.51	11.06	188.67	11.56	196.82	12.06	204.98	12.56	213.14	13.06	221.29	13.56
139.89	8.57	148.05	9.07	156.20	9.57	164.36	10.07	172.52	10.57	180.67	11.07	188.83	11.57	196.99	12.07	205.14	12.57	213.30	13.07	221.46	13.57
140.05	8.58	148.21	9.08	156.37	9.58	164.52	10.08	172.68	10.58	180.84	11.08	188.99	11.58	197.15	12.08	205.31	12.58	213.46	13.08	221.62	13.58
140.22	8.59	148.37	9.09	156.53	9.59	164.69	10.09	172.84	10.59	181.00	11.09	189.16	11.59	197.31	12.09	205.47	12.59	213.63	13.09	221.78	13.59
140.38	8.60	148.54	9.10	156.69	9.60	164.85	10.10	173.01	10.60	181.16	11.10	189.32	11.60	197.48	12.10	205.63	12.60	213.79	13.10	221.95	13.60
140.54	8.61	148.70	9.11	156.86	9.61	165.01	10.11	173.17	10.61	181.33	11.11	189.48	11.61	197.64	12.11	205.80	12.61	213.95	13.11	222.11	13.61
140.71	8.62	148.86	9.12	157.02	9.62	165.18	10.12	173.33	10.62	181.49	11.12	189.65	11.62	197.80	12.12	205.96	12.62	214.12	13.12	222.27	13.62
140.87	8.63	149.03	9.13	157.18	9.63	165.34	10.13	173.50	10.63	181.65	11.13	189.81	11.63	197.97	12.13	206.12	12.63	214.28	13.13	222.44	13.63
141.03	8.64	149.19	9.14	157.35	9.64	165.50	10.14	173.66	10.64	181.82	11.14	189.97	11.64	198.13	12.14	206.29	12.64	214.44	13.14	222.60	13.64
141.20	8.65	149.35	9.15	157.51	9.65	165.67	10.15	173.82	10.65	181.98	11.15	190.14	11.65	198.29	12.15	206.45	12.65	214.61	13.15	222.76	13.65
141.36	8.66	149.52	9.16	157.67	9.66	165.83	10.16	173.99	10.66	182.14	11.16	190.30	11.66	198.46	12.16	206.61	12.66	214.77	13.16	222.93	13.66
141.52	8.67	149.68	9.17	157.84	9.67	165.99	10.17	174.15	10.67	182.31	11.17	190.46	11.67	198.62	12.17	206.77	12.67	214.93	13.17	223.09	13.67
141.69	8.68	149.84	9.18	158.00	9.68	166.16	10.18	174.31	10.68	182.47	11.18	190.62	11.68	198.78	12.18	206.94	12.68	215.09	13.18	223.25	13.68
141.85	8.69	150.00	9.19	158.16	9.69	166.32	10.19	174.47	10.69	182.63	11.19	190.79	11.69	198.94	12.19	207.10	12.69	215.26	13.19	223.41	13.69
142.01	8.70	150.17	9.20	158.32	9.70	166.48	10.20	174.64	10.70	182.79	11.20	190.95	11.70	199.11	12.20	207.26	12.70	215.42	13.20	223.58	13.70
142.17	8.71	150.33	9.21	158.49	9.71	166.64	10.21	174.80	10.71	182.96	11.21	191.11	11.71	199.27	12.21	207.43	12.71	215.58	13.21	223.74	13.71
142.34	8.72	150.49	9.22	158.65	9.72	166.81	10.22	174.96	10.72	183.12	11.22	191.28	11.72	199.43	12.22	207.59	12.72	215.75	13.22	223.90	13.72
142.50	8.73	150.66	9.23	158.81	9.73	166.97	10.23	175.13	10.73	183.28	11.23	191.44	11.73	199.60	12.23	207.75	12.73	215.91	13.23	224.07	13.73
142.66	8.74	150.82	9.24	158.98	9.74	167.13	10.24	175.29	10.74	183.45	11.24	191.60	11.74	199.76	12.24	207.92	12.74	216.07	13.24	224.23	13.74

* These tables were effective at the time of publication.

FEDERAL SOCIAL SECURITY-MEDICARE TAX TABLE—6.13% Employee Tax Deduction (continued)

$ Wages less than	$ Tax	$ Wages less than	$ Tax	$ Wages less than	$ Tax	$ Wages less than	$ Tax	$ Wages less than	$ Tax	$ Wages less than	$ Tax	$ Wages less than	$ Tax	$ Wages less than	$ Tax	$ Wages less than	$ Tax	$ Wages less than	$ Tax	$ Wages less than	$ Tax
224.39	13.75	233.37	14.30	242.34	14.85	251.31	15.40	260.28	15.95	269.25	16.50	278.23	17.05	287.20	17.60	296.17	18.15	305.14	18.70	314.12	19.25
224.56	13.76	233.53	14.31	242.50	14.86	251.47	15.41	260.45	15.96	269.42	16.51	278.39	17.06	287.36	17.61	296.33	18.16	305.31	18.71	314.28	19.26
224.72	13.77	233.69	14.32	242.66	14.87	251.64	15.42	260.61	15.97	269.58	16.52	278.55	17.07	287.53	17.62	296.50	18.17	305.47	18.72	314.44	19.27
224.88	13.78	233.85	14.33	242.83	14.88	251.80	15.43	260.77	15.98	269.74	16.53	278.72	17.08	287.69	17.63	296.66	18.18	305.63	18.73	314.61	19.28
225.05	13.79	234.02	14.34	242.99	14.89	251.96	15.44	260.93	15.99	269.91	16.54	278.88	17.09	287.85	17.64	296.82	18.19	305.80	18.74	314.77	19.29
225.21	13.80	234.18	14.35	243.15	14.90	252.13	15.45	261.10	16.00	270.07	16.55	279.04	17.10	288.01	17.65	296.99	18.20	305.96	18.75	314.93	19.30
225.37	13.81	234.34	14.36	243.32	14.91	252.29	15.46	261.26	16.01	270.23	16.56	279.21	17.11	288.18	17.66	297.15	18.21	306.12	18.76	315.09	19.31
225.54	13.82	234.51	14.37	243.48	14.92	252.45	15.47	261.42	16.02	270.40	16.57	279.37	17.12	288.34	17.67	297.31	18.22	306.29	18.77	315.26	19.32
225.70	13.83	234.67	14.38	243.64	14.93	252.62	15.48	261.59	16.03	270.56	16.58	279.53	17.13	288.50	17.68	297.48	18.23	306.45	18.78	315.42	19.33
225.86	13.84	234.83	14.39	243.81	14.94	252.78	15.49	261.75	16.04	270.72	16.59	279.70	17.14	288.67	17.69	297.64	18.24	306.61	18.79	315.58	19.34
226.02	13.85	235.00	14.40	243.97	14.95	252.94	15.50	261.91	16.05	270.89	16.60	279.86	17.15	288.83	17.70	297.80	18.25	306.77	18.80	315.75	19.35
226.19	13.86	235.16	14.41	244.13	14.96	253.10	15.51	262.08	16.06	271.05	16.61	280.02	17.16	288.99	17.71	297.97	18.26	306.94	18.81	315.91	19.36
226.35	13.87	235.32	14.42	244.30	14.97	253.27	15.52	262.24	16.07	271.21	16.62	280.18	17.17	289.16	17.72	298.13	18.27	307.10	18.82	316.07	19.37
226.51	13.88	235.49	14.43	244.46	14.98	253.43	15.53	262.40	16.08	271.38	16.63	280.35	17.18	289.32	17.73	298.29	18.28	307.26	18.83	316.24	19.38
226.68	13.89	235.65	14.44	244.62	14.99	253.59	15.54	262.57	16.09	271.54	16.64	280.51	17.19	289.48	17.74	298.46	18.29	307.43	18.84	316.40	19.39
226.84	13.90	235.81	14.45	244.78	15.00	253.76	15.55	262.73	16.10	271.70	16.65	280.67	17.20	289.65	17.75	298.62	18.30	307.59	18.85	316.56	19.40
227.00	13.91	235.98	14.46	244.95	15.01	253.92	15.56	262.89	16.11	271.86	16.66	280.84	17.21	289.81	17.76	298.78	18.31	307.75	18.86	316.73	19.41
227.17	13.92	236.14	14.47	245.11	15.02	254.08	15.57	263.06	16.12	272.03	16.67	281.00	17.22	289.97	17.77	298.94	18.32	307.92	18.87	316.89	19.42
227.33	13.93	236.30	14.48	245.27	15.03	254.25	15.58	263.22	16.13	272.19	16.68	281.16	17.23	290.14	17.78	299.11	18.33	308.08	18.88	317.05	19.43
227.49	13.94	236.47	14.49	245.44	15.04	254.41	15.59	263.38	16.14	272.35	16.69	281.33	17.24	290.30	17.79	299.27	18.34	308.24	18.89	317.22	19.44
227.66	13.95	236.63	14.50	245.60	15.05	254.57	15.60	263.54	16.15	272.52	16.70	281.49	17.25	290.46	17.80	299.43	18.35	308.41	18.90	317.38	19.45
227.82	13.96	236.79	14.51	245.76	15.06	254.74	15.61	263.71	16.16	272.68	16.71	281.65	17.26	290.62	17.81	299.60	18.36	308.57	18.91	317.54	19.46
227.98	13.97	236.95	14.52	245.93	15.07	254.90	15.62	263.87	16.17	272.84	16.72	281.82	17.27	290.79	17.82	299.76	18.37	308.73	18.92	317.70	19.47
228.15	13.98	237.12	14.53	246.09	15.08	255.06	15.63	264.03	16.18	273.01	16.73	281.98	17.28	290.95	17.83	299.92	18.38	308.90	18.93	317.87	19.48
228.31	13.99	237.28	14.54	246.25	15.09	255.23	15.64	264.20	16.19	273.17	16.74	282.14	17.29	291.11	17.84	300.09	18.39	309.06	18.94	318.03	19.49
228.47	14.00	237.44	14.55	246.42	15.10	255.39	15.65	264.36	16.20	273.33	16.75	282.31	17.30	291.28	17.85	300.25	18.40	309.22	18.95	318.19	19.50
228.63	14.01	237.61	14.56	246.58	15.11	255.55	15.66	264.52	16.21	273.50	16.76	282.47	17.31	291.44	17.86	300.41	18.41	309.39	18.96	318.36	19.51
228.80	14.02	237.77	14.57	246.74	15.12	255.71	15.67	264.69	16.22	273.66	16.77	282.63	17.32	291.60	17.87	300.58	18.42	309.55	18.97	318.52	19.52
228.96	14.03	237.93	14.58	246.91	15.13	255.88	15.68	264.85	16.23	273.82	16.78	282.79	17.33	291.77	17.88	300.74	18.43	309.71	18.98	318.68	19.53
229.12	14.04	238.10	14.59	247.07	15.14	256.04	15.69	265.01	16.24	273.99	16.79	282.96	17.34	291.93	17.89	300.90	18.44	309.87	18.99	318.85	19.54
229.29	14.05	238.26	14.60	247.23	15.15	256.20	15.70	265.18	16.25	274.15	16.80	283.12	17.35	292.09	17.90	301.07	18.45	310.04	19.00	319.01	19.55
229.45	14.06	238.42	14.61	247.39	15.16	256.37	15.71	265.34	16.26	274.31	16.81	283.28	17.36	292.26	17.91	301.23	18.46	310.20	19.01	319.17	19.56
229.61	14.07	238.59	14.62	247.56	15.17	256.53	15.72	265.50	16.27	274.47	16.82	283.45	17.37	292.42	17.92	301.39	18.47	310.36	19.02	319.34	19.57
229.78	14.08	238.75	14.63	247.72	15.18	256.69	15.73	265.67	16.28	274.64	16.83	283.61	17.38	292.58	17.93	301.55	18.48	310.53	19.03	319.50	19.58
229.94	14.09	238.91	14.64	247.88	15.19	256.86	15.74	265.83	16.29	274.80	16.84	283.77	17.39	292.75	17.94	301.72	18.49	310.69	19.04	319.66	19.59
230.10	14.10	239.08	14.65	248.05	15.20	257.02	15.75	265.99	16.30	274.96	16.85	283.94	17.40	292.91	17.95	301.88	18.50	310.85	19.05	319.83	19.60
230.27	14.11	239.24	14.66	248.21	15.21	257.18	15.76	266.16	16.31	275.13	16.86	284.10	17.41	293.07	17.96	302.04	18.51	311.02	19.06	319.99	19.61
230.43	14.12	239.40	14.67	248.37	15.22	257.35	15.77	266.32	16.32	275.29	16.87	284.26	17.42	293.24	17.97	302.21	18.52	311.18	19.07	320.15	19.62
230.59	14.13	239.56	14.68	248.54	15.23	257.51	15.78	266.48	16.33	275.45	16.88	284.43	17.43	293.40	17.98	302.37	18.53	311.34	19.08	320.31	19.63
230.76	14.14	239.73	14.69	248.70	15.24	257.67	15.79	266.64	16.34	275.62	16.89	284.59	17.44	293.56	17.99	302.53	18.54	311.51	19.09	320.48	19.64
230.92	14.15	239.89	14.70	248.86	15.25	257.84	15.80	266.81	16.35	275.78	16.90	284.75	17.45	293.72	18.00	302.70	18.55	311.67	19.10	320.64	19.65
231.08	14.16	240.05	14.71	249.03	15.26	258.00	15.81	266.97	16.36	275.94	16.91	284.92	17.46	293.89	18.01	302.86	18.56	311.83	19.11	320.80	19.66
231.24	14.17	240.22	14.72	249.19	15.27	258.16	15.82	267.13	16.37	276.11	16.92	285.08	17.47	294.05	18.02	303.02	18.57	312.00	19.12	320.97	19.67
231.41	14.18	240.38	14.73	249.35	15.28	258.32	15.83	267.30	16.38	276.27	16.93	285.24	17.48	294.21	18.03	303.19	18.58	312.16	19.13	321.13	19.68
231.57	14.19	240.54	14.74	249.52	15.29	258.49	15.84	267.46	16.39	276.43	16.94	285.40	17.49	294.38	18.04	303.35	18.59	312.32	19.14	321.29	19.69
231.73	14.20	240.71	14.75	249.68	15.30	258.65	15.85	267.62	16.40	276.60	16.95	285.57	17.50	294.54	18.05	303.51	18.60	312.48	19.15	321.46	19.70
231.90	14.21	240.87	14.76	249.84	15.31	258.81	15.86	267.79	16.41	276.76	16.96	285.73	17.51	294.70	18.06	303.68	18.61	312.65	19.16	321.62	19.71
232.06	14.22	241.03	14.77	250.00	15.32	258.98	15.87	267.95	16.42	276.92	16.97	285.89	17.52	294.87	18.07	303.84	18.62	312.81	19.17	321.78	19.72
232.22	14.23	241.20	14.78	250.17	15.33	259.14	15.88	268.11	16.43	277.08	16.98	286.06	17.53	295.03	18.08	304.00	18.63	312.97	19.18	321.95	19.73
232.39	14.24	241.36	14.79	250.33	15.34	259.30	15.89	268.28	16.44	277.25	16.99	286.22	17.54	295.19	18.09	304.16	18.64	313.14	19.19	322.11	19.74
232.55	14.25	241.52	14.80	250.49	15.35	259.47	15.90	268.44	16.45	277.41	17.00	286.38	17.55	295.36	18.10	304.33	18.65	313.30	19.20	322.27	19.75
232.71	14.26	241.69	14.81	250.66	15.36	259.63	15.91	268.60	16.46	277.57	17.01	286.55	17.56	295.52	18.11	304.49	18.66	313.46	19.21	322.44	19.76
232.88	14.27	241.85	14.82	250.82	15.37	259.79	15.92	268.77	16.47	277.74	17.02	286.71	17.57	295.68	18.12	304.65	18.67	313.63	19.22	322.60	19.77
233.04	14.28	242.01	14.83	250.98	15.38	259.96	15.93	268.93	16.48	277.90	17.03	286.87	17.58	295.85	18.13	304.82	18.68	313.79	19.23	322.76	19.78
233.20	14.29	242.17	14.84	251.15	15.39	260.12	15.94	269.09	16.49	278.06	17.04	287.04	17.59	296.01	18.14	304.98	18.69	313.95	19.24	322.93	19.79

(continued)

FEDERAL SOCIAL SECURITY-MEDICARE TAX TABLE—6.13% Employee Tax Deduction (continued)

$ Wages less than	$ Tax	$ Wages less than	$ Tax	$ Wages less than	$ Tax	$ Wages less than	$ Tax	$ Wages less than	$ Tax	$ Wages less than	$ Tax	$ Wages less than	$ Tax	$ Wages less than	$ Tax	$ Wages less than	$ Tax	$ Wages less than	$ Tax	$ Wages less than	$ Tax
323.09	19.80	332.06	20.35	341.03	20.90	350.00	21.45	358.98	22.00	367.95	22.55	376.92	23.10	381.82	23.40	390.79	23.95	399.76	24.50	408.73	25.05
323.25	19.81	332.22	20.36	341.20	20.91	350.17	21.46	359.14	22.01	368.11	22.56	377.08	23.11	381.98	23.41	390.95	23.96	399.92	24.51	408.90	25.06
323.41	19.82	332.39	20.37	341.36	20.92	350.33	21.47	359.30	22.02	368.28	22.57	377.25	23.12	382.14	23.42	391.11	23.97	400.09	24.52	409.06	25.07
323.58	19.83	332.55	20.38	341.52	20.93	350.49	21.48	359.47	22.03	368.44	22.58	377.41	23.13	382.31	23.43	391.28	23.98	400.25	24.53	409.22	25.08
323.74	19.84	332.71	20.39	341.69	20.94	350.66	21.49	359.63	22.04	368.60	22.59	377.57	23.14	382.47	23.44	391.44	23.99	400.41	24.54	409.39	25.09
323.90	19.85	332.88	20.40	341.85	20.95	350.82	21.50	359.79	22.05	368.77	22.60	377.74	23.15	382.63	23.45	391.60	24.00	400.58	24.55	409.55	25.10
324.07	19.86	333.04	20.41	342.01	20.96	350.98	21.51	359.96	22.06	368.93	22.61	377.90	23.16	382.79	23.46	391.77	24.01	400.74	24.56	409.71	25.11
324.23	19.87	333.20	20.42	342.17	20.97	351.15	21.52	360.12	22.07	369.09	22.62	378.06	23.17	382.96	23.47	391.93	24.02	400.90	24.57	409.87	25.12
324.39	19.88	333.37	20.43	342.34	20.98	351.31	21.53	360.28	22.08	369.25	22.63	378.23	23.18	383.12	23.48	392.09	24.03	401.07	24.58	410.04	25.13
324.56	19.89	333.53	20.44	342.50	20.99	351.47	21.54	360.45	22.09	369.42	22.64	378.39	23.19	383.28	23.49	392.26	24.04	401.23	24.59	410.20	25.14
324.72	19.90	333.69	20.45	342.66	21.00	351.64	21.55	360.61	22.10	369.58	22.65	378.55	23.20	383.45	23.50	392.42	24.05	401.39	24.60	410.36	25.15
324.88	19.91	333.85	20.46	342.83	21.01	351.80	21.56	360.77	22.11	369.74	22.66	378.72	23.21	383.61	23.51	392.58	24.06	401.55	24.61	410.53	25.16
325.05	19.92	334.02	20.47	342.99	21.02	351.96	21.57	360.93	22.12	369.91	22.67	378.88	23.22	383.77	23.52	392.75	24.07	401.72	24.62	410.69	25.17
325.21	19.93	334.18	20.48	343.15	21.03	352.13	21.58	361.10	22.13	370.07	22.68	379.04	23.23	383.94	23.53	392.91	24.08	401.88	24.63	410.85	25.18
325.37	19.94	334.34	20.49	343.32	21.04	352.29	21.59	361.26	22.14	370.23	22.69	379.21	23.24	384.10	23.54	393.07	24.09	402.04	24.64	411.02	25.19
325.54	19.95	334.51	20.50	343.48	21.05	352.45	21.60	361.42	22.15	370.40	22.70	379.37	23.25	384.26	23.55	393.24	24.10	402.21	24.65	411.18	25.20
325.70	19.96	334.67	20.51	343.64	21.06	352.62	21.61	361.59	22.16	370.56	22.71	379.53	23.26	384.43	23.56	393.40	24.11	402.37	24.66	411.34	25.21
325.86	19.97	334.83	20.52	343.81	21.07	352.78	21.62	361.75	22.17	370.72	22.72	379.70	23.27	384.59	23.57	393.56	24.12	402.53	24.67	411.51	25.22
326.02	19.98	335.00	20.53	343.97	21.08	352.94	21.63	361.91	22.18	370.89	22.73	379.86	23.28	384.75	23.58	393.72	24.13	402.70	24.68	411.67	25.23
326.19	19.99	335.16	20.54	344.13	21.09	353.10	21.64	362.08	22.19	371.05	22.74	380.02	23.29	384.92	23.59	393.89	24.14	402.86	24.69	411.83	25.24
326.35	20.00	335.32	20.55	344.30	21.10	353.27	21.65	362.24	22.20	371.21	22.75	380.18	23.30	385.08	23.60	394.05	24.15	403.02	24.70	412.00	25.25
326.51	20.01	335.49	20.56	344.46	21.11	353.43	21.66	362.40	22.21	371.38	22.76	380.35	23.31	385.24	23.61	394.21	24.16	403.19	24.71	412.16	25.26
326.68	20.02	335.65	20.57	344.62	21.12	353.59	21.67	362.57	22.22	371.54	22.77	380.51	23.32	385.40	23.62	394.38	24.17	403.35	24.72	412.32	25.27
326.84	20.03	335.81	20.58	344.78	21.13	353.76	21.68	362.73	22.23	371.70	22.78	380.67	23.33	385.57	23.63	394.54	24.18	403.51	24.73	412.48	25.28
327.00	20.04	335.98	20.59	344.95	21.14	353.92	21.69	362.89	22.24	371.86	22.79	380.84	23.34	385.73	23.64	394.70	24.19	403.68	24.74	412.65	25.29
327.17	20.05	336.14	20.60	345.11	21.15	354.08	21.70	363.06	22.25	372.03	22.80	381.00	23.35	385.89	23.65	394.87	24.20	403.84	24.75	412.81	25.30
327.33	20.06	336.30	20.61	345.27	21.16	354.25	21.71	363.22	22.26	372.19	22.81	381.16	23.36	386.06	23.66	395.03	24.21	404.00	24.76	412.97	25.31
327.49	20.07	336.47	20.62	345.44	21.17	354.41	21.72	363.38	22.27	372.35	22.82	381.33	23.37	386.22	23.67	395.19	24.22	404.16	24.77	413.14	25.32
327.66	20.08	336.63	20.63	345.60	21.18	354.57	21.73	363.54	22.28	372.52	22.83	381.49	23.38	386.38	23.68	395.36	24.23	404.33	24.78	413.30	25.33
327.82	20.09	336.79	20.64	345.76	21.19	354.74	21.74	363.71	22.29	372.68	22.84	381.65	23.39	386.55	23.69	395.52	24.24	404.49	24.79	413.46	25.34
327.98	20.10	336.95	20.65	345.93	21.20	354.90	21.75	363.87	22.30	372.84	22.85	381.82	23.40	386.71	23.70	395.68	24.25	404.65	24.80	413.63	25.35
328.15	20.11	337.12	20.66	346.09	21.21	355.06	21.76	364.03	22.31	373.01	22.86	381.98	23.41	386.87	23.71	395.85	24.26	404.82	24.81	413.79	25.36
328.31	20.12	337.28	20.67	346.25	21.22	355.23	21.77	364.20	22.32	373.17	22.87	382.14	23.42	387.04	23.72	396.01	24.27	404.98	24.82	413.95	25.37
328.47	20.13	337.44	20.68	346.42	21.23	355.39	21.78	364.36	22.33	373.33	22.88	382.31	23.43	387.20	23.73	396.17	24.28	405.14	24.83	414.12	25.38
328.63	20.14	337.61	20.69	346.58	21.24	355.55	21.79	364.52	22.34	373.50	22.89	382.47	23.44	387.36	23.74	396.33	24.29	405.31	24.84	414.28	25.39
328.80	20.15	337.77	20.70	346.74	21.25	355.71	21.80	364.69	22.35	373.66	22.90	382.63	23.45	387.53	23.75	396.50	24.30	405.47	24.85	414.44	25.40
328.96	20.16	337.93	20.71	346.91	21.26	355.88	21.81	364.85	22.36	373.82	22.91	382.79	23.46	387.69	23.76	396.66	24.31	405.63	24.86	414.61	25.41
329.12	20.17	338.10	20.72	347.07	21.27	356.04	21.82	365.01	22.37	373.99	22.92	382.96	23.47	387.85	23.77	396.82	24.32	405.80	24.87	414.77	25.42
329.29	20.18	338.26	20.73	347.23	21.28	356.20	21.83	365.18	22.38	374.15	22.93	383.12	23.48	388.01	23.78	396.99	24.33	405.96	24.88	414.93	25.43
329.45	20.19	338.42	20.74	347.39	21.29	356.37	21.84	365.34	22.39	374.31	22.94	383.28	23.49	388.18	23.79	397.15	24.34	406.12	24.89	415.09	25.44
329.61	20.20	338.59	20.75	347.56	21.30	356.53	21.85	365.50	22.40	374.47	22.95	383.45	23.50	388.34	23.80	397.31	24.35	406.29	24.90	415.26	25.45
329.78	20.21	338.75	20.76	347.72	21.31	356.69	21.86	365.67	22.41	374.64	22.96	383.61	23.51	388.50	23.81	397.48	24.36	406.45	24.91	415.42	25.46
329.94	20.22	338.91	20.77	347.88	21.32	356.86	21.87	365.83	22.42	374.80	22.97	383.77	23.52	388.67	23.82	397.64	24.37	406.61	24.92	415.58	25.47
330.10	20.23	339.08	20.78	348.05	21.33	357.02	21.88	365.99	22.43	374.96	22.98	383.94	23.53	388.83	23.83	397.80	24.38	406.77	24.93	415.75	25.48
330.27	20.24	339.24	20.79	348.21	21.34	357.18	21.89	366.16	22.44	375.13	22.99	384.10	23.54	388.99	23.84	397.97	24.39	406.94	24.94	415.91	25.49
330.43	20.25	339.40	20.80	348.37	21.35	357.35	21.90	366.32	22.45	375.29	23.00	384.26	23.55	389.16	23.85	398.13	24.40	407.10	24.95	416.07	25.50
330.59	20.26	339.56	20.81	348.54	21.36	357.51	21.91	366.48	22.46	375.45	23.01	384.43	23.56	389.32	23.86	398.29	24.41	407.26	24.96	416.24	25.51
330.76	20.27	339.73	20.82	348.70	21.37	357.67	21.92	366.64	22.47	375.62	23.02	384.59	23.57	389.48	23.87	398.46	24.42	407.43	24.97	416.40	25.52
330.92	20.28	339.89	20.83	348.86	21.38	357.84	21.93	366.81	22.48	375.78	23.03	384.75	23.58	389.65	23.88	398.62	24.43	407.59	24.98	416.56	25.53
331.08	20.29	340.05	20.84	349.03	21.39	358.00	21.94	366.97	22.49	375.94	23.04	384.92	23.59	389.81	23.89	398.78	24.44	407.75	24.99	416.73	25.54
331.24	20.30	340.22	20.85	349.19	21.40	358.16	21.95	367.13	22.50	376.11	23.05	385.08	23.60	389.97	23.90	398.94	24.45	407.92	25.00	416.89	25.55
331.41	20.31	340.38	20.86	349.35	21.41	358.32	21.96	367.30	22.51	376.27	23.06	385.24	23.61	390.14	23.91	399.11	24.46	408.08	25.01	417.05	25.56
331.57	20.32	340.54	20.87	349.52	21.42	358.49	21.97	367.46	22.52	376.43	23.07	385.40	23.62	390.30	23.92	399.27	24.47	408.24	25.02	417.22	25.57
331.73	20.33	340.71	20.88	349.68	21.43	358.65	21.98	367.62	22.53	376.60	23.08	385.57	23.63	390.46	23.93	399.43	24.48	408.41	25.03	417.38	25.58
331.90	20.34	340.87	20.89	349.84	21.44	358.81	21.99	367.79	22.54	376.76	23.09	385.73	23.64	390.62	23.94	399.60	24.49	408.57	25.04	417.54	25.59

(continued)

FEDERAL SOCIAL SECURITY-MEDICARE TAX TABLE—6.13% Employee Tax Deduction (concluded)

$ Wages less than	$ Tax	$ Wages less than	$ Tax	$ Wages less than	$ Tax	$ Wages less than	$ Tax	$ Wages less than	$ Tax	$ Wages less than	$ Tax	$ Wages less than	$ Tax	$ Wages less than	$ Tax	$ Wages less than	$ Tax	$ Wages less than	$ Tax	$ Wages less than	$ Tax
417.70	25.60	426.68	26.15	435.65	26.70	444.62	27.25	453.59	27.80	462.57	28.35	471.54	28.90	480.51	29.45	489.48	30.00	498.46	30.55	507.43	31.10
417.87	25.61	426.84	26.16	435.81	26.71	444.78	27.26	453.76	27.81	462.73	28.36	471.70	28.91	480.67	29.46	489.65	30.01	498.62	30.56	507.59	31.11
418.03	25.62	427.00	26.17	435.98	26.72	444.95	27.27	453.92	27.82	462.89	28.37	471.86	28.92	480.84	29.47	489.81	30.02	498.78	30.57	507.75	31.12
418.19	25.63	427.17	26.18	436.14	26.73	445.11	27.28	454.08	27.83	463.06	28.38	472.03	28.93	481.00	29.48	489.97	30.03	498.94	30.58	507.92	31.13
418.36	25.64	427.33	26.19	436.30	26.74	445.27	27.29	454.25	27.84	463.22	28.39	472.19	28.94	481.16	29.49	490.14	30.04	499.11	30.59	508.08	31.14
418.52	25.65	427.49	26.20	436.47	26.75	445.44	27.30	454.41	27.85	463.38	28.40	472.35	28.95	481.33	29.50	490.30	30.05	499.27	30.60	508.24	31.15
418.68	25.66	427.66	26.21	436.63	26.76	445.60	27.31	454.57	27.86	463.54	28.41	472.52	28.96	481.49	29.51	490.46	30.06	499.43	30.61	508.41	31.16
418.85	25.67	427.82	26.22	436.79	26.77	445.76	27.32	454.74	27.87	463.71	28.42	472.68	28.97	481.65	29.52	490.62	30.07	499.60	30.62	508.57	31.17
419.01	25.68	427.98	26.23	436.95	26.78	445.93	27.33	454.90	27.88	463.87	28.43	472.84	28.98	481.82	29.53	490.79	30.08	499.76	30.63	508.73	31.18
419.17	25.69	428.15	26.24	437.12	26.79	446.09	27.34	455.06	27.89	464.03	28.44	473.01	28.99	481.98	29.54	490.95	30.09	499.92	30.64	508.90	31.19
419.34	25.70	428.31	26.25	437.28	26.80	446.25	27.35	455.23	27.90	464.20	28.45	473.17	29.00	482.14	29.55	491.11	30.10	500.09	30.65	509.06	31.20
419.50	25.71	428.47	26.26	437.44	26.81	446.42	27.36	455.39	27.91	464.36	28.46	473.33	29.01	482.31	29.56	491.28	30.11	500.25	30.66	509.22	31.21
419.66	25.72	428.63	26.27	437.61	26.82	446.58	27.37	455.55	27.92	464.52	28.47	473.50	29.02	482.47	29.57	491.44	30.12	500.41	30.67	509.39	31.22
419.83	25.73	428.80	26.28	437.77	26.83	446.74	27.38	455.71	27.93	464.69	28.48	473.66	29.03	482.63	29.58	491.60	30.13	500.58	30.68	509.55	31.23
419.99	25.74	423.96	26.29	437.93	26.84	446.91	27.39	455.88	27.94	464.85	28.49	473.82	29.04	482.79	29.59	491.77	30.14	500.74	30.69	509.71	31.24
420.15	25.75	429.12	26.30	438.10	26.85	447.07	27.40	456.04	27.95	465.01	28.50	473.99	29.05	482.96	29.60	491.93	30.15	500.90	30.70	509.87	31.25
420.31	25.76	429.29	26.31	438.26	26.86	447.23	27.41	456.20	27.96	465.18	28.51	474.15	29.06	483.12	29.61	492.09	30.16	501.07	30.71	510.04	31.26
420.48	25.77	429.45	26.32	438.42	26.87	447.39	27.42	456.37	27.97	465.34	28.52	474.31	29.07	483.28	29.62	492.26	30.17	501.23	30.72	510.20	31.27
420.64	25.78	429.61	26.33	438.59	26.88	447.56	27.43	456.53	27.98	465.50	28.53	474.47	29.08	483.45	29.63	492.42	30.18	501.39	30.73	510.36	31.28
420.80	25.79	429.78	26.34	438.75	26.89	447.72	27.44	456.69	27.99	465.67	28.54	474.64	29.09	483.61	29.64	492.58	30.19	501.55	30.74	510.53	31.29
420.97	25.80	429.94	26.35	438.91	26.90	447.88	27.45	456.86	28.00	465.83	28.55	474.80	29.10	483.77	29.65	492.75	30.20	501.72	30.75	510.69	31.30
421.13	25.81	430.10	26.36	439.08	26.91	448.05	27.46	457.02	28.01	465.99	28.56	474.96	29.11	483.94	29.66	492.91	30.21	501.88	30.76	510.85	31.31
421.29	25.82	430.27	26.37	439.24	26.92	448.21	27.47	457.18	28.02	466.16	28.57	475.13	29.12	484.10	29.67	493.07	30.22	502.04	30.77	511.02	31.32
421.46	25.83	430.43	26.38	439.40	26.93	448.37	27.48	457.35	28.03	466.32	28.58	475.29	29.13	484.26	29.68	493.24	30.23	502.21	30.78	511.18	31.33
421.62	25.84	430.59	26.39	439.56	26.94	448.54	27.49	457.51	28.04	466.48	28.59	475.45	29.14	484.43	29.69	493.40	30.24	502.37	30.79	511.34	31.34
421.78	25.85	430.76	26.40	439.73	26.95	448.70	27.50	457.67	28.05	466.64	28.60	475.62	29.15	484.59	29.70	493.56	30.25	502.53	30.80	511.51	31.35
421.95	25.86	430.92	26.41	439.89	26.96	448.86	27.51	457.84	28.06	466.81	28.61	475.78	29.16	484.75	29.71	493.72	30.26	502.70	30.81	511.67	31.36
422.11	25.87	431.08	26.42	440.05	26.97	449.03	27.52	458.00	28.07	466.97	28.62	475.94	29.17	484.92	29.72	493.89	30.27	502.86	30.82	511.83	31.37
422.27	25.88	431.24	26.43	440.22	26.98	449.19	27.53	458.16	28.08	467.13	28.63	476.11	29.18	485.08	29.73	494.05	30.28	503.02	30.83	512.00	31.38
422.44	25.89	431.41	26.44	440.38	26.99	449.35	27.54	458.32	28.09	467.30	28.64	476.27	29.19	485.24	29.74	494.21	30.29	503.19	30.84	512.16	31.39
422.60	25.90	431.57	26.45	440.54	27.00	449.52	27.55	458.49	28.10	467.46	28.65	476.43	29.20	485.40	29.75	494.38	30.30	503.35	30.85	512.32	31.40
422.76	25.91	431.73	26.46	440.71	27.01	449.68	27.56	458.65	28.11	467.62	28.66	476.60	29.21	485.57	29.76	494.54	30.31	503.51	30.86	512.48	31.41
422.93	25.92	431.90	26.47	440.87	27.02	449.84	27.57	458.81	28.12	467.79	28.67	476.76	29.22	485.73	29.77	494.70	30.32	503.68	30.87	512.65	31.42
423.09	25.93	432.06	26.48	441.03	27.03	450.00	27.58	458.98	28.13	467.95	28.68	476.92	29.23	485.89	29.78	494.87	30.33	503.84	30.88	512.81	31.43
423.25	25.94	432.22	26.49	441.20	27.04	450.17	27.59	459.14	28.14	468.11	28.69	477.08	29.24	486.06	29.79	495.03	30.34	504.00	30.89	512.97	31.44
423.41	25.95	432.39	26.50	441.36	27.05	450.33	27.60	459.30	28.15	468.28	28.70	477.25	29.25	486.22	29.80	495.19	30.35	504.16	30.90	513.14	31.45
423.58	25.96	432.55	26.51	441.52	27.06	450.49	27.61	459.47	28.16	468.44	28.71	477.41	29.26	486.38	29.81	495.36	30.36	504.33	30.91	513.30	31.46
423.74	25.97	432.71	26.52	441.69	27.07	450.66	27.62	459.63	28.17	468.60	28.72	477.57	29.27	486.55	29.82	495.52	30.37	504.49	30.92	513.46	31.47
423.90	25.98	432.88	26.53	441.85	27.08	450.82	27.63	459.79	28.18	468.77	28.73	477.74	29.28	486.71	29.83	495.68	30.38	504.65	30.93	513.63	31.48
424.07	25.99	433.04	26.54	442.01	27.09	450.98	27.64	459.96	28.19	468.93	28.74	477.90	29.29	486.87	29.84	495.85	30.39	504.82	30.94	513.79	31.49
424.23	26.00	433.20	26.55	442.17	27.10	451.15	27.65	460.12	28.20	469.09	28.75	478.06	29.30	487.04	29.85	496.01	30.40	504.98	30.95	513.95	31.50
424.39	26.01	433.37	26.56	442.34	27.11	451.31	27.66	460.28	28.21	469.25	28.76	478.23	29.31	487.20	29.86	496.17	30.41	505.14	30.96	514.12	31.51
424.56	26.02	433.53	26.57	442.50	27.12	451.47	27.67	460.45	28.22	469.42	28.77	478.39	29.32	487.36	29.87	496.33	30.42	505.31	30.97	514.28	31.52
424.72	26.03	433.69	26.58	442.66	27.13	451.64	27.68	460.61	28.23	469.58	28.78	478.55	29.33	487.53	29.88	496.50	30.43	505.47	30.98	514.44	31.53
424.88	26.04	433.85	26.59	442.83	27.14	451.80	27.69	460.77	28.24	469.74	28.79	478.72	29.34	487.69	29.89	496.66	30.44	505.63	30.99	514.61	31.54
425.05	26.05	434.02	26.60	442.99	27.15	451.96	27.70	460.93	28.25	469.91	28.80	478.88	29.35	487.85	29.90	496.82	30.45	505.80	31.00	514.77	31.55
425.21	26.06	434.18	26.61	443.15	27.16	452.13	27.71	461.10	28.26	470.07	28.81	479.04	29.36	488.01	29.91	496.99	30.46	505.96	31.01	514.93	31.56
425.37	26.07	434.34	26.62	443.32	27.17	452.29	27.72	461.26	28.27	470.23	28.82	479.21	29.37	488.18	29.92	497.15	30.47	506.12	31.02	515.09	31.57
425.54	26.08	434.51	26.63	443.48	27.18	452.45	27.73	461.42	28.28	470.40	28.83	479.37	29.38	488.34	29.93	497.31	30.48	506.29	31.03	515.26	31.58
425.70	26.09	434.67	26.64	443.64	27.19	452.62	27.74	461.59	28.29	470.56	28.84	479.53	29.39	488.50	29.94	497.48	30.49	506.45	31.04	515.42	31.59
425.86	26.10	434.83	26.65	443.81	27.20	452.78	27.75	461.75	28.30	470.72	28.85	479.70	29.40	488.67	29.95	497.64	30.50	506.61	31.05	515.58	31.60
426.02	26.11	435.00	26.66	443.97	27.21	452.94	27.76	461.91	28.31	470.89	28.86	479.86	29.41	488.83	29.96	497.80	30.51	506.77	31.06	515.75	31.61
426.19	26.12	435.16	26.67	444.13	27.22	453.10	27.77	462.08	28.32	471.05	28.87	480.02	29.42	488.99	29.97	497.97	30.52	506.94	31.07	515.91	31.62
426.35	26.13	435.32	26.68	444.30	27.23	453.27	27.78	462.24	28.33	471.21	28.88	480.18	29.43	489.16	29.98	498.13	30.53	507.10	31.08	516.07	31.63
426.51	26.14	435.49	26.69	444.46	27.24	453.43	27.79	462.40	28.34	471.38	28.89	480.35	29.44	489.32	29.99	498.29	30.54	507.26	31.09	516.24	31.64